TRADITION IN SCULPTURE

UXORI, FILIO, FILIÆ

TRADITION

IN

SCULPTURE

by ALEC MILLER

THE STUDIO PUBLICATIONS: LONDON & NEW YORK

Printed in England by Edmund Evans, Ltd., London,
and published in London
by The Studio, Ltd., 66 Chandos Place, W.C.2,
and in New York City
by The Studio Publications Inc., 381 Fourth Avenue

CONTENTS

INTRODUCTION

THERE is a very intimidating comment by William Blake, written as marginalia on his copy of Sir Joshua Reynolds' *Discourses on Art*—and Blake's capitals give it peculiar emphasis :—

" To Generalise is to be an Idiot, to Particularise is the alone Distinction of Merit—General Knowledges are those Knowledges that Idiots possess."

One may well tremble before such a direct and challenging generalization !—though comfort may be found, perhaps, in a dictum of Justice O. W. Holmes : " No generalization is wholly true—not even this one." Indeed, that thought may usefully be recalled throughout the reading of this book, which has many generalizations, though I hope it is not therefore " a tale told by an idiot ". The scale of the book is not large, and the subject is wide ; so the aim has been to sketch in the salient features of sculptural history, and, in doing this, statements of general, rather than of particular, accuracy are almost inevitable. But even generalizations need not be lacking in substantial truth ; what is essential is that they should be recognized as such, and not taken to be precise statements of scientific fact. It is likely enough that there are definite statements in this book more open to challenge than are many of the generalizations.

If I assert that Egyptian sculpture is pervaded by a religious significance, and has an impressive sense of permanence—that Greek sculpture glorifies and idealizes Man and his physical beauty—that Roman sculpture records unflinchingly the outlook of a more realist race—that the sculpture of the thirteenth century has a spiritual beauty never again known in art : these are generalizations which are almost unchallengeable, but they are not the whole truth about the subject. The attempt to make accurate statements of date as to when such and such changes took place might readily lead to a false appearance of precision, because there are always exceptions and vital changes may arise almost imperceptibly. Dates, therefore, are here reduced to a minimum. They may be left to those exacting critics whom Socrates calls " the conquering rabble of the over-wise " ; and when required, they can always be found in a textbook

In considering Art History there seem to be opposing schools—one school building on data collected with scientific precision, annotated, classified and fitted with care into a scheme, as if art were something distinct and separate from the other activities of man ; so that its development is traced and its changes noted without particular relation to the intellectual atmosphere of the age and race. Such histories are apt to trace the rise, the apogee, and the decline of each nation and period of art as if there were valid and final standards of judgment and a universally accepted type of art.

The other school, violently reacting from the precise and factual, has abandoned statement for interpretation ; as Lange did, for instance, when he saw in the gay smiles of the Aeginetan sculptures " the expression of the cheerful heroism of the Greeks, which defeated Persia ". March Phillips' *Works of Man* and Elie Faure's *Histoire de l'Art* are both brilliantly suggestive on the interpretative side ; though Vernon Lee, while admitting the *Works of Man* to be " suggestive and delightfully appreciative ", yet calls the book " the reductio ad absurdum " of art criticism ! And it is true that after a few chapters of Faure one longs for some simple, concrete fact or date to give one a foothold in the continuous stream of eloquent and luminous interpretation. Yet, as T. R. Glover says : " History is hard to interpret if we look back on it : it is useless unless we try to interpret it."[1]

As a craftsman I have approached the subject of sculpture with the single aim of understanding and explaining the course and the vicissitudes of its development. The causes which effected the changes are sometimes new techniques, and sometimes new ideas, or both together ; and to trace these ideas may be more revealing, and even more precise, than to give dates. One who sets out to give instruction is answerable not so much for the rightness of his views (for time and new factors may change these) as for their uprightness ; they should be sincerely and even vehemently held and believed, because, as Plato makes Socrates say, " I assure you, there is a far greater risk in the purchase of instruction than in that of food ". A reader who takes this risk may find in this book . . . lacunæ certainly, perhaps prejudices, and some personal and individual views about the technique of sculpture ; and yet the endeavour throughout has been to stimulate interest and to integrate sculpture with the other achievements of man which make up history. The lacunæ are twofold : intentional, and unintentional. The latter arise from the same cause as Dr. Johnson's confusion of the pastern and the hock of a horse—ignorance. The intentional gaps are mainly caused by the scale of this book ; for to mention even the groups or schools of sculptors whose work has had influence and impressed each its generation would turn this to a catalogue ; and to list individual sculptors would be futile and impossible. This is neither a manual of technique nor a history, but only an approach to sculpture from the angle of a working craftsman. I have tried to study certain representative works and outstanding individualities, and from these to deduce the characteristics and trace the animating spirit of the time. Michelangelo dominated toweringly over his generation (and perhaps unfortunately, in the next) : Bandinelli's " Hercules and Cacus " and the works of Ammanati, *et al.*, may be left undisturbed. So Houdon, Canova and Flaxman : different as they were, and representing opposing tendencies of realism and classicism, yet they and their work are the important sculptural facts of the eighteenth century.

Prejudices or " imperfect sympathies " are inevitable, though often

[1] " The Ancient World."

they are defensible. I have tried to view with detachment some works, famous or notorious, with which I am personally out of sympathy owing to my training and experience, yet which demand and deserve study and comment. Many of the critics of today hand out æsthetic judgments as if they were the " tables of the Law ", only a little more final than the Ten Commandments, and (a grave danger !) as abrogating all the æsthetic experience and judgments of the past. I cannot, without enlarging and rewriting this book, defend all the judgments herein ; but the intention is to explain them and to show the bases on which they are made. I have lived long enough to have seen the reversal of almost every critical judgment applied to artists and writers as the century opened, and no æsthetic criticism is here made because it conforms to current views and ideas. We may well recall the wise words of Leonardo : " The artist is never eccentric; he has no intellectual superstitions ; he imitates, he innovates, never abjures the old because it is old, nor the new because it is new, but finds in each something of the present moment." And is it not significant that one of the distinguishing marks of great art is that, in some strange way, it is of no date and of all time ? To one who has watched artists, writers, and critics, once hailed as " new " and " modern " vanish into the limbo of things that were, and who remembers the days of " L'Art Nouveau ", it is, at once, clear and comforting to realize that " modern " may change from being an epithet to become an epitaph.

To have read and studied many histories of art, and to have had long practice in many kinds of sculpture, are not in themselves an adequate preparation for writing this book. Yet such studies are useful. My own long technical experience convinces me, for instance, that the suggestion made in an important and scholarly book on mediæval sculpture, that a certain wooden sculptural effigy is " perhaps a preliminary model for a final statue in stone or alabaster ", is untenable ; for here the learned authors suggest that a sculptor or carver might use a tough, fibrous, and rather intractable material (English oak) to make a preliminary model for a statue in stone or alabaster, both of which, as carving materials, require much less time and skill than wood. Scholarship is a fine accomplishment ; yet the absence of first-hand technical knowledge is a great handicap in dealing with an art like sculpture, where concept, design, and technique all merge. Another issue is raised by the art historian who uses the current comminatory adjective " photographic " to describe Greek sculpture, and dismisses the Phidian Zeus as " a horror ". This is the dire result of arbitrarily assuming that his twentieth century æsthetics are universally valid—an untenable position, such as may have been in the mind of AE when, with acute Irish wit, he said : " Experts should be on tap, but not on top ".

This book attempts to approach the subject of sculpture much as a mediæval mason sculptor might have done, had he been versed in past history and able to look four or five centuries ahead. The technique of sculpture was a comparatively simple affair till the advent of electrical devices, and reducing- and enlarging-machinery ; and a student must bear in mind that technique and material are an integral part of sculpture, and that it cannot be usefully studied except through an understanding of materials and processes, or interpreted except as an aspect of history. " The history of art has suffered as much as any history by trenchant and absolute divisions. Pagan and Christian art are sometimes harshly opposed, and the Renaissance is represented as a fashion which set in at a definite period. That is the superficial view : the deeper view is that which preserves the identity of European culture. The two are really continuous and there is a sense in which it may be said that the Renaissance was an uninterrupted effort of the Middle Age—that it was ever taking place." These wise and salutary words from Pater's essay on Winckelmann[1] may fittingly be remembered by any who read this sketch.

And if the divisions between the art of one country and another are at times tenuous and indeterminate, and different styles and periods are treated as equally important, yet the attempt has been made to seize and separate the active and salient characteristics of each age and interpret them in terms of sculpture. For instance, the technical excellence and rhetorical splendour of Baroque sculpture cannot conceal its spiritual poverty ; but it is nevertheless very important as the art of its age and place, precisely because it forces on one's attention the fact that the characteristic qualities and standards of a nation and a period while valid for that nation and period, are not necessarily valid for another age.

Inevitably, personal convictions and predilections tend to draw one into sympathy with certain kinds of sculpture ; and I make no pretence to have achieved either complete knowledge or complete, unbiased detachment. But I have tried hard to avoid ambiguity, believing in Huxley's dictum :—" Be clear, though you may be convicted of error."

As my experience and studies have been wholly with European and American sculpture this survey is limited to the Western world. In the wide field of Oriental Sculpture I recognize that there is much that is beautiful, and some that is almost overpoweringly so—but it is outside the range and scale of this book and I could add nothing on this subject other than at second hand.

[1] " The Renaissance "

" Sculpture is the reduction of any shapeless mass of solid matter into an intended shape." RUSKIN : ARATRA PENTELICI

DEFINITIONS & PROCESSES

THE most casual observer, straying through a museum of sculpture, must have noticed that an Egyptian statue is different from a Greek one : that a mediæval statue is different from either : and that a statue by Michelangelo is different from any other. To trace and record the causes of all those differences would involve writing a history of civilization from Egypt to the Renaissance, tracing especially the development of religion, philosophy and art from their common origin in man's desire to find a means of expression.

In a brief review, the tracing of the threads of civilization must necessarily be sketchy, but it is essential that the reader should understand, and, for the time being accept, the point of view that Art is one manifestation of the human spirit working in the mind of man, and that the attempt to study this manifestation as an isolated aspect of man's activity is fatal to any real understanding, not only of art, but of any aspect of man's achievement.

Looking at four statues of four epochs, their salient characteristics might be stated thus. The Egyptian one, is the most stylized. Its forms are less closely copied from nature, it has what are called " conventions " of form, and an apparent simplicity of surface.

The Greek Apollo is more human. The forms are more nearly those of nature, and if a nude man of good physique stood beside it in the same attitude the approximation to nature would be seen to be nearer than is that of the Egyptian figure. The face is less individualized than is the body.

The mediæval statue is heavily draped. The body beneath the drapery is less perfectly understood than in the Greek one, and some angularity of figure is visible beneath the drapery, which being heavy suggests a Northern origin. The face is not very individualized though the generalization is different from that of the Greek.

In a statue of Michelangelo's the face is highly expressive of individuality and of emotion. The figure has neither the stylized convention of the Egyptian, nor the serene, idealized realism of the Greek statue, nor has it the simple expressiveness of the mediæval Madonna. It is indeed the personification of emotion, but it has no appearance of realism because the physical structure is enlarged and hypertrophied beyond Nature. The shape of the block is simple and the form compact within it.

A student of sculpture, might make some such observations as these, even though he did not express them articulately, and gradually it might dawn upon him that these figures were but carved history, differing only from written history in their being unconscious and

10

unprejudiced expressions of their time and creators. And so it becomes plain that if one would understand a work of sculpture one must realize that it is but the expressive flowering of a certain kind of social culture, and that every change or development is indicative of changed social conditions, new philosophies, different religious points of view, and changing tools and materials. The briefest sketch therefore of a history of sculpture must concern itself with many aspects of life and thought not immediately artistic. A history of art which assumes that changes of form are accidental and fortuitous is of little use.

It is, of course, true that Art is not solely a product of the age which produces it, but that it has a life and vitality of its own, just as we are not only the product of our immediate parents but have roots which go far back to a distant ancestry. In art the analogue is tradition which is handed on through changes and generations. This book, therefore, is an attempt to trace this inheritance of tradition and also the forces which moulded life and thought so that it was expressed in those sculptured forms in wood and stone, marble and bronze.

It is intended for students and craftsmen, especially for students and workers in the craft of sculpture, and in the subsidiary crafts allied to architecture. It will deal also with the technique of the craft, though it is intended primarily as a historical sketch and interpretation and not as a technical treatise. But it is impossible to understand sculpture without some knowledge of the processes by which it is made, and some insight into the thought processes which generated it.

One essential distinction to be realized is that there are two kinds of sculpture : *Plastic Sculpture*, which is a soft material like clay or wax squeezed with the fingers or modelled into shape with tools, and *Carved Sculpture*, which is cut into shape with tools from a hard material.

All the processes of modelling in clay and wax have been admirably and elaborately described in many text books, and are taught in most art schools. The reader is referred especially to *Modelling* by Lanteri, and *Modelling and Sculpture* by Albert Toft. But the distinction between these two kinds of sculpture is so little realized, even in art schools, and by writers on sculpture, that it may be useful to try and state it in clear terms. A well known English writer on sculpture told me that he had taught " sculpture " in an art school for seventeen years without realizing this vital distinction !

The first step towards making a modelled figure statue is to make in wire or piping an " armature "—which is really a skeleton. This armature is made as nearly as possible in the action in which the finished figure has been conceived (this conception having been previously arrived at in the artist's mind, either by (a) contemplation, or (b) visually with the aid of drawings, or (c) from reference to a living model, or (d) by a combination of all these). The armature is therefore an abstract of the action of the figure—it is the figure reduced to its simplest terms. On this is built up with soft clay or wax, forms following more or less closely the actual muscular construction of the figure. This process of building up from

11

almost linear curves to solid forms is, as good modellers like Lanteri and St. Gaudens always insist, a process of addition, and students are rightly urged not to build up clay and then cut it down but to build up with great care till the true form of the figure, conceived mentally, or actually before the sculptor in a living model, has been reached. The conception has then been realized, " matter has been reduced to an intended shape ". The further processes of reproducing this clay or wax into a more permanent material are reproductive processes and not actually " sculpture ". All these processes of casting in plaster, terra-cotta, or metals are mechanical, and though they require great skill, judgment and manual dexterity, they are essentially not creative but duplicating processes. These processes have often been described, and the reader desirous of studying or experimenting will find all the necessary information in many books. There must be no confusion then in the mind as to the qualities and characteristics of this modelled sculpture. Its surfaces and forms are such as have arisen from the addition of pieces of clay. It has been built up from within, outwards, and it should bear quite distinctively the evidences of the material and the processes of its making, for such evidences are the mark of good crafts-manship.

Carved sculpture is that in which the conceived form is approached from without, inwards, by the process of attrition or cutting away. The beginning of a statue in wood or stone is not a skeleton but a roughly rectangular three-dimensional block of solid substance within the bounds of which lies the figure or form conceived by the sculptor. Again the sculptor may have mentally visualized this conception in different ways. He may, like the Eastern artist, have conceived it entirely by meditation and contemplation, or he may have conceived it with the aid of drawings and studies from a living model or even by a combination of all these ending in a clay, or other sketch model embodying what he has (a) contemplated (b) observed in the living model (c) drawn and then transferred into the preliminary model, or he may carve directly without any such aids.

The process of carved sculpture is just the freeing of the statue from the enclosing block, cutting away all the material that is not wanted, and if the sculptor stops cutting down when he has reached the pre-conceived form, his end is achieved. Again " matter has been reduced to an intended shape " and the form is there revealed in a more or less permanent material. Now it should be obvious that the qualities inherent in good modelled sculpture, plasticity and soft and ductile forms, are qualities entirely foreign to a hard material and to the process of chiselling. So much is this true that it may be said that a plastic model is essentially a wrong preparation for a carved statue especially if the translation into the stone, marble or wood is largely mechanical. Yet the realization of these differing qualities has been almost entirely lost and is constantly ignored by artists, teachers, and critics. Especially has this been so since the development and elaboration of the " pointing machine " with the aid of which skilled workmen are constantly employed in translating the plastic qualities of the sculptor's clay model into material in which these very qualities are always false and often ridiculous and even monstrous. It is not necessary to suggest or imply that carved sculpture is essentially better than modelled sculpture (though the fact that the modellers themselves, called on to personify their craft in a symbolic figure, always give the figure a hammer and chisels and never spatula or modelling tools would almost warrant the suggestion).

The distinction between the two types of sculpture as " plastic " and " glyptic " was first made by Ruskin in 1870 in *Aratra Pentelici*. " Clay, being ductile, lends itself to all softness of line ; being easily frangible it would be ridiculous to give it sharp edges. So that a blunt and massive rendering of graceful gesture will be its natural function : but as it can be pinched or pulled, or twisted in a moment into projection which it would take hours of chiselling to get in stone, it will also properly be used for all fantastic and grotesque form not involving sharp edges . . ." " What is true of chalk and charcoal for painters, is equally true of clay for sculptors ; they are most precious materials for true masters, but tempt false ones into fatal license. . . . " "The modern system of modelling the work in clay ; getting it into form by machinery and by the hands of subordinates ; and touching it at last if indeed the (so-called) sculptor touch it at all, only to correct their inefficiencies, renders the production of good work in marble or stone a physical impossibility. The first result is that the sculptor thinks in clay instead of marble, and loses his instinctive sense of the proper treatment of a brittle substance. The second is that neither he nor the public recognize the touch of the chisel as expressive of personal feeling or power, and that nothing is looked for except mechanical polish."

The first and great thing then is to realize clearly in one's mind in studying sculpture that these processes produce two entirely different kinds of work. In the whole history of the art no carved statue, from the time of Egypt till Michelangelo, ever looks like clay, or has qualities not natural to the chisel and the material, and similarly almost all modern sculpture has essentially the qualities of plastic modelling though its material may be stone, marble, or bronze. Bronze does indeed occupy a sort of intermediate place between modelling and carving. The mind realizes, on looking at a bronze figure, that though it is a hard material, it was once soft and molten and that it was when molten that it was poured into the mould and took the impress of its shape. So that it may reasonably be urged that soft and ductile modelled qualities are not actually false in bronze, or other metal castings. The modern treatment of bronze is almost entirely plastic. It may, however, be noted that ancient bronzes, Egyptian, Greek and mediæval, have an entirely different quality from either modelled or carved work of the same period. Greek bronzes, if well preserved, have a metallic firmness of surface entirely different from that of Greek carved marbles, and rightly so. It is only necessary to compare say, the bronze head from Beneventum in the Louvre or the Boy Victor at Munich with any Phidian or contemporary marble, to see that

13

to a Greek artist a bronze figure was never a replica of a marble one, but an entirely different problem solved in a different way.

Probably Greek bronze casting was not technically so perfect as modern casting, and so the sculptor had to do much more work on the bronze, filing, grinding and engraving, whereas with the modern " cire perdue " process of casting bronze the surfaces are rarely worked on at all by the artist.   .

This is a technical question which has not yet received the attention it deserves from classical scholars and archæologists.[1]

It is urgent that these technical and æsthetic distinctions should be understood, for the failure to do so has perverted taste and prevented real understanding of the true qualities of craftsmanship ; and, aided by the development of mechanism, has created among the craftsmen themselves a vicious distinction between creators and artizan copiers, in which undue emphasis is given to the plastic creator while the translator is counted off into a heap of mechanism. This wrong distinction and division has been a great loss to both groups. The sculptors are apt to be led astray by the facile ease of handling clay—and the marble carvers spend their lives copying other people's conceptions, and translating into marble qualities often false to that material. The failure to understand these distinctions has lessened the value of much writing on the subject of sculpture. It is still rare, even in the best known histories of sculpture that the illustrations record in what material the work has been made, and generally it is assumed that in the whole course of sculpture, the clay model has been a necessary and inevitable preliminary. A few writers have recently realised the distinction and write with enthusiasm of sculpture *en taille directe*, as if it were a modern thing ; forgetting, apparently, that great numbers of the marbles of antiquity, and certainly all the hundreds of thousands of mediæval ecclesiastical statues, were conceived and carved directly in the stone, wood, or marble by the craftsmen who built and adorned these buildings. Consequently almost all carved sculpture from antiquity to the Renaissance has that true technical beauty which is born of the instinctive feeling for the stone and the chisel, and if the clay model was used as a preliminary, it never influenced the sculptor's innate and traditional carved stylism. How far astray we have been led in this matter may be seen in an important history of American sculpture, the writer of which is himself a distinguished sculptor.

One of the illustrations reproduces a portrait bust in marble and especial praise is given to " the perfection of the marble cutting ; for though executed in marble the effect is of such perfect mastery that the face and neck appear plastic, as if responsive like wax to the pressure of the artist's thumb ", and later he refers to this plastic quality as " the acme of modern marble cutting ". These are really quite contradictory statements. " The perfection of marble cutting " is to preserve the firmness of

[1] The late Stanley Casson has since written an interesting and illuminating study of tools and technique and its bearing on Greek Art : " The Technique of Early Greek Sculpture."

14

the material, not to falsify it. Every mediæval sculptor knew this, and it is incarnate in all the work of the greatest from Egypt and Phidias to Michelangelo. In another English history of sculpture with many varied and beautiful illustrations the writer jumps from Greco-Roman sculpture to the Renaissance, with only a casual remark about the " rude grandeur " of the middle ages ! One might as well talk of the " rude grandeur " of the Taj-Mahal or of the Parthenon !

A few words on the actual technique of carving may be useful—they are the outcome of forty years of daily experience in the processes. Wood is a more difficult medium for sculpture than any of the softer stones. The grain of wood, especially of strongly fibred woods like oak and teak is more compelling, and the deep recesses are difficult of access in spite of the fact that wood carving tools are much more elaborately shaped and curved and more numerous, than those required for carving stone. Fundamentally the process of removing the unwanted material is the same with both materials, though it is safer to carve wood as much as possible across the fibres of grain, while stone may usually be cut in any direction. Wood is mentioned here because it is not only one of the oldest materials for sculpture, but one of the best, and is too much neglected today.

Stone carving tools have varied but little since the discovery of metals. Two or three hammers of different weights, " pitchers " and " points " for rough work, then claw or toothed tools, and chisels, with a few gouges; these are all that are needed for the actual carving of a statue in any of the oolithic, lime, or sand stones, or in marble. Granite and all igneous stones require stronger tools, differently tempered, and work is much slower, while the hardness and extreme brittleness of the material compel compactness and simplification of form. But most modern work is done in one or another of the " free " stones, or in marble, Carrara, Sicilian or Pentelic.

As the work of various epochs and countries is considered, reference will constantly be made to the relation between material and technique, but for the present let us grasp firmly the fact that virtually all the sculpture of the past is *carved sculpture* and let us consider for a moment Ruskin's definition : " The reduction of any shapeless mass of solid matter to an intended shape ". This, it may be observed, is pure æstheticism : it includes as sculpture a chipped flint, a clay pot, and the Sphinx, a pie crust and the Victoria Memorial, a totem pole, and those angels of the " Monument-alists " which have added a new terror to death.

So the definition, though it shows Ruskin's acute analytical power, and is immensely suggestive, must be narrowed for the purpose of this sketch, by the addition of something like this—" which is either imitative of nature, or has meaning ". For a block of stone, hewn by the quarryman to his " intended shape " is not yet sculpture, and does not become so till the artist has shaped it into expressiveness and so filled it with beauty and meaning. All past sculpture has been largely representational, even though it is not all equally imitative of natural forms, and it is surely significant that the ancient Egyptian hieroglyph for sculpture means " to make alive "

15

and a sculptor was " a maker alive ". There is today a marked revolt against representation in art, and a tendency to despise such art as tends towards realism. But even the so-called " abstract " or " non-representational " art of today attempts to convey its meaning by descriptive or expressive titles, and thus makes its art, as it was for Paleolithic Man, a mode of speech—" a means of transferring emotion " (Tolstoy's definition of Art). Dante calls sculpture " Visible speech ", an epithet which exactly describes the mediæval attitude to art

The implication, and sometimes the claim of the non-representative, non-imitative artist, is that here is a way of escape from the descent to the unimaginative commonplace involved in the pursuit of realism. But indeed there are many other ways of escape from the commonplace. The unimaginative realism of the Nurse Cavell in London, or of the stone soldiers of the American Civil War memorials, is immeasurably different from the imaginative reality of the Demeter in the British Museum, whose steadfast eyes induce in us a hushed reverence. Her power to move us comes, not because she resembles a woman, nor yet because of her serene beauty, but because her creator, some Cnidan Greek of the third century B.C., charged the marble with his own deep feeling and his own emotion. As one looks at this moving " Mother Earth " from which we come, and to which we go, one recalls Meredith's lines :

" Death, shall I shrink from loving thee ?
Into the breast that gives the rose
Shall I with shuddering fall ? "

It is quite possible that the course of art may set away from representation, but unless the whole psychology of man changes I cannot see that art can ever become entirely abstract, for when it does it will have become private and esoteric, and be no longer a means of communicating emotion, though it is obvious that to follow the path of unselective factual representation leads inevitably into a cul de sac.

" When the grasp on the bow was decision, and arrow and hand, and eye—were one." MEREDITH

PRIMITIVE SCULPTURE

ARCHÆOLOGY is the science which begins where geology ends, and has been aptly described as " History as workmen made it ".

The study of archæology involves the interpretation of remains and data covering many thousands, perhaps millions, of years. The mere " brute facts " of science are but the raw material to be related to other facts and so given deeper significance.

The enduring value of all records, sculptured, painted or written, is incalculable: indeed to destroy any work on which man has laboured is to commit a murder ; to the interpreter there are no " dead " men, no " past " ages, for what we call the past is only the roots of the present.

Civilization requires communities, and art, like religion, is a manifestation of one phase of the social instinct which leads to the formation of communities. The roots of art go deep down into magic, use and religion. This close relation of art with religion in totemism and animism must be borne in mind, and we do well to regard the works of these earliest artists as the visible monuments of a dawning religious emotion.

The element of magic in artistic representation is perhaps at the root of that dread of being represented in effigy, which is so widespread, and which certain religions, as the Jewish and Mohammedan, have taken into account, by forbidding any representation in painting or sculpture of the human figure. We have to recognize how deeply rooted is the mystical element.

As Professor Reinach says : " Primitive men did not merely seek to occupy their leisure or to fix their visual memories in order to gain from their companions admiration for their dexterity. The severe choice which presided over their artistic activity implies, for this same activity, some object less trite than those which have been alleged up to the present. They knew what they were doing, and why they did it—they were not idlers or dreamers inscribing or painting any familiar silhouette, no matter what, following the fancy of the moment."

The element of use or efficiency may well have been the result of experiment—the discovery that a flint arrowhead which had been chipped into perfect symmetry carried farther than a less skilfully balanced one, would tend to give an incentive for the exercise of skill ; and it is significant that it was in the fourth glacial period of the reindeer hunters, of which the Magdalenian peoples have left us such magnificent examples of painting in caves, of carved bone, and ivory, and of exquisitely chipped flints, that prehistoric man's art attained to its greatest height of vivid and powerful skill in representation. Sir Arthur Evans notes—" In their most developed

17

stage, as illustrated by the bulk of the figures in the cave of Altamira itself, and others in France and Spain these primeval frescoes display not only a consummate mastery of natural design, but an extraordinary technical resource. In single animals the tints composed of red and yellow ochre and charcoal are varied from black to dark and ruddy brown, or brilliant orange, and so by fine gradations to paler nuances—outlines are brought out by white incised lines—and in the culminating phase of this art we find even impressionist works—the galloping herds of horses, from the Chaumont Grotto, depicting the leader, in each case in front of his troop, and its serried line, straight as that of a well-drilled battalion—in perspective rendering. The whole *must* be taken to be a faithful memory sketch of an exciting episode of prairie life."

Art of such vividness, depicted with such technical skill, was surely a highly developed art behind which lay a long period of groping and study.

Perhaps one explanation of the development of this high standard of skill is to be found in the fact that these artists were first of all hunters, and the trained rapidity of vision, certainty of hand, and acute selective emphasis so characteristic of their art, was the result of the fact that they were men feebly armed against many dangers, whose very lives were dependent on alert faculties, quickened perceptions and instantaneous action. Only thus could they live at all, and the hunter's eye and hand was also that of the artist. Representations of the human figure are rare until a slightly later date, though there is a sculptured stone relief of a " steatopygous woman " in the Dordogne which may belong to the age of the cave paintings, and in the Tuc d'Audoubert cave are two bisons modelled in clay which show great skill and virile modelling.

Professor G. Elliot Smith insists that these representations of fat women were not in any way meant as indicating that primitive women were normally steatopygous. " The aim was to reproduce the female form in such a way that all of the characters associated with the functions of reproduction were intensified even to the stage of gross exaggeration." " The artists were modelling symbols to express a definite magical purpose and not simply trying to portray the human form." Small figurines were worn as amulets and it seems clear that this sculpture originated not in a desire to make beautiful or decorative objects—but to make objects which would give their possessor magical power.

Paleolithic man seemed less interested in his own species than in animals. It is possible that the animals depicted were totems—which are described by Sir J. G. Frazer as "a class of material objects, which a savage regards with superstitious respect, believing that there exists between him and every member of the class an intimate and altogether special relation."[1]

If these pictured animals were the cave man's totems, then Paleolithic man had in him the germs of religious emotion such as underlay the religious systems of the Egyptians, the Chaldeans and the Greeks, and

[1] " Totemism." Sir J. G. Frazer.

from their burial customs one is forced to deduce that these Paleolithic people believed that the dead went to some ghostly world and continued some sort of ghostly existence.

The succeeding age seems in Europe at least to be widely separated by a long period in which there are no discoverable traces of man. Neolithic artistic skill was in no way comparable with that of its predecessors. Craftsmen worked hard stones and polished them into suitable shapes for use as hammers and implements, but there is no trace in their works of the hunter-artist's eye nor is there evidence that any trace of Paleolithic man's brilliant observation and skill was known, even as a remote tradition. Neolithic man was a farmer or a shepherd, a weaver or a potter. He was less dependent on rapidity of perception and action, and these essentially artistic faculties died of atrophy.

With the decay of Paleolithic art, no great pictorial art arose in the world until after many centuries it emerged once more in Egypt and Crete, under the incentive of the new civilization due to the discovery of metals.

Neolithic sculpture and art is decorative rather than representational and a comparison of the menhir from Aveyron (France) with the woman of Dordogne shows the wholly different approach to art. It is inconceivable that the carver of the menhir thought he was making a semblance of a woman ; the decorative stylism is crude, but it is quite deliberate, and in these two differing sculptures are the germs of the two great divisions in art—the narrative and pictorial, and the decorative and symbolical ; it is clear that the narrative is the older, but the two divisions persist throughout art history. But these Neolithics made a great contribution to the world and to the evolution of art.

They were the first builders and to them we owe the great art of architecture. The building of even the simplest dolmen—a sort of imitation cave, usually three monolith walls and a large roof stone, was only possible by the organized communal efforts of large numbers of men. The transition from the dolmen and the tumulus to the rock-cut tombs and the mastabas of Egypt is a simple development, so from the menhir to the obelisk with its story-telling hieroglyphics and to the commemorative or religious statue is a continuous process of gradual growth.

At this dawn of history there was the beginning of civilized life, requiring co-operative effort, and involving the handing on of the experience of one generation to the next, and so there was established that kind of continuity between the past and the present—broken and fitful as it may be at times—which is embodied in the word tradition. This inheritance of tradition (though too often derided today) is one of the marks of a high civilization, of a people, like the Egyptians and Babylonians who looked back to a past and forward to a future. They erected monuments of an almost indestructible character ; they covered them with pictured inscriptions to tell all succeeding generations of what they had accomplished. They did this, not only because they possessed the art of writing, but primarily because they had a dawning consciousness of the continuity of the heritage of tradition.

EGYPTIAN SCULPTURE

Mr CHESTERTON once wrote a history of England which recorded only one date, and that, as he observed with disarming candour, was probably wrong ! I had meant originally to follow his example because Egyptian chronology was for long a matter of controversy with wide discrepancies, particularly with regard to the dates of early dynasties. And for the purpose of this book, exact dating is of less importance than the endeavour to suggest the fundamental ideas which directed the inception and the development of Egyptian Art. But, as I understand that virtual agreement has now been reached among Egyptologists as to chronology, I give the dates as in Bædeker's *Egypt*, English Edition 1929 (Steindorff).

Menes, *c*. 3200 B.C. first dynasty

Old Kingdom, 2780-2270 B.C. third to sixth dynasty

Middle Kingdom, 2100-1790 B.C. eleventh and twelfth dynasty

New Kingdom, 1555-1150 B.C. eighteenth to twentieth dynasty

Late Dynastic Period to Persian conquest, 1150-525 B.C.

including Saite Period (twenty-sixth dynasty), 663-525 B.C.

These dates correspond closely to those given by Erman who also points out that Ancient Egypt was a small country, about the size of Belgium, with a population, according to Diodorus, of about seven million (today about five million).

The essential facts of Egyptian history which it is necessary to grasp and hold firmly are really only two vivid phrases : that of Herodotus, " Egypt is the gift of the Nile ", and that Egyptian civilization began in the North, so that " as one ascends the Nile one descends the stream of time ". (There was a return to the Delta in the New Kingdom.) The great significance of the Nile flood in the development of agriculture and civilization must always be remembered. It affected the whole life and religion of Egypt. At the first historic period of Egypt, the Old Kingdom, its art is found apparently fully developed and one is reminded of the myth of Athena springing fully grown and armed from the head of Zeus at a blow from the hammer of Hephæstus. And in this Old Kingdom art was produced in a civilization " unhelped by the electric current of foreign contact ", and it was on a vast scale, so that it has been said that from the third to the sixth dynasty, Egypt produced more statues than in all her subsequent history ! But it is inconceivable that art could reach the perfection of the early dynastic sculpture without a long period of training and development. Flinders Petrie demands 2000 years as necessary for

20

this time of development, which carries back the date of the early prehistoric work to about 5000 B.C. Of this prehistoric and predynastic work little need here be said.

There are small ivory figures in the Ashmolean Museum, and a number of small animal forms, mostly carved in ivory, though some are flint. There are engraved and incised slates and stones, the most striking being the large stone slabs found by Petrie at Koptos, and those represent the God Min, the procreative male principle. In these the figure and limbs are only suggested by incised lines while the slab itself is hardly shaped.

There are clay figures of women, of the type known as steatopygous, with enormous thighs, a phenomenon repeated in relatively modern Bushman primitive drawings. But if the predynastic representations of the human figure are often very crude, there was great skill shown in other arts. Hard stone vases were carved and ground with emery so truly that hardly any irregularity can be detected in their surfaces. Strangely enough it is in the pre- and early dynastic times that the hardest stones, diorite and porphyry, were used. Later, the Egyptians worked the softer stones, until by the twelfth dynasty serpentine and alabaster were chiefly used and the art of hard stone vase making was apparently lost.

It is strange and characteristic that when they made clay vases they often indicated on the surface whorls and spirals, a reminiscence of the spiral shells so often found in the stone, and this survival of the character- istics of one material into the decoration of another material is constantly met with in primitive art. There is an ivory mace in the British Museum which looks as if it were a translation into a ceremonial mace of a weapon made of spiked bones interlaced with thongs.

But by the time of the Old Kingdom the figure sculptors had reached the height of technical skill, and, indeed, they never in any succeeding age surpassed the vivid realism of this earlier work with its great distinction of personality. This personal and highly individualized portraiture is no accidental quality in Egyptian art : and the explanation of their pre- occupation with individual resemblance is to be found in their religious beliefs. For the almost illusive realism of these early sculptures was sought for a definite religious end. It was to persuade the soul, or spirit, of the dead to reside in the duplicated body of the statue. The hunger for personal immortality was already ancient, and the Egyptian, desirous above all this survival of the soul, made statues as auxiliary bodies in which the soul could live after the inevitable decay of the natural body. This is the central tenet of Egyptian religion, and thus it is that the element of almost illusive portraiture and its influence on the destiny of the soul, is the focus and the explanation of Egyptian sculpture. Egypt, though thousands of its statues have survived, was not a land peopled with statues. Most of these figures were closed up in tombs (as the people thought, forever) and all this beautiful vivid naturalism with its moving appeal was for the soul only and was not meant to be seen by any human eye. And it is hardly realized even yet how far they carried this pursuit of realism. These statues, when carved in wood or the softer stones, in chalk, limestone,

21

or sandstone, were coated with fine plaster and elaborately painted. The hard stone figures—granite, diorite, etc.—used for greater permanence, were less elaborately painted. The eyes were often made (as in the famous Sheikh El Beled and Nefret statues in Cairo) of white quartz with coloured stone or crystal irises. These eyes were fitted into the face with bronze eyelid settings, and real wigs and real clothes may have been added. The bodies and limbs were often treated rather summarily—these being the less variable element—the sculptors lavishing all their skill and delicacy of workmanship on the face. They thus achieved a beauty on the highest plane of reality, unsurpassed by any later art. The care taken to get exact portraiture may be seen in the fact that, even as early as the sixth dynasty, they sometimes took death masks in plaster or gypsum, presumably as a guide to the sculptor. A cast from one of those masks is in the British Museum.

The essentials of this Old Kingdom sculpture are thus summed up by Petrie :[1]

" The sculptors' work, and the painters', show the same sentiment, a rivalry of nature. They did not make a work of art to please the taste as such, but they rivalled nature as closely as possible : the form, the expression, the colouring, the glittering transparent eye, the grave smile, all are copied as if to make an artificial man. The painter mixed his half tints and his delicate shades, and dappled over the animals or figured the feathers of the birds in a manner never attempted in the later ages. The embalmer built up the semblance of a man in resins and cloth over his shrunken corpse to make him as nearly as possible what he was when alive. . . . In each direction man, then, set himself to supplement, to imitate, to rival, or to exceed the works of nature. Art as the gratification of an artificial taste and standard was scarcely in existence, but the simplicity, the vastness, the perfection and the beauty of the earliest works place them on a different level to all works of art and man's device in later ages. They are unique in their splendid power, which no self-conscious civilization has ever rivalled ; and in their enduring greatness they may last till all the feebler works of man have perished." All this elaborate care could, of course, only be for rich people ; the common labourer had to bury his dead in a pit on the margin of the desert, in the hope of a future, with only food for the journey and, at most, a rude clay figure for the abode of the soul. But the nemesis of all great ideas is apt to be their crystallization from form into formula, and perhaps it was inevitable that as religion changed and developed, this fine realism of the early sculptors should give way to more symbolism, and symbolism, being a formula for spiritual truth, rather than a vivifying idea, itself was gradually superseded by convention. But symbolism, though a formula, is a formula for a mystery, and in studying conventions one must distinguish between routine repetition and the self-imposed conventions of technique due to intractable materials.

[1] " History of Egypt."

The development of their religion had a definite bearing on Egyptian art not only at its birth, but throughout its whole course. Their religion began as a sort of fetishism, which gradually developed into a polytheistic animism. The ibis, the hawk, the vulture, the crocodile, the cat, were all worshipped as local totemistic deities. To give a certain nobility of form to these deities the heads only were animal, the bodies were usually human. It is strange that the Egyptian crocodile-headed creature who is represented as waiting to devour the condemned soul strongly resembles the wide-mouthed monster which represents Hell in all mediæval art. Having thus given form to the Gods the Egyptian artists were content endlessly to repeat these formulæ. This animism and the petrifying finality of definition in the forms of the gods narrowed the range of the artists and kept them from the search for new modes of expression and new forms in which to embody new and vital truths. Strangely enough, when the Greeks adopted part animal and part human forms to their deities, they chose to make the noblest part the human one, and the centaur, the satyr, and the river gods had animal bodies below the waist but human heads and trunks. It is characteristic that the Greeks added wings to the Egyptian human-headed Sphinx, though the winged lion is probably an Egyptian invention.

But if the pursuit of realism and their temperamental love of repetition and symbolism tended to prevent Egyptian sculptors from the search for that ideal quality so marked in Greek art, it gave other and very noble qualities to their work. The pursuit of realism, as we shall see, destroyed Greek art but the Egyptian pursuit of reality, perhaps because it was for a deep, instinctive religious end, gave the sculptors that mastery of technique which is so marked in the whole course of Egyptian art. This reverent religious sense gave to their work that deliberate reserve, while their conscious acceptance of the limitations of the material led them to subtle and beautiful simplifications of form. These great statues in granite and diorite, and the vast stone figures like the great Sphinx and the Colossi of Thebes have about them something of the eternal immobility of stone and nothing but the mastery of genius could have shaped diorite to that divine and impassive calm which pervades the great statue of Kephren at Cairo. If one understands that figure, and one of the more obviously realistic ones like Nefret, or the Sheikh el Beled, then one knows what those Old Kingdom sculptors did for art. Egyptian sculpture divides sharply into royal and official portraiture and the more humble genre portraits, but all are funerary and religious. The work of the twelfth dynasty is typical of the second great epoch of Egyptian art. It is of a more fixed and traditional type, but its noble and heroic style had not yet become a convention. It has a very beautiful reserve and is finished like a cameo. The black granite statues of Amenemhet III in the British Museum are typical examples of this period, and especially of exquisite finish and delicacy. These four statues are marvellously alike, every subtlety of contour in the face being reproduced in all. Portraiture with a conscious stylism and noble dignity can go no further. At the end of this middle period of Egyptian history occurred that troubled time known as the

" Hyksos " invasion and there was a foreign infiltration which left its mark on their art. After the long struggle which ended in the expulsion of those invaders, Egypt became definitely a great empire building state with, for the first time in history, a standing army, and (as the Hyksos had brought horses) chariots and horses became common subjects in Egyptian art. The religious ritual of the dead had changed. The little tomb chamber adjoining the actual sepulchre had become an elaborate and large tomb chapel, and the dead had become almost deified. As evidence that they were now regarded as eternally dwelling with the gods, the dead were often urged to intercede with the gods on behalf of the living, while little figures of wood, stone or faience were put in the tombs in large numbers to wait on the dead. These are the familiar " Shawabtis ". The small temple chapel was gradually enlarged till in the time of Amenhotep III nearly all the elements of the Christian basilica were to be found there. There was a higher central area to the pillared nave, and the " clerestory " thus made, already foreshadowed in Old Kingdom building, was filled with fretted stone or alabaster to admit light.

The vast colossi on the plain of Thebes are of this Pharaoh. These were originally about 70 feet high and weighed at least 700 tons. They were monoliths and must have been conveyed some 500 miles from the quartzite quarries of Gebel-el-Ahmar near Cairo. The son of this Amenhotep III was the famous heretic Akhenaton, who sought to destroy the animal polytheism of the earlier religion and to worship the sun as the source of all life. Beginning in the reign of Amenhotep III, and contemporaneously with Akhenaton and his new point of view, there arose a fresh and less conventional art, and, especially in decorative painting, a phase of vivid naturalism, something akin to that desire for truthful representation which made Cromwell want to be painted " wart and all ". So Akhenaton demanded less stylism and less formalism. This is seen in the many representations of himself and his wife Nefretiti in little intimate domestic scenes. Akhenaton is generally represented with the curious limp stance of a delicate man, (he was probably epileptic) and both he and Nefretiti show a strange and abnormal development of thigh. These characteristics are to be seen in most of the reliefs showing them together. In the small limestone statue of Nefretiti in the British Museum the strange thighs are most marked, and it can be no accidental characteristic, for the quality of the carving is accomplished to the point of exquisiteness. As early as the eighteenth dynasty, the bodily characteristics of the King tended to set a standard type, and were often copied into other official portrait sculpture. In the reign of Akhenaton for the first time in Egyptian art the foot was drawn from the outer side with the toes which belong to it. This innovation survived, though in the priestly revival after Akhenaton's death a great effort was made to re-establish the orthodoxy of art as well as of religion. Many representations of Akhenaton show not only realistic skill, but even caricature, in which all the characteristics of face and figure are boldly exaggerated, and in the tender and lovely torso of one of the daughters there is an exquisite sensitiveness rivalling Greek work at its finest. Another

Neolithic sculpture is decorative rather than representational and its deliberate convention contrasts with the attempted realism of the Paleolithics.

1. PALEOLITHIC STONE CARVING OF WOMAN FROM THE DORDOGNE

2. NEOLITHIC STONE MENHIR FROM SAINT-SERNIN, AVEYRON

PRIMITIVE SCULPTURE

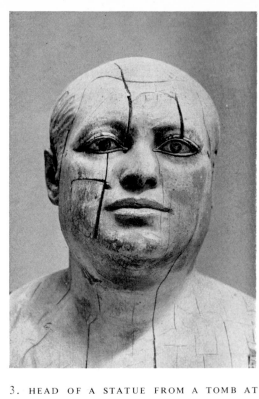

3. HEAD OF A STATUE FROM A TOMB AT
SAKKARA : ACACIA WOOD : OLD KINGDOM,
FIFTH DYNASTY *c*.2600 B.C. CAIRO MUSEUM

The search for realism.
The head, above, shows
almost illusive realism, highly
individualised. Note the
asymmetry of the nose, the
inset eyes.
The surface
was originally coated
with gesso and painted ;
the glass or quartz eyes
set in bronze rims.

4. STATUE OF A NOBLEMAN: BLACK GRANITE :
DYNASTIES ONE-THREE: BRITISH MUSEUM

5. STATUE OF KEPHREN
DIORITE
FOURTH DYNASTY *c*.2800 B.C.
CAIRO MUSEUM

The head is more
realistic and individual
than the figure which is
not freed from the
throne at any point, a
convention partly due to
the brittle intractability
of the material.

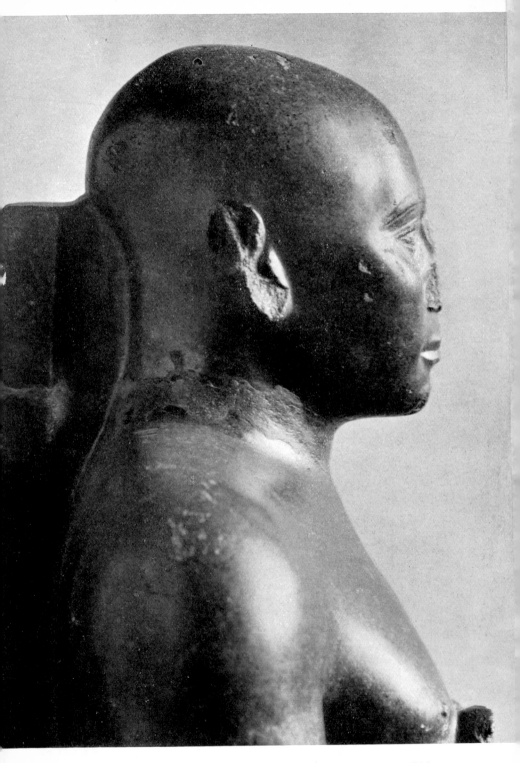

6. PORTRAIT OF A MAN: GREEN BASALT: SAITIC PERIOD AFTER 700 B.C.

The attempted return to the realism of the Old Kingdom sculpture.

7. ROYAL HEAD: RED SAND-
STONE: MIDDLE KINGDOM,
TWELFTH DYNASTY: THE LOUVRE.

8. RIGHT: HEAD OF AMENEMHET
III: OBSIDIAN: MIDDLE KINGDOM,
LATE TWELFTH DYNASTY: COL-
LECTION, M. C. S. GULBENKIAN

EGYPTIAN SCULPTURE

9. TORSO OF A DAUGHTER
OF AKHENATON: LIMESTONE:
NEW KINGDOM, EIGHTEENTH
DYNASTY: FROM EL AMARNA:
UNIVERSITY COLLEGE, LONDON

10. FIGURE OF AN EARLY
SUMERIAN ROYAL PERSONAGE
OR OFFICIAL: STONE:
BEFORE 2500 B.C.: FROM
TELL LO: BRITISH MUSEUM

11. HEADLESS STANDING
GUDEA FROM CHALDEA:
BASALT:
c.3000 B.C.: THE LOUVRE

12. HEAD OF GUDEA:
DIORITE: THE LOUVRE

Granite and restricted tools
were factors in determining
the simplifications of surfaces
which give such marked style
to the Gudea statues. It would
seem almost as if a hard and
difficult medium did, of itself,
give a dignity to sculpture.

13. SEATED GUDEA FROM CHALDEA
DIORITE: *c.*2500 B.C. : THE LOUVRE

BABYLONIA AND ASSYRIA

14. SPHINX DE MENEPHTAH: RED GRANITE: NINETEENTH DYNASTY: THE LOUVRE

15. FACADE OF THE GREAT TEMPLE,
ABU-SIMBEL: NINETEENTH DYNASTY
c.1250 B.C.   SANDSTONE

The gigantic scale of the sandstone carvings of Rameses III. A simplified and architectonic style suitable to the scale, much less realistic than life-sized statues. Kingly but cold and formal.

curious point was that Akhenaton reiterated the old belief that the seat of the mind was in the heart and abdomen and that the controlling power was the spoken " Word " ; perhaps herein lay the germ of the Greek doctrine of the " Logos ". Like Mycerinus he might be said to have lived " Ennobling that dull pomp, the life of Kings, by contemplation of diviner things ". Yet this great king and fine thinker is summarily dismissed by R. H. Hall as " a foolish idealist and pacifist " ! Flinders Petrie says that " after Akhenaton everything is descent ", a generalization which has to except many beautiful examples, especially of the nineteenth and twenty-sixth dynasties.

Fine examples of the work of the New Kingdom are to be seen in the British Museum. There are four black granite statues of the lion-headed goddess Sekhmet of the most perfect, if slightly conventional style, and a red granite monument of Thothmes III, with figures in relief, which is remarkable for the very subtle simplification of forms adopted by the sculptor to suit the intractable material. As examples of carving in a hard and very difficult material these can hardly be rivalled by any later art. The freer treatment of wood is well shown in three life-sized statues of the nineteenth dynasty which still show traces of paint and though the eye sockets are empty, the eyes were evidently inserted separately and were probably of quartz and crystal. The eyebrows are deeply sunk channels which must have been filled with a dark substance—glass or enamel. Of the eighteenth dynasty there is a group of a priest and his wife in limestone, and here the sculptor has allowed himself the utmost delicacy of detail, though still adhering to the conventional flat joining up of planes, so necessary in hard granite or basalt, so much less necessary in this soft and even-grained limestone. This dynasty is the period of great priestly power, for after Akhenaton the priests assumed control not only of the religious and sacerdotal functions, but they even usurped kingly powers. The people were impoverished, though one person in every fifty was a temple slave. The state priesthood owned half a million cattle, 169 towns, a large fleet, and 53 shipyards.[1] This immense priestly power was, as Erman[2] says, " maintained by the religious fanaticism of a decaying nation ", and it is typical that in the tomb paintings " barren religious representations then took the place of the old bright pictures of daily life ". The power of the rich priestly class which constituted the nobility may be traced in the vast and splendid architecture at Karnak, Abu Simbel and Luxor. A certain cold formalism is evident in much of the sculpture, as in the Menephtah statue (the Pharaoh of the hard heart) and even the great scale and fine craftsmanship can hardly atone for the lack of feeling and intensity.

Flinders Petrie shows clearly that the great schools of sculpture arose and flourished for many centuries at the places where the material was quarried and he argues, with a true craftsman's instinct, that men who learned sculpture on soft lime or sandstone would be helpless on granite

[1] Breasted, " History of Egypt."

[2] A. Erman, " Life in Ancient Egypt."

25

and diorite. From this and from pictorial representation of their transit, he assumes that statues were generally carved where the stone was quarried and were seldom worked *in situ*. The main schools were : the Basalt, Diorite and Hardstone Carvers of the Eastern Desert, the Limestone School of Memphis and Middle Egypt, the Quartzite Sandstone School of Gebel el Ahmar, and the Nubian Sandstone School, which provided the main works of the eighteenth and nineteenth dynasties in Upper Egypt. It seems clear that the work in hard stone is on the whole finer than that in lime and sandstone, as if the intractability of the material had imposed a severe nobility of style on the carvers. A notable instance of this is the twelfth dynasty head carved in obsidian, than which nothing nobler has been done in portraiture in the history of art. Perhaps it is even possible that some of this skill was inherited and transmitted through generations. Artists had a high status and Erman notes that the longest genealogy which has been found is of a family of artists. The great Rameses at Turin shows the hardstone sculpture of the Empire at its highest, while the colossal statues of the same Pharaoh at Abu Simbel are much more formal and expressionless. From the nineteenth dynasty onwards this cold mechanical style becomes commoner, though its course was inter-rupted by what is called the Saite Revival. This was in the twenty-sixth dynasty (seventh and sixth centuries, B.C.) when, after a period of tur-bulence, there was a sort of Renaissance (like the Greek archaistic revival) under the rule of a dynasty who originated as Princes of Sais.

At this time the people looked back to the period of the Old Kingdom as the finest days in the life and history of Egypt, and they tried to recapture in their art the fresh and vivid realism of those ancient days. The sculptures of the Old Kingdom were studied afresh and some works of unique beauty were produced. But even the skilful copying of a long past style, aided by that wistful, retrospective spirit which revived old religious forms of worship and art, could not produce works of vital and enduring power, though it did produce some works of great beauty, and perhaps for the first time in history there appeared a strange quality which can only be described as " elaborate elegance ". These *soignée*, exquisite women of of the Saite reliefs have about them something of the graceful artificiality of the shepherdesses of eighteenth century French art, but at the best it was a revived, derivative art and seeking its inspiration at second hand, as it were, it lacked the enduring force of great art, which Antæus-like, draws its vitality from contact with nature. All great art has a certain timeless quality and by this may be known ; words like realism, archaism, artifici-ality, should not arise as one contemplates it.

This art of Egypt remained almost untouched by outside influences, though in Ptolemaic times the curved archaic smile of early Greek sculpture was carefully copied. The view that Egyptian art remained fixed and static for forty centuries is commonly held, but a very little study shows it to be quite untrue. Plato in the fourth century B.C. visited Egypt and to his Greek mind he found Egyptian art monstrous and monotonously alike, though he admired this changeless quality. On returning to Greece he wrote the *Laws* in which he recalls the Egyptian outlook :

" Long ago they appear to have recognized the very principle of which we are now speaking—that their young citizens must be habituated to forms and strains of virtue. These they fixed, and exhibited patterns of them in their temples ; no painter, no artist is allowed to innovate, or to leave the traditional forms and invent others. To this day no alteration is allowed either in their arts or music at all ; and you will find that their works of art are painted or moulded in the same forms that they had ten thousand years ago—their ancient paintings and sculptures are not a whit better or worse than their work of today, but made with just the same skill."

Cleinias : " How extraordinary "

Plato : " How wise and worthy of a great legislator."

That view of Egyptian art persists to this day though it is rather less than half true. Gibbon characteristically dismissed all Egyptian art as " contemptible " ! Professor Huxley in the nineteenth century praised Old Kingdom sculpture but added that " the priests got hold of it and petrified it ". E. F. Benson in 1921 attacked it thus :

" There was something old and evil in Egypt, as tired as Ecclesiastes ; it preached Vanitas Vanitatis—its relentless hands reared the pyramids, which must stand forever as monuments of unimaginative construction and lost labour. . . . What monsters, to an Attic pilgrim, were these gods, conceived not in the kindly image of humanity, but as out of some incestuous menagerie. As by some disordered dream of a religious maniac, the hawk-faced god had a cobra for symbol of his divinity ; a cow, a cat or a lion had mated with a man and the offspring sat there bleak and appalling. This gigantic and hopeless art, bound hand and foot by the fetters of hieratic tradition, could do no more than multiply monoliths, incredulous of its own greatness, and untinged with the living colour of humanity."[1] Such did Egyptian art seem to the ancient and to the modern Hellene. This attitude, though hallowed by age and supported by the great name of Plato, is nevertheless not the whole truth and a closer acquaintance with Egyptian art shows that it underwent many changes and modifications. A point to be noted is that few writers about Egyptian art have recognized adequately its unique technical excellence, which in certain respects is unparalleled. Little is known of the tools and processes of Egyptian sculptors. Granite hammers were used to bruise the stone and gradually free it ; chisels of copper, and possibly in late times of iron, were fixed in wooden handles and used with a wooden mallet. For wood sculpture a small adze would seem to have been the principal tool, and the wood was generally acacia or sycamore. A round wooden mallet is in the Metropolitan Museum, New York, and if it were laid on a modern stonemason's " banker ", it would pass for a worn mallet of today. The museum also has two copper " points " and a copper chisel about an inch wide of the twelfth and nineteenth dynasties, presumably used for stone carving.

[1] E. F. Benson " Family Affairs."

Stone was broken out of the quarries by pounding with granite hammers along a marked line. Limestone and granite were split by drilling holes, driving in wood wedges and swelling these with water, just as is done today. (This at least in late dynastic times.) Emery and other abrasives were largely used. Indeed, a head such as the twelfth dynasty obsidian head, (see illustration, plate 8), must have been largely done by persistent abrasion, for, obsidian being volcanic glass, only a volcano would melt it, and the best tempered steel tools of today will not cut it. Drills were much used and even tubular drills with jewel points for working hard stones. (Interesting details about tools and technique are to be found in Petrie's *Pyramids and Temples of Gizeh*.) Flinders Petrie in *Seventy Years in Archæology* tells of his finding at Naucratis a collection of iron chisels which could be dated about 600 B.C., which he sent to the British Museum, only later to find that the authorities there had thrown them out as " ugly things ". A strange story, and a grave misjudgment and loss !

As a rough generalization, Egyptian art was most realistic in its earlier stages, and its course for four or five thousand years was a gradual progress towards convention. This passage from form to formula was noted by Champollion in the striking phrase " Egyptian Art knew only decay ". But though the conspicuous realism of Old and Middle Kingdom sculpture was never again found till the epoch of Græco-Roman portraiture, there is some subtle but vital difference between the realism of these two great schools of sculpture. So also there is a strange difference between the realism of the Saite period, which might be described as being concerned with the exterior aspect of the face, its bony ridges, tendons and muscles, while the earlier sculptors, searching for a clearness of definition with a passionate desire for truth of representation, not for its own sake, but to make a recognizable dwelling place for the soul, created the noblest realistic sculpture in history. This question as to the limits of realism in art will recur again and again in considering the development of every great epoch of sculpture, but no sketch, however slight, of Egyptian sculpture can ignore the cardinal fact that the pursuit of realism for a definite religious end is its central idea, and gives to the whole art of Egypt its deep significance and spiritual power.

And it is to be remembered that this art of Egypt was probably the first national art to arise on the earth. It thus acquires an added significance. Whether we accept or reject the theory of the diffusion of all culture from the Nile Basin, we are forced to recognize the claim that in Egypt life first reached a high standard of culture, and that the motive force behind all her great achievement in cultured life—in architecture, which still conveys a deep religious sense—in sculpture, which still moves us by its profound reverence and technical beauty—in literature (it is the origin and inspiration of some of the greatest passages in the Psalms)—was that sense of spiritual values which was the soul of Egypt and through which her art must be studied if we would know and understand it.

" Babylon is taken, Bel is confounded, Merodach is broken in pieces ;
for out of the North there cometh up a nation against her, which shall
make her land desolate, and none shall dwell therein."

BABYLONIAN & ASSYRIAN

MESOPOTAMIA—the Greek name for that vast country " between the
rivers " Tigris and Euphrates—offers strange differences from the land of
Egypt—that country of one river, one race, one religion, one almost
changeless culture, and solemn, hieratic art. The sculpture of Mesopotamia
divides more readily into epochs and shows more marked differences,
though its course covers a shorter period, than that of Egypt. The two
thousand five hundred years of this great civilization, the records of which
are left not only in their art, but in actual written inscriptions in cuneiform
writing—perhaps a graphic invention of the Sumerians, a non-Semitic
race, who occupied the northern portion of the land—yield a great deal
of historical data, especially with regard to temple building, and rebuilding.
These works, it would seem, were often regarded by the priest-kings as
of more significance and importance than military achievements. In
religion, science, literature, commerce and art the Babylonian peoples
exerted a powerful influence on the world. Even our watches are a reminder
to us that it is to Babylonian science that we owe the division into sixties
by which time is still calculated.

The twenty-five centuries are usually divided into three epochs :

1. First Ancient Babylonian Kingdom, about eighteen hundred
years, beginning *c.* 3000 B.C.

2. The Assyrian Ascendancy of six hundred years, *c.* 1200—600 B.C.

3. The Late Babylonian Epoch, a brief period of great building
activity and glory under Nebuchadnezzar, of about sixty years, after which
it was absorbed into the Empire of Persia.

Bab-ilu, The Gate of the God, was the traditional home of Abraham
and has been known to the whole Western World since the days of
Herodotus. The Macedonian Alexander the Great died there in 323 B.C.
Like that of Egypt, this Mesopotamian culture was based on agricultural
richness ; two or three wheat crops—the yield often three hundredfold—
could be raised in one year. There was little stone for building or sculpture,
but excellent clay was to be had everywhere from the rich alluvial soil.
This was sun-baked into bricks, and Babylonian or Chaldean architecture
was almost wholly brick building, faced either with glazed faience, or with
thin stone slabs. Their architecture consisted almost wholly of palaces and
fortifications. These sun-baked brick buildings decayed rapidly when
cities were deserted. Xenophon on the famous retreat of the ten thousand
traversed the site of Nineveh only two hundred years after its destruction
and found nothing but ruins—a deserted city the name and memory of
which had been forgotten. The perishable nature of Babylonian building

is perhaps the chief reason why it has had so little enduring effect on the architecture of the world. Incidentally the plan of the great Assyrian palace at Khorsabad is a rambling rabbit warren, compared to the symmetry and mystery of an Egyptian temple. In the more mountainous regions of the North the Assyrians had stone, and vast quantities of alabaster, a soft and easily carved stone, much used for their relief sculpture. From the earliest ages these Mesopotamian sculptors worked in the hard stones such as granite and diorite—which, with copper for tools, could be traded from the Arabian shore of the Persian Gulf—as well as in such local stone as could be found. Of the sculpture of the earlier Babylonian period the most remarkable and significant are twelve statues in black diorite of a certain Gudea of Lagash, who was a priest-king about 2450 B.C. These were found at Tell lo much broken so that only two of the heads could be fitted to the bodies. They are typical works of sculpture in a hard and difficult medium. The squat proportions, the compactness and entire absence of projections, the smoothly rubbed surfaces are all indications of a stylism forced on the sculptors by the intractability of the material. Much of the carving must have been done by bruising with flint or granite hammers. It is possible they had bronze chisels, though little is yet known as to the possibility of tempering and hardening copper so that it could cut so hard a material ; the sharp details of the eyes and features suggest the use of metal chisels. Copper was known and common in Egypt, but it is not known from what source the Babylonians got the tin required to make bronze tools. A very hard alloy of copper must have been used. Iron was unknown till about the time of the Assyrians. As late as Homer it was so rare that a piece or iron constituted one of the prizes at the funeral games of Patroclus. Emery or some such abrasive was used to finish the surfaces.

On one of the statues is an inscription recording how the diorite of which it is made was fetched in ships from distant Sinai. The quarries from which Gudea fetched his diorite were probably the same as the Egyptians used—and perhaps too the tools and technique were also similar—yet the results were wholly different. Sumerian statues were commemorative rather than religious in intention, and conventional in form. For them, unlike the Egyptian, no realistic image was needed to enable the soul to recognize its habitation. These Gudea statues were meant to be, as it were, his deputies. " They were to stand before Nin-girsu for ever, a visible incorporation of Gudea's worship and prayer." This kingly and warlike art with its brutal strength, its fierce and almost truculent definition of muscles, is strangely different from the quiet art of the Egyptian whose wish was to live with the gods, and " None can come there but he whose heart is true and does right ". These sculptures of Gudea have been much studied and even almost copied by some modern sculptors interested in problems of simplification of form, but stylisms arising from simplifications due to material can never be dissociated from that material, and to assimilate and copy these broad and simple surfaces into any other material is to miss their implications and distort their meaning. The flat surfaces of these Gudean statues are often covered with cuneiform inscriptions, and on one of the statues of Gudea as architect there is engraved on the flat slab on his knees the plan of a temple. (A brilliant modern use of inscriptions running uninterruptedly across sculptured forms is to be found in the sculpture by Lee Lawrie on the State Capitol at Lincoln, Nebraska, which, though in no sense imitative, yet owes much to Mesopotamian sculpture). Hammurabi *c.* 2000 B.C., whose portrait in a stone bas-relief may be seen in the British Museum, is the great king and law-giver whose codification of laws inscribed on a granite stele was set up beside his statue as " The King of Righteousness, who established the heart of the land in Righteousness ". He is perhaps the Amraphel of Shinar, referred to in Genesis, chapter 14.

Of the period of Assyrian Ascendancy, 1200-600 B.C., the statue of Assur-Nasir-Pal III, found by Layard and now in the British Museum, is typical. The heavy robe with its elaborate fringes, which completely obscures the figure underneath, the stolid immobile pillar-like figure, is in marked contrast to the work of the Sumerian sculptors of the Lagash statues. The eyebrows are rendered by deep sinkings, but probably these were once filled—as in Egyptian work—with a black bituminous paste or enamel. In the relief sculpture of the same King with a winged Deity, the legs are nude and the anatomy is entirely decorative and conventional, bearing little relation to anatomical structure, though it conveys an impression of strength and power. But these Mesopotamians considered it shameful to be unclad, so that no study of the figure was possible to the sculptors. The heavy draperies were probably partly ceremonial and partly necessary owing to the capricious climatic conditions. The features usually show the fierce semitic nose, hard frowning eyes and elaborately curled beards, and these works of the time of Assur-Nasir-Pal, both statues and reliefs, are stamped with the ferocity of the race. The Semitic Assyrians were hampered by the Hebraic uncompromising prohibition of portraiture in any form. They made many images but no likenessess. The same head did duty for the great winged bulls or lions which guarded their palace entrances. The Assyrian passion was to glorify the power and cruelty of war—the great eagle's wings symbolized his swiftness, the lion and the bull symbolized his strength and fierceness.

A pitiless blood lust pervades almost all Assyrian sculpture, for which there is no parallel in Egyptian or any succeeding work. Most of this Assyrian work is in softer stone and the long series of relief sculptures in the British Museum are in alabaster. This is in marked contrast to the earlier Babylonian sculpture which was usually in imported hard stone, like granite and diorite. But the Assyrians worked also in hard stones. They invented a sort of compromise between sculpture in the round and in relief. The most interesting examples of this are the great limestone monsters, guardians of the gateway to the palace of Assur-Nasir-Pal. These have the head of a bearded man, the body of a lion, and wings of a giant bird. They have great dignity and an impressive nobility, and are remarkable for their very skilful adaptation to relief, by the addition to the body of a fifth leg ! Seen from the side as relief sculpture they show four legs in the traditional animal walking movement. Seen from the front they show two fore legs and look like the front view of a human-headed animal represented in the round. It is a brilliant device and wholly successful. In true relief sculpture—as the long series in the British Museum show—these Assyrians excelled ; and, in the whole course of the history of sculpture, it would be hard to rival and impossible to excel their skill in the representation of animals. The subjects represented are monotonously restricted, kings hunting, kings killing, kings offering sacrifice, the horses with elaborate trappings, the hunted animals, running, wounded and dying, the carving always vigorous and conveying an impression of power. The relief treatment is at once decorative and pictorial ; decorative in its design and in the delighted preoccupation with trappings, tassels, fringes and such details ; pictorial in its freedom and movement. This whole series of reliefs is in strange and significant contrast to contemporary Egyptian work under the Princes of Sais, which looked back to Old Kingdom models and reinterpreted these with great delicacy and refinement. All this Assyrian work is always adequate narrative sculpture and tells the story with complete success, even though the subjects are restricted and sometimes revolting, as in the wounded lioness and the lion vomiting blood in the relief in the British Museum. The bronze gates from the palace of Shalmaneser show that, as early as the ninth century B.C., these artists could do vivid and skilful representations of the military expeditions of that King. These were hammered in raised relief in sheet bronze, the relief being hammered from the back and finished from the front, the method still used by metal workers and known as repoussé. Of the last Babylonian period under the Nebuchadnezzars the best known of its achievements are the so-called Hanging Gardens of Babylon—one of the seven wonders of the Ancient World. Their architecture was impressive in form and rich and beautiful in colour. The use of glazed bricks brilliantly coloured and with designs and animals modelled in relief show architectural sculpture at a very high standard. The superb bulls and winged dragons on the Ishtar gate of Babylon in moulded brick and coloured glaze are works of great skill and dignity. The treatment of wings is always beautiful and distinctive and has great decorative effect. In this and in the treatment of animals in relief, they are supreme. Women hardly exist in their art at any period and all their art is directed towards the glorification of kings and the enrichment of kings' palaces. War, hunting and killing are the constantly recurring themes, and superb as is their skill, the ever-present ferocity and the monotony of type and subject lessen the appeal, and we turn with a sense of relief to the true Semitic mode of expression, their great creative art of literature. Iron was the fact behind their vast military power, and iron remains their fitting symbol. In the books of Nahum and Zephaniah may still be read the pæans of praise at the destruction of this great Assyrian empire. " Thy shepherds slumber, O king of Assyria, Thy nobles shall dwell in the dust ! Thy people is scattered upon the mountains, and no man gathereth them."

16. LION FROM THE SIDE OF A DOORWAY IN THE PALACE OF ASSUR-NASIR-PAL: TWENTYSECOND–TWENTYFOURTH DYNASTY, 885–860 B.C.: BRITISH MUSEUM

A comparison of these two great lions shows and typifies the two different peoples. The Egyptian lion is powerful and serenely watchful—a true guardian of temple or palace. The Assyrian lion is striding out fiercely to meet and destroy any possible foe.

17. LION FROM THE TEMPLE OF SOLEB : RED GRANITE : EIGHTEENTH DYNASTY *c.*1400 B.C. : BRITISH MUSEUM

BABYLONIA AND ASSYRIA

In Egyptian reliefs, especially of the Rameses, the difference in scale of the various figures is so great that it is obviously a symbolic convention attributing immense power to the king. Whether due to a studied effort at perspective or simply a device to give prominence to the king an illusive suggestion of distance is achieved in Assyrian reliefs by the lesser variation in size of the figures. The stolid, immobile, pillar-like figure is typical of the period of Assyrian ascendancy, 1200-600 B.C., and in marked contrast to the work of the Sumerian sculptors of the Lagash statues. The features usually show the fierce semitic nose, hard frowning eyes and elaborately curled beards, stamped with the ferocity of the race. These Mesopotamians considered it shameful to be unclad, so that no study of the figure was possible to the sculptors. The heavy draperies which completely obscured the figure underneath were probably partly ceremonial and partly necessary owing to the capricious climatic conditions. This is the only statue in the round surviving.

18. BAS-RELIEF PALACE OF ASSURBANIPAL AT KUYUNJIK, NINEVEH : 668–626

19. ASSYRIAN PRIEST-KING :
   BRITISH MUSEUM

BRITISH MUSEUM

ASSYRIA

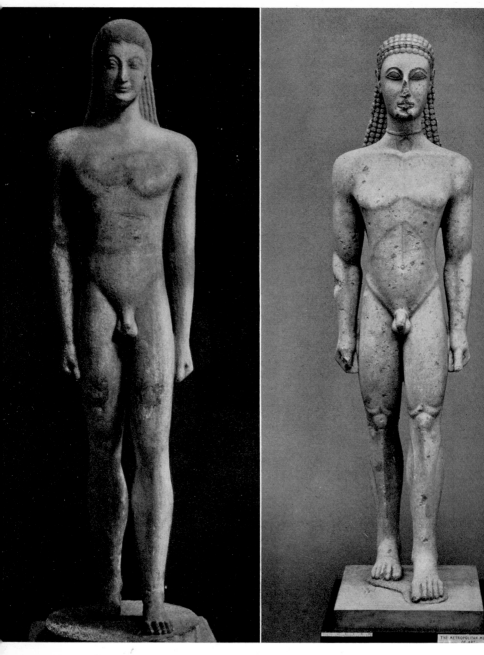

20. EARLY KOUROS TYPE FIGURE:
SIXTH CENTURY B.C.
ATHENS NATIONAL MUSEUM

21. YOUTH: MARBLE:
c. 615 B.C. ATTIC WORK:
METROPOLITAN MUSEUM OF ART, NEW YO

Early Greek figures show Egyptian action and detail giving way to quadrature and to a more living form.   We have the superb personification of the
heroic Greek spirit, expressed with splendid technique in the Apollo of
Olympia.

22. APOLLO FROM THE WEST GABLE OF THE TEMPLE OF ZEUS :
MARBLE : *c.*460 B.C.
MUSEUM OF OLYMPIA

THE RISE OF GREEK SCULPTURE

23. DORYPHORUS: MARBLE:
MUSEO NAZIONALE, NAPLES

This statue
was said to have been made
by Polycleitus
as a canon of proportion
for athletic figures.

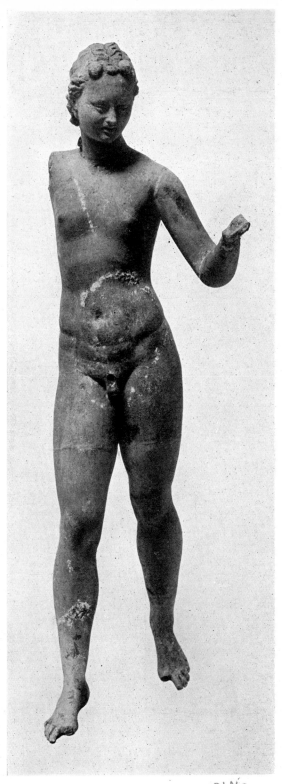

24. EROS: TERRA-COTTA:
MUSEUM OF FINE ARTS,
BOSTON

The Hellenistic pre-occupation
with hermaphroditism and
other abnormal forms ;
dwarfs, athletes with very
exaggerated muscles, etc.

25.   ARCHAIC   FIGURE
FOUND   NEAR   THE
PARTHENON: STONE :
SIXTH   CENTURY   B.C.
ACROPOLIS   MUSEUM,
ATHENS

26.   DEMETER OF CNIDUS : LATE GREEK : BRITISH MUSEUM

This is perhaps the most Christian of all Greek statues, very
similar in pose and action to the early type.   The head was
carved separately in a different marble.

27.   EARLY DEMETER *c.* 480 B.C. : ALTES MUSEUM, BERLIN

28.   ZEUS OR ÆSCULAPIUS : MARBLE
MUSEUM OF FINE ARTS, BOSTON

29. THE OLYMPIAN ZEUS: MARBLE

The evolving of a noble type.   All
these suggest a similarity, tending
towards the Christ in mediæval art.
Technically they have beautiful
qualities of chiselling.   Note the
scale, the variety of depth in the
waved hair of the Zeus on the right.

31. MICHELANGELO (1475–1564) : GOD CREATING THE SUN AND THE MOON (DETAIL) : SISTINE CHAPEL : THE VATICAN, ROME

30. ZEUS FROM OTRICOLI : MARBLE : THE VATICAN, ROME

In the Sistine Chapel, the God who with a superb gesture divides the night from the day and with the touch of a mighty forefinger creates Adam, is but an echo of the great Zeus type, first conceived by Greek artists.

32.   THE FRIEZE OF THE PARTHENON (DETAIL) : BRITISH MUSEUM

We can form no conception of the beauty and effectiveness of the Parthenon,
other Greek sculptures, until we imagine their position, their colour and the bri
sunlight of Greece.   Today as one studies the pedimental groups in the Bri
Museum the exquisite finish of the group, *The Three Fates*, is most striki
There are even drill holes in the wrists and neck where gilt bracelets and neck
were added.   No trace of colour survives, yet at the height of 40 feet, lit o
by reflection from below, the colour was important and some of the delicacy
modelling must have been sacrificed.   The Parthenon was completed in 432 i

33. THE THREE FATES: FROM THE EASTERN PEDI-
MENT   OF   THE   PARTHENON :   BRITISH   MUSEUM

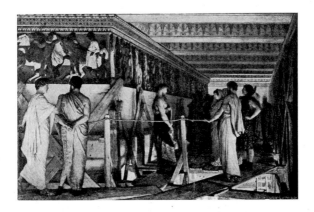

34. L. ALMA TADEMA: PHIDIAS AT THE PARTHENON

PHIDIAN SCULPTURE

35. FRIEZE OF THE PARTHENON (DETAIL): ACROPOLIS MUSEUM, ATHENS

Compare this exquisitely designed and carved drapery with that on the opposite page, where the even regularity of the folds of drapery and the almost mechanical repetition of the horse's mane betray a general clumsiness of handling. Obviously this is the work of a much more skilled carver. Probably the whole scheme of the frieze was designed by a master and carved by assistants of varying skill. The frieze was almost certainly not carved *in situ*.

36. FRIEZE OF THE PARTHENON (DETAIL) ACROPOLIS MUSEUM, ATHENS. 37. THESEUS OR DIONYSOS : EAST GABLE OF THE PARTHENON : MARBLE : BRITISH MUSEUM

PHIDIAN SCULPTURE

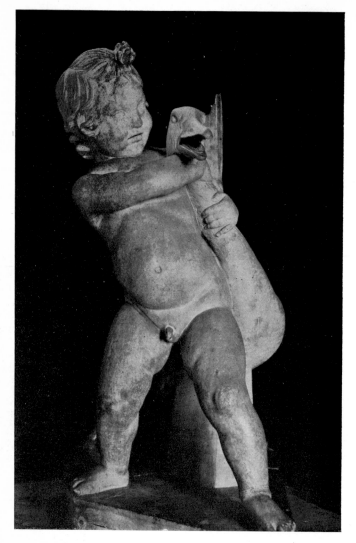

38. BOY WITH GOOSE : LATE GREEK : MARBLE

39. GIRL WITH PIGEONS : GREEK RELIEF : MARBLE
THE METROPOLITAN MUSEUM OF ART, NEW YORK

Later Greek work shows a perfect understanding of the forms and anatomy of childhood.   The relief, of an earlier period, while tender and expressive in feeling yet ignores, or fails to understand, the proportions of childhood.

THE RISE OF GREEK SCULPTURE

CIVILIZATIONS overlap and dovetail so that in even a slight historical sketch one must constantly retrace one's steps. During the last thousand years B.C. while Egypt pursued her own course with characteristic Eastern aloofness, new civilizations arose, flourished, and died, and during that time there was born or grew to power and fruitfulness, all the vital ideas in art, literature, drama, philosophy, science, politics and culture which have transformed the world. The " closed valley " civilization of Egypt steadily declined, and this land which gave the world its first and greatest noble and reverent art became at last only the granary of Rome. Babylon, Assyria, Persia, Greece arose and fell, Egypt held her own course, timeless and ageless. Theocracy—empire—vassal-state—colony—yet still EGYPT. But during the six centuries from the time of Cambyses, Western Europe saw an entire revolution in civilization by that race whose name still stands as a synonym for culture, for the world is still divided into Greeks and Barbarians.

Primitive man, assailed by the forces of nature, sometimes evil, some-times beneficent, endeavoured to placate the evil forces and to make use of the beneficent ones, by means which led to the origin of both ritual and art. If it were possible to propitiate the spirits which controlled these forces he felt more at home in this strange and terrible world. The Egyptians having personified these forces into a hierachy of half-animal gods, and given them material form or embodiment, the Greeks trans-formed these Gods by idealizing and humanizing them into fair and clearly conceived personalities. Egyptian sculpture is permanently signifi-cant because it was the art of making a durable dwelling place for the soul. Greek sculpture arose out of the entirely different desire to give bodily form to ideas of the gods and we shall fail entirely to understand their art if these underlying ideas are forgotten. It is strange how a great and revolutionary idea may be passed by. For instance, in a very able modern history of sculpture, after remarking on the multiplicity of Greek gods and the fact that they were conceived in human form, the writers continue, " To represent these divinities, the sculptor had only to create the loveliest human forms he could imagine ". The " only " is puzzling. As if it were easy ! What the Greeks had to do and did do was (to quote Miss Jane Harrison)[1] " to *think* the gods into human shape ". When that miraculous transformation was accomplished, the task of the Greek artist was to give form to these thoughts. And the artist's task was almost as great an

[1] " Introductory Studies in Greek Art."

intellectual labour as that of the philosopher. It involved long, conscious and entirely original study, untrammelled by the authoritarianism of the ancient civilizations, and as this study led the philosophers to the discovery of man, and to an examination of his powers, actual and potential, so it led the artists to the great discovery of the form of man, in its noblest and most ideal aspect, and finally the labours of both together led to the dethronement of these gods, then to their contraction into half-human heroes, and finally to their complete humanization—and so to the apotheosis of man.

The Egyptian made a statue as a dwelling place for the soul. The Greek made a statue as an archetype of a god. Behind all the marvellous sculptures of Greece, in spite of their apparent externalism, there was, latent in the Greek mind, a belief that the ultimate realities are spiritual and ideal. To the Egyptian the soul wandered homeless if the visible habitations, the body, and the statue, were destroyed ; the conception of the undying soul is here, though it is limited by the earthiness which required a material dwelling place. To a late Greek like Socrates the spirit could not be destroyed by any circumstances. " How shall we bury you ? " asked Crito. " As you please " he answered " only you must catch me first and not let me escape you ". (Phædo) This revolution in thought was accompanied by an equally complete revolution in art ; and by the time Socrates had effected his great revolution in thought by directing philosophy towards the powers and the destiny of man, instead of looking backward to find the beginnings of things, as did the earlier Greek philosophers, Greek sculptors had turned from the portrayal of gods to the representation of men. The Greeks were in all these things experimental and intellectual. They inherited traditions from Egypt, Babylon, Persia and Crete, and with the power of genius fused these elements into a noble national style and by applying rational and intellectual tests to all the problems of art, architecture, science and life they produced a new and beautiful art and moulded the whole course of the world. In matters of thought they disengaged speculation from priestly and theological guidance, and for the arbitrary deductions of authority they substituted the positive inductions of research. This intellectual curiosity and high courage changed sculpture in one brief century from the conventionally articulated derivative and half Egyptian Kouroi of Sunium and Tenea to the noble and majestic Apollo of Olympia ; and that same sceptical and experimental intellectualism which created Greece—and gives her external significance— in the end destroyed her art, her religion and her national life.

The investigations and discoveries of Henry Schliemann in the latter half of the nineteenth century changed the whole approach to the study of Hellenic art and life. Till then it had seemed to many that Greek culture was an invention of their own, that it had no distant origins or parentage. Schliemann finally destroyed this false idea—opened up a new world for investigation—and made it clear that the historic Greeks had been preceded by Greek ancestors of some kindred race who possessed wealth and skill and a highly developed culture. Schliemann's own story of his work in his books on Tiryns, Troy and Mycenæ is a record of splendid achievement, and his studies put back the origins of Greek art to a period nearly fifteen hundred years before the date suggested for the origins of Greek culture by Grote c. 800 B.C. Later investigation has shown that this Ægean pre-Hellenic civilization had left its mark far and wide in the basin of the Mediterranean and that Egyptian art had been influenced by it, and showed a close intercourse between the older and the newer civilization. Following on Schliemann, Sir Arthur Evans explored Crete and showed that island to be the home of this great Ægean culture, so Crete has been appropriately called " the stepping stone to Greece ". This civilization had outposts on the mainland at Mycenæ and Tiryns, and somewhere about 1400 B.C., invaders from the North—perhaps with iron, as Professor Burrows suggests—swept down and destroyed almost every vestige of this race and its works. Perhaps this total destruction is one reason why the art and life of the classical Greeks seems hardly, if at all, influenced by this earlier culture. They seem to have owed very little to foreign influence and to have built up their own civilization. This pre-Hellenic art is entirely different from any art known to Greece. There is little sculpture, though Sir Arthur Evans found a superb bull in plaster relief (gesso duro) of which the head was complete and it shows a mastery of modelling which gives it a place among the great animal sculptures of any age. The great frescoes of the Palace of Minos show brilliant skill in naturalistic rendering particularly of flowers and animals and the grace and beauty of the cup-bearing youth shows artistic power of the highest degree. There is also some glazed faience of animals in relief which shows the same brilliant naturalistic skill in drawing and modelling, but nothing of this inheritance seems to have passed to the Greeks.

In contrast with the comparative uniformity of Egyptian life and art, conservative, hieratic, and coherent, Greek art and culture developed in local communities, each separate, and with local characteristics, but held together by certain unifying principles and ideas. It will not be possible, owing to the scale of this book, to discuss fully the differences and characteristics of the various schools of Greek sculpture. The important thing is to keep clear in our minds the unifying principles and ideas which give Greek art its unique perfection. The differences are most marked in the earlier stages and are generally the result of contacts with other races. The works of the Eastern Ægean are touched with Orientalism. The whole early art of Greece owes much to Egypt, but from the assimilation of various influences, side by side with courageous experimentalism, a great national style was gradually developed. But before this could happen certain age-old conventions had to be broken down. Every standing Egyptian portrait statue stood on a vertical medial line, and faced front-wards. The left leg of all standing statues was forward. The weight of the figure was equally divided, that is, there was no pelvic movement and though the heel of the left foot was forward almost to the toes of the right foot, an imaginary frontal vertical line would still divide the figure exactly equally. It was Greek artists who first broke through this convention. Gradually the Greek artist broke every convention, every formula of previous art, and developed his own principle that every foumla is hampering and, in some degree, false, and so he led the way to the unprecedented freedom of Hellenic art.

Intellectual adventuring was foreign to the rigid theocracies of Egypt and Mesopotamia ; it was characteristic of the Greeks. By the latter part of the seventh century B.C., the sculptors were making large limestone statues, the so-called Kouroi or Apollos which although plainly derived from Egyptian models were at first much less accomplished in technique than their prototypes. They often show a squareness of form which suggests that the sculptors worked by outlining the figure on two surfaces of the block and cutting through till the shapes intersected, then some attempt was made to round the forms from these two aspects into a truer semblance of a figure. This quadrature is very marked in the Apollo of Sunium. It was not long however before this squareness disappeared and the Apollo of Tenea in Munich, and the Strangford Apollo in the British Museum, are entirely free from this faulty and tentative technique, and stand with slim figures and delicate limbs, though still bound by the frontal and medial line conventions.

The Korai, or Maidens of the same period, are entirely similar in action and in the conventional attitude, but are as invariably draped as the Apollos are nude. These draperies are very complex in arrangement, and represent skilfully a thin and clinging material which reveals vividly the body and legs beneath. Some figures, like the Hera of Samos (Louvre), show a pillar-like simplicity of outline which suggests a derivation from a tree trunk. We know from Pausanius that some of the oldest and most sacred statues were of wood, and were probably little more than tree trunks slightly shaped. A good deal of learned nonsense has been written about the " flat planes " of wood carving being copied into stone by Greek sculptors, and the Branchidæ figures are often instanced as examples. Flat planes are however no more natural and inevitable in woodcarving than in stone or marble carving. It is quite probable that Greek architecture developed from wooden building, and that the forms of wood construction are inherent in Doric architecture, but it is not likely that forms and conventions natural to wood should long continue to be copied by the carvers of stone statues or the makers of Greek architecture. To carve the Hera of Samos in wood would require many more tools, much more elaborately shaped and delicately sharpened than would be required to carve it in stone or marble, and it is unlikely that any Greek marble statue is a true copy of a wooden figure.

No wooden statues have survived from Greece, though great numbers survived into our era, and were seen by Pausanias in the second century A.D. Most of these were of very early date. Pausanias' *Travels in Greece* (that delightful and interesting Bædeker) provides ample evidence of the extensive use of wood for sculpture, and it is especially interesting to note that he mentions particularly that the two oldest athlete statues at Olympia were of wood. Many of these were primitive, but among the hundreds of

36

wooden statues mentioned by Pausanias are others not at all primitive, and they are often described very fully. The woods used are oak, apple, pear, olive, and even ebony, and occasionally he notes—in his careful way —that he " cannot distinguish the wood as the statues are dressed in real draperies " ! How far these wooden statues differed from statues in stone or marble is quite conjectural. In Egypt they were very similar, but perhaps the adventurous Greek carver found a greater freedom in wood than in stone.

The Greek Apollos or Kouroi bear a marked resemblance to Egyptian statues, chiefly in the frontal pose and limited action ; but there is a singular difference of spirit—already something of Greek candour and truth-seeking—and, it must be said, of clumsiness and rude force. The forms, especially of the later Egyptian statues, are suave and tranquil, untroubled by that passion for life which is so clear in Dorian and early Ionian art. It was here and at this moment that Western art took that decisive step which led to the great achievements of Attic art, the Parthenon marbles, so charged with vital power, so filled with that fusion of form and spirit which makes things immortal. Perhaps, indeed, the ultimate greatness of Greek art is not so much in the height to which it attained in that great fifth century, as in the fine spiritual and intellectual effort of the previous century, by which alone that supreme beauty was achieved. It is this sense of effort, this passion for form which makes the earlier sculptures so significant, not so much for what they achieve, splendid though that is, but for what they imply and portend. Those tranquil Korai with curved archaic smile, the Apollos of Sunium and Tenea, the sculptures of Ægina have broken definitely with the conventions of Egypt and Asia and show that the artists are adventuring into new paths. A generation later the wonderful Apollo of Olympia turns his head and raises his arm in a sort of benediction, a noble gesture, significant of the immense stride taken by the breaking down of the rigid medial line and frontal conventions. The ready-made formula is rejected, the traditional symbolic attitude refused, the symbol, so important in Egyptian art, is now made subservient to the thing symbolized. These Greek artists may have learned technical processes from the ancient East, but they did not for long copy the matured artistic style of the older civilization, but launched out towards their own solution of the problem of giving form to ideas.

Professor Beazley, writing of the vases of the Eastern and Western schools, points a contrast in a passage which seems also applicable to Eastern sculpture as compared with Western. " The East is conservative, the West experimental. The East is content with the ancient monsters of the Orient, the West invents new. The East likes uniform rows of animals, a whole row of goats, another of deer, the West mixes its animals. The East is decorative, the West is narrative. The East having no tale to tell retains filling ornaments and needs no inscriptions, the West ends by clearing the ground for action and for word."[1] The sculptors of the

[1] " Cambridge Ancient History " Vol. 4.

Olympian pediments took the last step leading to the noble, idealized forms of classical art with its unprecedented freedom and beauty. They even experimented with the problems of violent action. Such violence came again into Greek sculpture after Praxiteles, when the artists explored the possibilities of the sensual and the sensational, but it was hardly known before the Olympian work, and it is very significant that the next generation was a period of poise, and Phidian sculptors allowed but little action, limiting violent action almost to contests of men with half-animal centaurs (perhaps consciously typifying the struggle of Greece against barbarism.)

Individual portraiture was rare. In a long series of grave reliefs covering perhaps two centuries and bearing what were regarded as representations of persons, often even with names added, there is hardly a trace of individuality. There were two types for men—the youthful and the bearded —and one type for women ; so, contrary to the usually accepted view, it is in Greek sculpture that one finds men and women reduced to a pattern —especially in the faces. The bodies tend to have more variety. This may have arisen from the Greek idea of disciplining the outward semblance of life towards a preconceived ideal type. The result was portraiture strangely different from the vividly personal characterization of the early Egyptian sculptors. Even the prancing horsemen of the Parthenon frieze are unindividualized and move rhythmically rather than violently and not till its later stages did Greek art turn to violence and emotionalism. In the great ages they set up those statues of gods and heroes for contemplation and admiration, and next to their beauty, their most striking characteristic is their serenity. No Greek statue has a more consummate technique than the great Olympian Apollo. Those hard, firm contours are instinct with the sense of the chisel and the stone. The simplicity of the treatment of the drapery is not due to any deliberate archaism, or lack of imitative skill ; but is a conscious, or subconscious, convention, exquisitely adapted to marble carving. Indeed, all the sculptures on the Olympian temple are characterized by a perfect understanding of a carving technique, as distinct from a modelled or plastic technique ; they show conclusively that primitiveness is not implicit in direct carving. Before a work like this Apollo one is left breathless. It seems not to have been made, but to have been born. Later though it is, by several centuries, than the Homeric poems, there is much of the same godlike spirit in this figure, and as in the *Iliad* and the *Odyssey* there is also here a heroic quality which typifies and idealizes the expansion of a great civilization—the dawn of human freedom.

We shall appreciate and understand the culmination of the Greek genius in the great fifth century, only according as we see clearly all that is implied in those wonderful works of the earlier age. For those works, in stone, marble and bronze, are charged with power and beauty—the embodiment of the spirit of Hellas.

PHIDIAN SCULPTURE

ONE may well pause before attempting to write of Phidian sculpture.
The superlatives have been exhausted.

How can one hope to add words of value to a subject which has
stirred the critical imagination and called forth the eloquence of some of
the greatest writers, from Lucian to Pater ? One cannot think of the
Olympian Zeus without recalling that profound phrase of Quintilian's
regarding it : " whose beauty seems to have added something to the
received religion, so adequate is the majesty of the work to the Godhead
it expressed ". Lucian, Pliny, and Dio Chrysostom have all praised this
statue in memorable words, and descriptions of it are known from many
ancient writers. No trace of the statue has survived, save a blackened
rent on the stone base where it stood ; which recalls the legend of antiquity, that when Phidias had completed the statue he prayed the god to
send him down some sign of favourable recognition, and suddenly a
thunderbolt fell through the open roof and struck the temple floor,
leaving this blackened rent. The story is significant. How different must
this Zeus have been from the solemnly passive Kephren! The Greek
artist, by seizing on an eternal idea and giving it form, made a type which
is immortal. And though our knowledge of the Phidian Zeus is limited to
descriptions in literature, to reproductions on coins, and to several marble
heads—the Otricoli Zeus, the Æsculapius from Melos in the British
Museum, and a noble head in Boston—yet all these suggest a similarity of
head, and there emerges clearly a grand, benignant type which had not
appeared in art before, and which has constantly reappeared in Christian
art. Once again the Greek artist has created a new type. The mediæval
sculptors, desiring to embody in stone the idea of the Eternal Father,
recreated this same type, though in a narrower and harder manner. The
Phidian amplitude of form gave place to a type which is at once more
spiritual and yet more stern and severe. There is some profound meaning
in the way the broad and ample forms of the greatest classical sculpture
are narrowed and refined in Christian sculpture. The wide and serene brow
of pagan art is narrowed and heightened and filled with thought in the
Beau Dieu. The noble nose forms in Phidian art, which show no bony
structure, shrink in the Christian figures to narrower and harsher ridges ;
while the Phidian treatment of the eye, in which the upper eyelid is but
slightly indicated in the deep shadow of the gently arched sockets, is
changed to an eye truer to the form of nature, but yet less noble than the
ancient. The mediæval sculptor knew little or nothing of classical art, but
both unconsciously embodied the intellectual atmosphere of their ages.

39

At the Renaissance, when men turned again to the study of classical art, the idea of God the Father was embodied in stone and paint in forms strangely similar to that of the Phidian Father of the Gods. So, also, with the athletic types. The Diadumenos, Doryphorus, the Discobolus, are all embodiments of qualities deeply sought after in Greek life ; courage, temperance and friendship ; and these statues remain to this day, not only examples of almost unattainable physical beauty, but also the unconscious elucidation of their age and race, if we but learn to read them rightly. One of the marks of Greek greatness is this power of creating permanent types.

It is surely not mere coincidence that, during the fifth century in Greece, a broad conception of the powers and potentialities of man took shape for the first time, and that at the same moment the sculptors achieved the realization in marble of the noblest conception of human form. Phidias was almost exactly contemporary with Sophocles and there is a striking similarity in conception between the characters of the great tragic dramas Œdipus, Ajax, Antigone, and the noble and heroic forms of the Parthenon pediments ; the Theseus, the Fates and Demeter and Persephone. These profoundly moving Greek conceptions, embodied in words and marble were achieved partly by audacious philosophical speculation and partly by acute æsthetic perception. The majestic beauty of the Antigone, with its great chorus in praise of Man, has its contemporary counterpart in the Phidian Athena Parthenos. Both dramatist and sculptor were glorifying man, and their work is stamped with the freshness, directness and simplicity which characterize the creations of genius. Never before in its history had such types been made.

The Theseus (so-called) of the Parthenon—the one presumably Phidian figure which is almost complete, and not headless—is extraordinarily noble ; and noble in a profoundly intellectual way. The enlargement and glorification of parts of the body, like the great pectorals, and the attenuation of the abdominal parts, show it to be not merely an athletic type copied in marble, but rather a hero with a conscious ennoblement of the parts of the physical body which suggests Godhead—the head and the heart.

In the Greek statues gods, heroes and men merge almost imperceptibly into each other. There is here no sharp cleavage like that which, in Egyptian sculpture, separates the frank realism of the Sheikh or the Scribe from the awe-inspiring aloofness of the kingly Kephren or the Colossi. All Greek sculpture, like all Egyptian sculpture, was religious in the sense that it was used for the decoration of temples ; and the importance of art to Greek religion lay in the idea that the God who was not clearly imagined, apprehended or embodied, was nothing. In Christian art the image is but a symbol. In Greek art the statue of the God was the seat of the " unseen power " of the Deity. But the artists gradually widened the scope of their art by including in it life in all levels of existence—men, women, centaurs, horses—and by finding beauty not only in gods and heroes, but in all living things. They dared to think freely, and they were insatiably curious, refusing to be bound by ideas or forms inherited from the ancient theocracies of the East. They analysed and meditated on the old answers to problems of human conduct and destiny and they first grasped the conception of a unity throughout the visible and invisible universe. At the same time they searched out new problems in form, studying life and nature with open eyes and reinforcing these studies by new scientific anatomical observation : so they achieved those noble and gracious human forms which to this day are unequalled.

This wide range of outlook is beautifully touched on in Hegel (Caird's translation) : " If the first paradise was the paradise of nature, this is the second, the higher paradise of the human spirit which, in its fair naturalness, freedom, depth and brightness, here comes forth like a bride out of her chamber. The first wild majesty of the rise of spiritual life in the East is here circumscribed by the dignity of form, and softened into beauty. Its depth shows itself no longer in confusion, obscurity and inflation, but lies open before us in simple clearness. Its brightness is not a childish play, but covers a sadness which knows the hardness of fate, but is not by that knowledge driven out of freedom and measure ".

This intellectual pioneering often extended boundaries by breaking them down. The gulf between Gods and men was bridged by the Heroes. Ethics and æsthetics were not separated in the Greek mind. A work of art was great if it embodied a great idea. The greatest work of art was that which embodied the noblest idea. Ethics and politics were equally indeterminately enclosed. Plato's *Republic* purports to be a political treatise concerning the search for justice : it might equally be described as an ethical treatise on education. Aristotle, it is true, wrote separate treatises, one on ethics and one on politics ; but the one is simply the first instalment of the other. This breaking down of divisions was really part of the process of making definitions. Clearly defined distinction was the aim even though it was reached by widening boundaries and extending previous definitions. No quality is more marked in the fifth century Greek sculpture than its exquisitely clear definitions, its clarity of statement. In Greek life the State was the entity, the individual the fragment : so in art they did not emphasize one fact but regarded and generalized all, as a means of representing one all-encompassing conception. As Plato courageously set out to follow " whithersoever the argument may lead us," so Phidias and his contemporary artists embraced within the compass of their art all life known or imagined by them—gods, goddesses, heroes, old men, pretty maidens, horses, bullocks, centaurs, amazons, satyrs—and touched them all with beauty and with that ennobling spirit which, while it observes nature and human forms, yet removes the representation from our common clay. It might almost be said that the only form ignored was that of the human baby. In the subjects involving the representation of infancy, as in the Eirene and the Infant Plutus, or the Hermes with the Infant Dionysus, the forms of the child bear no resemblance to the strangely un-adult proportions of infancy, and are merely youthful forms ludicrously reduced in scale. Not till the later age of Hellenistic sculpture did artists understand or re-create the engaging proportions of childhood.

Of the great chryselephantine statues made by Phidias and his colleagues none have survived. But contemporary descriptions and representations on coins give indications of their impressive beauty. The Lenormant and Varvakeion statuettes may give at least a hint of the majesty of the Athena Parthenos (as a newspaper print may give a hint of a beautiful picture). The statue was 40 feet high, made on a core of wood, the face and arms of ivory and the drapery of hammered gold. Pausanias, who saw it in the time of Marcus Aurelius, described it briefly : " This work of art is in ivory and gold. The statue of Athena is of full length and on her breast is the head of Medusa worked in ivory ; and in one hand she has a Victory—four cubits high—in the other hand a spear, and at her feet a shield, and near the spear a dragon which perhaps is Erichthonius." And of one of the Great Phidian statues Dio Chrysostum has written these moving words : " Methinks if one who is heavy laden of soul, who hath drained the cup of misfortune and sorrow in life, and whom sweet sleep visiteth no more, were to stand before this figure he would forget all the griefs and hardships that fall upon the life of man." And there is the story that 800 years after Phidias, Alaric and his Goths were scared from their raid on the Acropolis by the sight of the great protective goddess—Athena Promachos.

The Parthenon was rededicated as a Christian church in 435 A. D. (just as Byzantium was rising to power) and it remained a Christian church for a thousand years. The statue of Athena was rededicated as a Christian Virgin and survived as such till the fifth century A. D. Yet all that a recent and widely read Art historian says of the Athena Parthenos is that " it must have been a horror " ! He had, of course, the advantage of not seeing it. The comments and judgments of those who saw the statue and the Parthenon seem more explicable, and one may recall Shelley's tribute. A point which must not be forgotten in any study of architectural sculpture is its position. It must be remembered that the frieze should be seen from below ; that it was coloured, that bits, bridles and trappings were added in gilt bronze, and that it was lit entirely by reflection from the white marble stylobate below. It is only necessary to take a plaster cast— even on a reduced scale—lighting it from below, to see how the whole rhythm of the composition is changed. It is a further evidence of the sculptor's skill and care that the relief is much deeper at the top which was in shadow.

The wonderful technical excellence of Parthenon or Phidian sculpture is apt to be forgotten in admiration of its noble beauties of form. Yet, though all the sculptors were adequately equipped technically, a study of the 480 feet of the Parthenon frieze shows several different styles and personal techniques.[1] The suggestion of a modern critic that the frieze was modelled and then copied by carvers (the usual modern method) may, I think, be dismissed until evidence is produced. Since the introduction of the pointing-machine, and the consequent division of sculptors into modellers

[1] See the large scale photographs published in "The Acropolis." Weyhe, New York, 1932.

42

and carvers (the first supposedly " artists," and the second only " work-men "), it is too often forgotten that carving, if one is traditionally trained to it, is an easy technique, and consequently modelling as a preliminary is largely a waste of time. The whole treatment of the frieze suggests direct carving. A carved relief tends to have many points of the design on or near the outer surface, the approach to the design being from the outer surface to the background. A modelled relief tends to have a flat background and many parts of the design near to it, because modelling begins from the background, and only occasionally reaches the full relief of the outer surface. Trained to his work, the Greek carver, like the mediæval carver, would readily tackle problems of direct carving, which would be difficult or impossible for the modeller accustomed to a medium which allows of endless experiment. The beautiful rhythmical draperies of the so-called " Three Fates " bear, to my mind, every evidence of being carved directly by a sculptor to whom the process of carving was so easy as to be almost instinctive. It has lately been urged that these figures were modelled nude, draped with real drapery, remodelled, cast in plaster, and then carved from the plaster models (the modern practice). And this wild conjecture is put forward by one whose whole point of attack on scholars and writers about Greek sculpture is that their analyses and criticisms are purely conjectural ! Until contemporary Greek evidence to the contrary is produced, one may continue to believe that the Parthenon sculpture, with its large nobility of style, is the work of a group of men working under a great artist, in a tradi-tional manner, enthused by a common inspiration. The Parthenon was built during the general beautifying of Athens in the half century after the repulse and defeat of the Persians at Salamis. There was then a great outburst of nationalism—a sense of expanded freedom, and of rich civic life in which everyone shared—and we may well believe that artists and sculptors were in constant demand. There is no training in art so successful as that which comes from continuous work. Pliny suggests that the carving of marble appeared to be an older art than that of bronze casting, and surviving statues of the late seventh and sixth centuries B. C. confirm this. It is possible that the earliest Greek bronze statues were cast in sections from wooden models and afterwards fitted together as shown on the Foundry Vase in Berlin. But it is also possible that these were made, as was the early Egyptian statue of Pepi, from hammered plates of bronze and then rivetted together. The art of bronze hollow casting by the " cire perdue " process may have been known by the end of the sixth century and during the fifth century Greek craftsmen became expert bronze founders. As A. J. B. Wace says, " As bronze sculpture grew in popularity it was observed that bronze gave greater movement to the figure and consequently greater naturalism. It would follow almost inevitably that the bronze technique would exercise its influence on marble and stone sculpture which thus in its turn would tend to greater naturalism."[1] Pliny credits Lysistratos, the brother of Lysippus (fourth century), with

[1] " An Approach to Greek Sculpture ".

the discovery of the device of taking plaster casts from life, and so leading to a greater realism in portrait sculpture, (though this practice was known and used many centuries before by the Egyptians). But Mr. Wace's contention that accepting Pliny's statement means that " at least from the time of Lysippus onwards every sculptor working in marble or bronze made a clay model first " is surely to be taken with caution. A sculptor—or worker in marble accustomed to carving—would very easily be able to carve a statue, especially if it were of a traditional type, without making or getting someone else to make a clay preliminary model. It may seem strange to scholars and critics without carving experience, but it is both easier and quicker to carve from a clearly conceived mental image than to copy from clay or other model. In my own experience it has always taken longer to repeat a figure than to create one. Pliny can only have been quoting hearsay evidence. That Greek sculptors used callipers, compasses, and other measuring devices is obvious : but the most elaborate of these can have borne little or no resemblance to the modern pointing instrument.

The development of sculpture towards realism was probably due more to philosophical and psychological ideas, than to the technique of death or life masks and bronze casting. It was a part of the process of self-realization, and perhaps Socrates and Plato, with their insistence that the ultimate reality in man was not body but soul, had a greater influence on sculpture, and especially portrait sculpture, than the new or rediscovered technical processes of Lysistratus and Pasiteles. A technical point to be noted is that in the treatment of hair in portrait heads the tufts are usually much larger and simpler in marble than in bronze. When in marble the tufts of hair are small and with fine lines added (as in the marble athlete head in the Metropolitan Museum), it would suggest that it was a marble copy of a bronze original. The tools of the Greek sculptors seem to have been very similar to modern marble carving tools. Traces of claw or toothed tools are commonly found on Greek marbles, also marks of the point, the first tool after the rough shaping. Mr. S. Casson, in his valuable book on tools and technique, insists that the flat chisel was not known till comparatively late, but this tool is so simple an instrument that it is difficult to find a reason for the Greeks not having it. The use of emery abrasives is very obvious as some of the illustrations in Mr. Casson's book show conclusively. The back of the Hermes of Praxiteles shows marks of either a shallow gouge, or of a " bull-nosed " chisel. Probably the first rough shaping of a block was done by sawing ; the saw being the usual weighted, swinging, framed blade, without teeth, worked by hand and used with sand grit—and water : a method used today wherever stone or marble has to be cut without electrical power. and known as the " grub-saw." They also had drills and probably even the tubular drill.

The attack made on Greek art today is often that it is too realistic (the one great dread of the modern artist) ; though, curiously enough, it was never so " life-like " as early Egyptian sculpture, which has not yet been subjected to the same criticism. And what is meant by " realism " ? A plaster cast taken from life of a Greek youth posed like the Diadumenos or the Theseus would have borne little resemblance to the statues. Other qualities beside representation have entered into the statues, and they are in no sense mere transcripts from nature. It is these added qualities which make the statues less " life-like," but more real. A statue or any work of art is made " real " by the emotional intensity of the artist being charged into it ; as the *Odyssey* is more " real " than a gramophone record of an actual conversation. One great quality of fifth century Attic sculpture, serenity, is a quality which it shares with Egypt, and which is never again found in sculpture until the end of the twelfth century and during the thirteenth century in mediæval Europe.

The passion of the Greek was for self-realization, a passion which began as far back as the time when " Homer came to Hellas." This was the motive force of that great search for realities which probed the mysteries of nature and the depths of the human spirit. The Greek sculptors thus realized and recreated man in a noble mould, distinguishing their works by just that subtle difference that makes the Phidian Theseus nobler than the Sheikh-el-Beled or the Scribe. So they, first in the world, realized the forms of the gods not as beings with the heads of predatory animals, or giants, or gorgons, but as beings of more than human understanding, who had governing power over the world, who could be fitly represented only by such noble human forms as have the Melian Zeus—(or Æsculapius) the Olympian Apollo and the profoundly moving Demeter of Cnidus. This change is like the change wrought by Greek inductive science, by which the inheritance of Egyptian and Babylonian knowledge of the stars (studied by these earlier people for their supposed influence on human affairs) was developed, defined, and related to their great concept of the unity of Nature, thus forming the beginnings of the science of astronomy. Nomadic and desert people must have regarded the stars with awe, and the glories of the heavens been conducive to religious emotion. The Greek outlook was less religious but more truly scientific. On the other hand, it is to Greece that we owe the Platonic concept of dual worlds, the seen and the unseen. And there is a duality in the great Greek statues of the gods, so nobly human, and yet so charged with spirit that they move us profoundly today. The conscious pursuit of this strange quality of Beauty—by which one thing may be distinguished from another—so that this Beauty may be called the most real thing in the Universe, is one of the great gifts of Greece. Nothing was standardized. Greek religion had no creed—no fixed dogma—many priests—no episcopate. The solvent for all problems was the free play of reason and intelligence. This spirit of intellectual adventure, by which they broke " through custom to freedom," pervades all their work. The Greeks were free to go wrong, as we shall see ; while the Eastern artists, working to fixed formulæ, were not free. In the striking words of Faure, their sculpture " was born of freedom and was killed by it."

*" This is Cypris—not she of the people ; nay, venerate the goddess by her name
—the Heavenly Aphrodite. This statue is the offering of chaste Chrysogone, even
in the house of Amphicles, whose children and whose life were hers ! And
always year by year went well with them, who began each year with thy worship,
Lady—for mortals who care for the Immortals have themselves thereby
the better fortune."* THEOCRITUS : FOR A STATUE OF APHRODITE

LATER GREEK SCULPTURE

THE long and lovely decline (so-called) of Greek sculpture is traceable
in a succession of works which embody the spirit of their age, and stamp
that age with a greatness which was almost unquestioned until the twentieth century. The present generation, in a somewhat self-conscious revolt
back to primitiveness, has attacked the æsthetic conception from which
Greek work developed ; and today a small but persistent group of critics
derides and belittles the Greek achievement, and endeavours to destroy
the potent influence of classical art. This has been done subtly. In my own
lifetime, the so-called " apogee " of Greek sculpture has been pushed
further and further back : from the Medician Venus and the Versailles
Diana, to Praxitelean and Phidian work ; then to the Olympian work ;
thence to the Apollo of Tenea. And now it is the still more primitive
Apollos, as that of Sunium, which alone excite or are considered worthy
of admiration. Self-conscious sophistication seems to find disproportionate
pleasure in the passionate yet naive simplicity of archaic art. But critical
opinion is ever shifting. The sculptures themselves justify and elucidate the
thought and the age.

While Socrates with his relentless questioning was undermining
orthodox religion, ceaselessly searching for definitions (and it is significant
that he was a sculptor and the son of a sculptor, whose art is the art of
definition), Greek sculptors were turning from the representations of gods
towards those of intermediate type, the Heroes ; and thence to the portrayal of men. The 150 years which separate the Apollo of Olympia from
the Hermes of Praxiteles record a change in sculpture as great and as
significant as the changes in the religious ideas embodied in these two works.
The Olympian Apollo is noble, aloof and godlike. The Hermes is subtle,
sensuous and refined almost to the point of preciousness. The very slightly
curved medial line of the Apollo is in the Hermes replaced by an almost
violent double curve, and the drapery over the left arm of the Hermes so
startlingly resembles real drapery as to be almost illusive ; while that of the
Apollo is perfectly marble-like, exquisitely chiselled, yet with no attempt
at realism. The treatment of the hair in the Hermes is a treatment typical
only of marble carving, and indeed to copy it by modelling would be
almost impossible. It has every evidence of chiselling, and none of modelling or of bronze casting.

Greek sculpture in this interval has definitely started on that slippery slope which led to the pursuit of realistic verisimilitude (a kind of scientific realism), which ended in Græco-Roman portraiture—those portrait busts which seem like casts from life, except that they are so vivid and true ! And similarly Greek philosophy, which at the time of the making of the Apollo was exploring man's mind, charting his thoughts and guiding his aspirations, had, by the time of this triumphantly realistic portraiture, divided into two great groups, Epicureanism and Stoicism, which gradually degenerated into the glorification of pleasure, and the apotheosis of despair. It is true that Praxiteles' Cnidian Aphrodite profoundly shocked the religious susceptibilities of his age. In spite of the questioning of Socrates and the rationalizing of Euripides, the goddess of Love was still too sacred to be represented nude. Yet, once accepted, the nude Aphrodite soon became a common preoccupation of sculptors ; and indeed many of these statues are strangely lovely. The Medician Aphrodite is a very poor and conventional example of the type. The skill of the carving far outweighs the emotional capacity of the artist. Alexandria, where the acute and searching critical spirit endlessly worked over and refined all the characteristic Greek types in literature and art, produced some of the loveliest of these soft, very effeminate, yet, in their essence, nobly sculptural forms ; indeed, Alexandrian artists, with a strange power never before and never again found in nude sculpture, wrought softly rounded and sensuous bodies, while still preserving in them a sense of hard marble and chiselled definition. The Aphrodite of Cyrene, with its searching anatomical knowledge, its voluptuous femininity, its appeal to the senses, is yet far removed from a mere marble transcript of a beautiful human body.

Before this Alexandrian Hellenistic age Greek sculptors had turned towards the expression of heightened emotion and violent action. But their static and ineffectual representations were outdone by the work of the great tragedians, who created *living* impersonations of the Gods and Heroes, expressing joys and sorrows, pain and anguish, and so evoking in the spectators a powerful interest in their fortunes. In the great dramas the momentary creations of the actors have outlived the imperishable marble.

This change in the spirit of Greek art from contemplation to dramatic interest, from simplicity to complication, is usually regarded as a decline ; but perhaps it would be truer to regard it as a turning toward new paths, impelled by a desire to express more than marble would hold. The passion for speculation, which could find no adequate expression in form, turned towards philosophy, which became strong, searching and acute just when art turned from the expression of serene and noble power towards emotional rhetoric and violent action. In the Hellenistic age there is a marked change not only in sculptural style, but also in the subject matter of sculpture. The earlier preoccupation with type forms and with forms ideally generalized now gave way to much more individualized characterization. The change had been first from God to Hero, now it was from Hero to individual Man. Especially after Alexander, who was constantly portrayed by favourite sculptors, there was an immense preoccupation with what may be called " imaginary portraits." How far these were really imaginary is beyond the range of my knowledge. In certain well-known examples, as in the so-called Homer, which has made the blind bard vivid to countless generations, the type is obviously created, though marvellously individual. Others, like the Socrates, the Sophocles, the Demosthenes, the Plato and the Aristotle are surely less imaginary. Probably few are contemporary, yet they seem to be based on a tradition of personality, and even of exact knowledge. The bronze head, sometimes called " Aristotle," and sometimes just " A Philosopher," is a beautiful and arresting work. If these are not the lineaments of Aristotle, they are at least those of a man in whom profound thought and speculation seem to be working behind the furrowed brow. This is the head of a man capable of that widely ranging intelligence and critical observation which laid the foundations in so many fields of modern science. It is noteworthy also that in this head we have a beautiful example of bronze technique, offering interesting and illuminating comparisons, especially in the treatment of the hair, with the carved marble head of Demosthenes. Perhaps, as Mr. Roger Hinks suggests, these should be considered as noble inventions, " characters " in the Theophrastan sense, rather than exact portraits. This preoccupation with individuality coincided with a decline in religion, and so the forms and attributes of the gods underwent a great change. The life-giving power of the sun is typified in the Apollo Sauroctonus of Praxiteles as a slender androgynous youth playing with a lizard ! Eros, the once powerful and compelling god, becomes the child Cupid. Hera, no longer a noble matron, becomes a scold, and Aphrodite a courtesan. Dionysus, no longer the source of ecstatic creative activity, descends into the drunken Bacchus. Another change was the strange loss of vitality which resulted from the passion for generalization, in religious or cult statues, as distinct from individual portraiture. Statues like the Apollo Belvedere and Diana of Versailles are so completely generalized that their beauty is only a negation of defect. They are " faultily faultless, icily regular, splendidly null ; dead perfection, no more." Those suave generalities are entirely different from the work of the earlier and greater age—when the forms of gods and men were not so much generalised as transfigured.

The rhetorical violence of Pergamene sculpture is in strange contrast to fifth century work ; but it is still great sculpture, full of emotional power and romance, and carved with consummate skill. The great philosophers had sought for truth : the later sophists sought mainly for a dialectical victory. So, too, the great sculptors produced statues vividly conceived and passionately felt, while the later artists often turned out works of repeated pattern, devoid of feeling. Form again gave way to formula. Philosophy became no longer a rule of life, but a mere exercise in the practice of logical controversy—a sort of educational calisthenics.

The little baked clay figurines, which were meant to solace and charm the dead in their Bœotian tombs, are often exquisitely wrought. This was a sort of commercial art, probably inexpensive, of a common material, and easily duplicated ; yet how perfect ! They echo the light-hearted spirit of

40. NIKE UNTYING HER SANDAL   MARBLE : 425 B.C.
ACROPOLIS MUSEUM, ATHENS

There are two characteristic divisions of sculpture in which the Hellenistic sculptors produced work of unique interest and beauty. These are the nude Aphrodites which merge into genre sculpture of girls untying sandals, dressing and undressing ; and those portraits or imaginary portrait busts in which the personality of the subject is recorded in a way absolutely final. This thin flying drapery was made possible by a changed technique in a material capable of great delicacy.

LATER   GREEK

41. TRENTHAM MOURNING
WOMAN: LATE HELLENISTIC
OR GRECO-ROMAN : MARBLE :
BRITISH MUSEUM

42. FIGURINE : TERRA-COTTA:
BRITISH MUSEUM

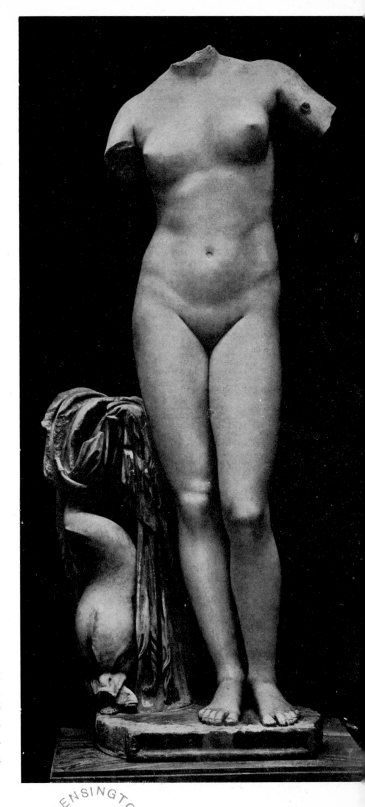

43. APHRODITE OF
CYRENE:
MUSEO NAZIONALE
DELLE TERME,
ROME

voluptuous, yet distin-
guished in style, com-
bining fleshy contours
with a sense of marble.

It is worthy remarking that if this Hermes is a Roman copy, where is there another " copy " carved with such consummate subtlety and skill?

45. A FURY, OR MEDUSA : MARBLE :
MUSEO LUDOVISI
BONCOMPAGNI ALLE TERME,
ROME

For the purposes of comparison
it matters little whether the
Hermes is the work of Praxiteles
or a copyist, Roman or other.
The very chippy treatment
of the hair and the scale of tufts
contrasts with the snakiness of
the fury, a beautiful technique of hair carving.
Much work on the head below has been done with the drill.

46. ATHLETE'S HEAD :
MARBLE :
THE METROPOLITAN MUSEUM
OF ART,
NEW YORK

LATER GREEK

Metallic and engraved treatment of hair. Compare with the crisp sharp edges of the chiselled marble hair, softened by time and weather erosion.

47. BERENICE :
BRONZE :
MUSEO NAZIONALE,
NAPLES

48. HEAD OF
PSYCHE :
GREEK : MARBLE :
MUSEO NAZIONALE,
NAPLES

An interesting comparison
may be made with the head
below. Note here the
impersonal quality of Greek
work, compared with
Roman, the formalized hair
compared with the more
realistic Roman treatment.

49. THE BLOND EPHEBE:
GREEK:
FIFTH CENTURY B.C. :
ACROPOLIS MUSEUM,
ATHENS

50. MAN'S HEAD:
ROMAN MARBLE :
THE METROPOLITAN
MUSEUM OF ART,
NEW YORK

GREEK

51. BEARDED BACCHUS
KNOWN AS BACCO INDIANA:
BRONZE :
MUSEO NAZIONALE, NAPLES

52. HELLENISTIC HEAD
GREEN SLATE :
THE BRITISH MUSEUM, LONDON

Hellenistic portraits
differ
from the even more realistic
Roman portraits,
or the Old Kingdom
Egyptian portraits,
because of some
touch of imaginative quality
which re-interprets the
personality rather than
merely reproduces the physical
features. Yet the direction
given to sculpture was
towards the cul-de-sac of
realism.
In the smooth hard slate,
the scale of hair tufts
and general treatment
differs from marble and
approximates to that of bronze.

53.   HERACLITUS, PHILOSOPHER OF EPHESUS: BRONZE: MUSEO NAZIONALE, NAPLES
showing change of scale in hairtufts, also engraved lines of hair—firm metallic forms.

GRÆCO-ROMAN

The Etruscans, who invaded Northern Italy in the ninth century B.C., brought with them inherited artistic traditions from Asia Minor and the Ægean. Added to it was their own indefinable yet very real personal note ; statues like the terra-cotta Apollo of Veii or the bronze Orator of Lake Trasimene are unquestionably works of great art.

54. THE ORATOR : ETRUSCAN BRONZE : R.MUSEO ARCHEOLOGICO, FLORENCE

55.   PUGILIST : BRONZE : MUSEO NAZIONALE DELLE TERME, ROME

With the Greco-Roman decline of athletics as a personal discipline, there arose the professional athlete, vicariously admired for his exaggerated muscles and prowess. This pugilist has a certain brutal power and shows good metallic treatment.

56. ALTARE ARA PACIS : PORTION OF RELIEF : MARBLE : UFFIZI, FLORENCE

It is interesting to compare the relief of the Altare Ara Pacis with the frieze of the Parthenon. Both record in relief sculpture a religious procession. But in the whole length of the Parthenon frieze there is little individuality ; only Greeks, tranquil and serene ; while the Roman frieze is obviously full of portraiture of patrician families. Also in the desire for completer realism, the relief has been deepened until it is unwieldy ; and the whole result though the carving is skilful and the sense of personality impressive somehow lacks the rhythmical beauty which makes the Parthenon frieze like a piece of martial and ceremonial music. Again, as in Greece the proportions of childhood are imperfectly understood.

57, 58. ROMAN HEADS : MARBLE : METRO-POLITAN MUSEUM OF ART, NEW YORK

Typical of the later portrait bust extended into almost half-length. Note the iris of the eye is indicated, not by painting, but by incised lines. Face well characterised, hair carelessly carved.

Apart from portraiture, Roman art records the decay of Roman life and not till the rise and growth of the new religion could a new and vital religious art appear. Christian art for a long time echoed Hellenistic and Roman forms, but gradually it developed its own iconography. Then the delicate and truthful realism, for instance, of late Roman painting, gave way to a harsh schematic stylism, which was to harden into the Byzantine formula. Compare the Byzantine Virgin and Child, opposite, with the York Madonna, plate 65.

59. ST. MICHAEL : IVORY : THIRD-SIXTH CENTURY : BRITISH MUSEUM

60.   THE   VIRGIN   AND   CHILD   ENTHRONED : IVORY   PLAQUE : BYZANTINE,
ELEVENTH CENTURY : STROGANOFF COLLECTION : CLEVELAND MUSEUM OF ART

MEDIÆVAL   SCULPTURE

61. MOSAIC : SEVENTH CENTURY : RAVENNA

Perhaps some of the rigidity, the hard formalism of Byzantine art, even in painting and in miniatures, is due to the technical restrictions of mosaic, which compelled the artist to adopt a severe outline and to avoid all chiaroscuro, except the simplest shading. Yet, within the limits imposed by the technique, nothing nobler in art has been done than these great mosaics ; and even today the very names of Augustine, Athanasius, Jerome, Chrysostom, Tertullian, recall to mind not so much personalities, but the tall, harsh, angular figures clad in heavy gilded vestments who look down on us in Ravenna, Constantinople and Monreale. These stern, rigid and uncompromising figures fitly represent the men who built up the great edifice of that Church which asserted its claim to supreme authority over every soul from slave to emperor.

Theocritus, in their vivid freshness. One, in the British Museum, of two women sitting together, vividly recalls the Fifteenth *Idyll*, with its two chattering women who venture among the crowds of Alexandria to make their way to the festival of Adonis, under Ptolemy Philadelphus. Theocritus here gives us a brilliantly vivid picture and one strikingly modern. The crisp and witty dialogue reads like the *New Yorker*, the complaints about maids, and grumbles at the smallness of suburban houses, the gibes at husbands—" the great big endless booby "—the difficulties of shopping, the new fashions in cloaks, the crowded streets, are all vividly recalled and suddenly that far off strange cosmopolitan city with its third of a million people, Alexandria, becomes for us a place of real people. We can almost see the great hall built especially for the festival and we can note, like the ancient historian, that the sculptured groups of tragedy and comedy are " dressed in real clothes " and perhaps like Atheneaus we admire this new realism. Perhaps these draperies were mainly for such decorative sculpture but that temple statues were often so dressed we know from Pausanius who many times records in his garrulous and delightful guide-book (written in the second century, A. D.) that he could not distinguish the material of the statues he came upon, because they were " dressed in a woollen tunic and cloak."

Greek sculpture, inheriting the later Egyptian tradition of well-defined conventions in figure sculpture, worked its way back to a complete realistic verisimilitude, similar to that of Old Kingdom Egyptian sculpture. The cycle was complete, and it was characteristic. Roman sculptors seized on this quality and carried the tendency still further. Yet the differences between Greek and Roman realism are greater than the resemblances, and nothing is gained by the comparison of one work of art with another except for the purpose of understanding both. The great achievements of Greek sculpture have left their impress on the whole course of civilization and culture, and though the noble idealism of earlier Greek art gave way to work in which the technical skill outweighed the thought, and though the intellectual freedom by which they discovered Man led in the end to sophistry, yet the audacity and strength of Greek reasoning renewed the intellectual life of Europe and gave us ideas of nature and mankind as a unity, and so prepared the way for that Roman empire whose strength lay in action rather than thought—and through them to the great concept of the Christian religion. Such a contribution to the culture of the world is inestimable. In the moving words of Gilbert Murray :

" It is a wondrous fabric, held together for an hour by some splendid grasp of human genius—not based on strong material foundations—they saw early the world that is behind the ordinary world of human strivings, more real and more intangible, and throughout their history somehow this ideal haunted the race, a vision perturbing their sight, unfitting them for continued empire, yet shedding strangely over their defeat a splendour denied to their conquerors."

Apollo, Pan and Love
And even Olympian Jove
Grew weak, for killing Truth
had glared on them.
SHELLEY'S " HELLAS "

ROMAN SCULPTURE

IT is not many years since a well-known professor of classical art said to me, in the sacred confines of the Ashmolean Museum : " There is no such thing as Roman art ; it is all either brought from Greece, or is the work of Greek artists exiled or enslaved in Rome." And he quoted approvingly the well-known phrase of Horace : " Captive Greece made captive her savage conqueror, and brought the arts to rustic Latium."

That attitude is much less common today ; at least it is recognized as only a dangerous half-truth. And by a curious irony the tendency of succeeding professors of classical art has been to call almost every hitherto accepted example of Greek sculpture " a Roman copy." Roman sculpture is recognized as a subject worthy of serious and persistent study. (The bibliography of Mrs. Strong's two volumes on Roman art is enormous). And one of the byways of the subject to which it is time scholars turned their attention is the tracing of the development of those schools of sculpture which produced the multitudinous statues hitherto called Greek originals and now so persistently labelled " Roman copy."

In the second century, B. C., the conquest of Hellas was completed by the sack of the great and rich city of Corinth ; but long before that Roman conquerors had brought back Greek sculptures to Rome (in one instance, ten thousand were brought from one island). Beside the influence of these examples, there was the long traditional inheritance from the Etruscans.

Etruscan art, unlike Greek art, was little concerned with legends of the gods, but was directed to concrete things, particularly funerary and commemorative portraiture. As with Egypt, the belief in a future life was the focus of their art, which was largely devoted to making lifelike memorials of the dead. Thus their art turned towards naturalism, which remained a marked characteristic during the whole course of Roman art.

Something in the Roman mind " savagely utilitarian " (as Pliny remarks of his countrymen) made them create few legends, and fewer of those " images " which, like the Greek types, have made a deep and permanent impression on the world ; although, improperly enough, it is by their Roman names that we know and recognize most of the Greek and some of the Egyptian divinities. The passion for realistic portraiture, which began with the Etruscans, reached a climax under the Empire, when the most typical sculptures were those noble and stately statues of the Emperors. So in architecture, beginning with the round hut of the peasant,

50

of wood, reeds and thatch, they evolved typical buildings like the Temple of Vesta and the Pantheon, which is just the round hut translated into marble and concrete and hollow tiles. But the Pantheon, though it was the abode of the gods, is less typical of Rome, her power and her skill, than are the vast Baths of Caracalla, or the palaces of the Cæsars. Their most typical buildings are not the sacred ones, but baths, fora, triumphal arches, aqueducts, viaducts. These are all more characteristic ; indeed a Roman aqueduct, like that at Segovia, with its vast scale, its enduring granite, its precious gift of water, its mere existence there—more than a thousand miles from Rome—is at once typical and symbolic. Greek trabeated architecture is static. Roman arcuated architecture as at Segovia is building in being ; it is almost in movement, each arch requiring its neighbour, till, at the end, the living thrust is carried by buttresses to earth. Greek energies were spent on discovering the laws of nature and of thought. Roman energy was bent on institutions. Greece may have *civilized* the world, even the Roman world ; but Rome *organized* it. The Greeks founded the City—the Romans the Nation.

The ideal of the Roman empire was to embrace in one orbit all communities of civilized men. Laws were adjusted and institutions changed, without discarding the old order. Indeed early Roman history is largely a record of adjusting the relations of conflicting orders, and the gradual admission of the unprivileged to equality of rights. So in architecture their peculiar gifts of adjustment and organization enabled them to fuse into a coherent style the hitherto entirely separate elements of the lintel and the arch. Out of this fusion arose the great Romanesque style, from which Gothic architecture was born. The Roman genius was for practical affairs. They were " realists " in every sense ; ready to use the arts, the tools and the ideas of other races and " desirable aliens " like the Greeks, turning all these gifts and forces towards their own practical ends with the skill of the Philistine. Their adaptability in widening precedents to meet new cases, in building new structures on old foundations, yet retaining all the old material that would serve, is characteristic. This is often true, not only in their gradual codifying of law and building up of a social structure, but also in actual building, where they many times re-used columns and capitals and material. Sometimes this re-used material was spoil from Greece or from the outposts of their Empire, sometimes it was Roman. This habit led to a curiously impersonal style of architectural sculpture, by which the sculptures on the Arch of Constantine, though mostly stolen from other earlier monuments, are so skilfully adapted and adjusted as to look homogeneous. This power of organizing and standardizing is seen even in Roman England. The Great Wall seems to be built of millions of stones worked fairly nearly into a standard size such as could be handled by two masons. Quoins and bonders of course were larger ; but the impression is distinctly that of a work of what is now called mass production. A Roman or an Egyptian would have understood Mr. Henry Ford, a Greek would not. And as one traces the structural plan and mosaic decoration of the Roman villa from Timgad and Carthage to Spain and

Chedworth and Bignor, one finds that it became as stereotyped as the villa of English suburbia. What results from this kind of organization is a high technical standard of workmanship, but never a great school or training ground of craftsmen. The " composite capital," using details of Ionic and Corinthian capitals in combination, as on the Arch of Titus, is another example of Roman adaptation, somewhat parallel to the fusion of the elements of the lintel and the arch in architecture. Yet this was quite different from the eclecticism of, for instance, Persian art ; because, with his power of synthesis, the Roman artist ennobled his borrowings, except in the case of the Corinthian order in architecture, which in Roman hands lost its Greek restraint and became too richly exuberant in all its detail. It is characteristic that the Romans were the first to use the columnar order of the Greeks as if it were a decorative rather than a structural feature. They thus established the idea of building for effect, rather than for purpose. Nevertheless, they used the Greek orders with spectacular effect.

It was against impalpable things that all the realist skill and might of Rome was helpless. For instance, Rome could never impose law on Ireland or on the Picts of Scotland ; and all her efforts to extirpate the new religion of Christianity were ineffectual. Rome could acquire and use beauty, but could seldom create new beauty. This failure to initiate is, perhaps, the mark of the parvenu. Rome was rich before she was civilized ; and, as with the nouveau-riche, her culture was largely bought ready-made. But although the traditions of Rome were largely adopted. they were held in high regard. The story is told of how Cicero, when Commissioner for Sicily, sought out the neglected and overgrown tomb of Archimedes, cleaned it and cleared it of weeds, re-cut on it the cylinder and the sphere—those symbols of the famous theorem—and so restored to Syracuse and the world the memory of her greatest citizen. And yet Cicero held it as a virtue in Pompey that " the historic fame of no city seduced him to sight-seeing, and the statues, pictures and adornments of Greek cities which others regarded as plunder he would not even look at." Ironically enough (for Cicero seems to agree with Pompey) it seems odd that future ages should call the guides to such historic cities and sights Cicerones ! The sense of inheritance is the mark of a critical and synthesising people, rather than of a creative people : and this historic sense led them to make those great monuments recording the exploits and victories of their famous generals and emperors, which are so characteristic of their art. The Greeks memorialized their conquests by symbolic groups of Centaurs and Lapiths. The Romans carved the lineaments and recognizable features and accoutrements of the actual personages ; thus, incidentally, providing for posterity a very valuable body of data of historic importance. They invented also the continuous narrative : as in the Column of Trajan, where a whole series of episodes in the Dacian campaign may be followed to this day.

This preoccupation with individual realism, this effort at complete verisimilitude, left little room for the emergence of the personality of the artist. Those personal touches by which, in other schools of sculpture, one can recognize and trace an artist and his school, are not to be found in

Roman art. There was, indeed, a curious sort of "Pre-Raphælite" movement under Augustus, which strove to imitate the forms of archaic Greece ; and later there was a revival of neo-Attic work. But, on the whole, both in historical and commemorative monuments and in portraiture (these two groups merge into each other) the outstanding quality is the individuality of the persons represented. This individuality is especially characteristic of portraits under the Republic ; while under Augustus there is a marked tendency in official portraiture towards a heroic and almost divinized representation. The bronze Augustus found at Meroe has in it something of the sustained nobility and impressive aloofness of the Egyptian Kephren—or the great Rameses at Turin. The quartz eyes inset in the Augustus head show a tendency towards realism which was carried still further under the late Emperors, when Roman sculptors achieved elaborate polychrome effects by using differently coloured marbles, with gilded hair and glass eyes carefully coloured ; in fact, they exploited every kind of material to gain their æsthetic effects and they aimed at a very complete realism. In its whole course, Roman portrait art achieved and maintained a very high level of excellence. A study of the sculptures in the Roman Court of the Metropolitan Museum, for instance, shows that in the portrayal of contemporary people they show far greater understanding and consequently a more interesting technique than in their copies of the Greek philosophers and poets which were in such demand and with which they may there be conveniently compared. In the portrait busts certain technical developments are noticeable. There is the gradual growth from the head and neck, till the bust becomes almost a half figure, and sometimes includes the arms. There is too the carved incision of the iris of the eye, and the elaborate polychrome effects of different marbles, waxed, gilded and polished. As Mr. R. Hinks says : " The determination to extract every particle of physiognomic significance was a Roman contribution to the art of portraiture " and, he adds : " The finest Antonine portraits show a technical brilliance and psychological insight which were never surpassed in Antiquity."[1] It was a great school of portraiture ; and, just as the later Fleming could make a work of art out of an ugly old man with a bulbous nose, so with the same unflinching realism the Roman sculptor could make, in the gilded bronze Vitellius, a record of a loathsomely sensual head, which is yet informed with vital " style " and touched with beauty. And one can trace and understand the cruelty and ferocity of Caracalla in that marble head in Rome, because the sculptor has, with burning passion, annihilated his material to express the character. And there is in the British Museum a bronze head of Hadrian remarkable for beauty of its metallic treatment, especially in the hair and beard ; a good deal of its detail seems to have been engraved after casting, and the whole effect is one of great delicacy and refinement. Compared with these vital works, an official statue like that of Marcus Aurelius on horseback seems quite lifeless and characterless.

[1] " Roman Heads."

New forces were at work. The old Olympian gods had been " rationalized " out of existence. Roman life and, consequently, Roman art were being marked by a great cleavage into Pagan and Christian, although the division was not at first clearly defined. Great conflicts were arising. Pagan civic power was being challenged by the spiritual power of the new and strange religion of Christianity. The healing spirit of Greek and Roman humanism, as known to Virgil and Cicero, was now pitted against the fierce and hard dogmatism of people who owed no allegiance to the state or to tradition. No great pagan art could arise in these early centuries A.D. ; the pagans had gods they no longer believed in and instead of the searching and serious rationalizing of Socrates and Euripides about the nature of the Gods, there was the laughing mockery of Lucian to whom Zeus was merely a comic figure. " All eclectics are sceptics," says Novalis, and eclecticism—" the creed of weary minds " (as Mahaffy calls it)—had laid hold of the dying Roman world in which the most living thing was the Christian church. These Christians had One new God, incarnate in the Son ; but they rarely represented Him in spite of, possibly because of, their compelling passion, deep conviction and spiritual fervour. In its great struggle with the new religion, paganism spiritualized itself by absorbing that last phase of ancient philosophical humanism, Neo-Platonism ; and thus set up a spiritual rival to the new religion. But strangely enough the Christians in turn absorbed Neo-Platonism, and thus cut the ground from under the feet of the pagan world. And so it was Greek intellectualism, rather than Roman rationalism, which was absorbed into the Christian religion. There was a real affinity between Platonism and Christianity. Socrates and Christ were unquestionably the two greatest religious teachers of the Western world. And in Plato and Paul each found the great interpreter. There was something not quite Greek in Socrates' individualism ; for instance, his passionate plea for the integrity of the individual soul in the *Apology*. He will not " conform " to the State ; and in this he asserts a new ethic—consistency to truth. As Christianity absorbed pagan religious ideas and philosophy, so also it absorbed Roman and Egyptian forms into its ritual ; and in the gradual development of Christian mythology the legends of the Saints often follow closely those of the pagan gods and heroes. The fusion of Christianity with Hellenism showed itself in the more naturalistic art of Alexandria ; while from Persia and the East came the use of symbolism, and Christians, being liable to suppression by the Roman State, seized on symbols and avoided open representation in art. The Fish and the monogram represented Christ ; the dove represented the holy Spirit ; the vine symbolized the church ; the phœnix, the resurrection, etc. Similarly, the earliest representations of Christ closely resemble the beardless classical Apollo, the halo, even, being occasionally omitted. Not till the second or third century was the bearded, long-haired Christ known. Again, David the psalmist and harpist is often indistinguishable from the pagan Orpheus. The change was often merely in the label.

So also did the everyday clothes of the Roman citizen become, almost without the Christians realizing it, the vestments of the new religion. What was originally purely secular dress gradually acquired a special significance, through being retained by a conservative and powerful clergy long after the clothes had become obsolete in the daily life of a Roman citizen. Dean Stanley has an interesting essay on this subject, in which he traces the names of ecclesiastical vestments to their Roman origins. For instance, the alb is just the Roman shirt (*camisa* whence *chemise*), which being a white garment, was called " alba " ; and the fact that the finest of these garments were at one time made in Dalmatia gives us the word " dalmatic." So also the garment worn *over* the fur or wool *pelisse* becomes, by a contraction of *super pelissa*, the " surplice." While the chasuble, originally a round blanket with a hole for the head in the middle, like the Mexican poncho, is named from *casa*, a house, because it enveloped the wearer ; much as a hat is (or used to be) vulgarly called a " tile."

Roman sculpture has constantly suffered by being compared with Greek sculpture. The Roman mind was untouched by the imaginative idealism of Greek art, hence the Roman sculptor failed to create a religious art which can move us today. This inability to make a great imaginative effort is Roman, and it is characteristic that Lucretius, who in his long and noble poem on the *Nature of Things*, " denied divinely the divine," is concerned only to show the ceaseless ebb and flow of nature, her inexhaustible energy alternating between life and death, and makes no mention of the impalpable spiritual forces which unite man to Nature. Rome—that city of gold—the far-flung Roman Empire—had behind it skill, organization, culture, but little spiritual purpose. The constant struggle for expansion, the necessity for organization, the search for power rather than for beauty, left little leisure for any wide intellectual advance, and this lack is visible in Roman art. In the preface to *Back to Methuselah*, Bernard Shaw says wisely : " Art has never been great except when it has been providing an iconography for a living religion." And he adds, " It has never been quite contemptible except when imitating the iconography when the religion had become a superstition." But in the narrower field of portraiture the Roman contribution is memorable and in no derogatory sense one might use of it the words of Horace to Licinius : " Safe in his golden mediocrity." And one might add : " This very mediocrity, so fine, so chastened, so certain, is in truth as inimitable as any other great artistic quality ; one must fall back on the word genius, and remember that genius does not confine itself within the borders of any theory but works its own will." (J. W. Mackail on Horace).[1]

[1] Latin Literature.

We Christians are but of yesterday—and already we fill the world! We have left you only your temples. TERTULLIAN, *c.* 200 A.D.

THE RISE OF CHRISTIAN ART

THE process of growth from a naturalistic and highly developed art to an art of abstract and schematic symbolism, was a reversal of the process by which Greek and classical art had grown. Only in Egypt had art begun with a realistic aim, and worked its way through realism to a more rigid stylism. The change from paganism to Christianity, though it wrought great differences in the lives and feelings of men, showed for a long time little change in the forms in which feeling was expressed. The art of the catacombs derives directly from classical art, but being largely the work of simple people intent on didacticism, it has not the skilful and assured technique of the Roman artists or of the painters of the " Aldo brandini marriage." The art, both in painting and sculpture, of the pagan Roman state was formal, pompous and accomplished ; in contrast to the restricted technique and elementary symbolism of the Christians. The beginnings of Christian sculpture and art, being probably secret, were not the work of skilled or trained artists. This new art was largely funerary and memorial, as was the Etruscan art from which was developed the art of Rome. It was not till the fourth century that Christian art could be openly displayed alongside of Roman pagan art, and it is both symptomatic and symbolic that in the fourth century the Altar of Victory was removed from the Senate—as the majority of the Senators were by then Christians. And the word " paganism " was by then used as meaning the religion of the peasants (pagani), thus reversing the conditions of several centuries earlier when the State, realizing that the claim to spiritual independence of the Christians was incompatible with their supreme Social Authority, endeavoured to extirpate the new and challenging religion. The removal of the Altar was an acknowledgment of the failure of this attempt.

From humble beginnings the church was rising to power and authority, and gradually a new art was developed. In certain aspects this art kept closely to ancient traditions and only slowly was there incorporated into it a whole series of new symbols. The changes were slight but they were significant. Just as the ritual of Christianity absorbed certain pagan forms and models, so too in the legends and mythology of Christian saints, as well as in the artistic presentation of them in painting and sculpture, one can trace their growth from the familiar models of pagan gods and heroes, though the outlines are now formalized and abstract. Some new elements crept in from Syria and the East ; but the marked characteristic of early Christian art is the gradual substitution of an abstract and schematic symbolism for the more concrete and realistic expression of classical art. And this more abstract art was developed beyond the rigid symbolism of Byzantine art, until it was brought by Duccio, Giotto and the mediæval carvers to that lovely spiritualized realism of the great age of Christian art, in the twelfth and thirteenth centuries when form and spirit became one.

The history of this thousand years between Constantine (who made Christianity the state religion, and founded its great capital in the east) and the apogee of Christian art is often dark, bloody and confused. Yet, in spite of endless wars, proscriptions and restrictions, the great edifice of the Church was built up, both materially and immaterially, and there arose two noble and imaginative artistic movements : the splendid development of the art of mosaic decoration, and the soaring and aspiring art of Gothic architecture. In the time of Constantine, what to a Roman citizen constituted the whole civilized world was under one vast political, social and ecclesiastical organization. The official adoption of Christianity was gradual. Even Constantine's coins bore both Christian and pagan emblems. And though it seemed easier to make a new Christian capital at Byzantium, rather than at Rome where pagan temples and statues insistently challenged attack, yet Byzantium, meant to be Christian and Latin, became Christian and Greek.

The brief episode of Julian the Apostate had no significant influence on art, perhaps mainly because Christian art was still almost entirely pagan in form in any case. The marble statue of Julian in the Louvre, though draped like the great figure of Sophocles in the Lateran, is formal and empty by comparison with it. Julian's desire to graft the ethical conceptions of stoicism at its best, on to a mystical interpretation of the old mythology made little appeal, and died at his death : and under Theodosius Christianity was completely reinstated. Yet the powerful and living fruits of pagan philosophies, as also of pagan art, lived on and vitalized thought and art. Augustine was saturated with Plato and neo-Platonism ; and it was characteristic of him that, after Alaric's sack of Rome in 410, he wrote the *De Civitate Dei*, to remind all Christians that there was a heavenly city which could not be attacked or sacked, which had no frontiers, and which embraced the faithful over all the world. The city-state ideals of Plato and Aristotle were still potent and had taken on a wider and more spiritual application to conceptions of society. With strange prescience Augustine realized that he stood between two civilizations and he first used the term *In hoc interim seculo*—the middle age—and laid the foundations for a true philosophy of history, asserted the reality of the spiritual life and its indestructibility. The Empires of the world might crumble and pass ; the things of the spirit remained.

A typical ivory relief of the emperor Flavius Honorius, exactly contemporary with Augustine, shows the emperor holding in his right hand a sort of labarum with the inscription IN NOMINE XPI VINCAS SEMPER, while in his left is the pagan Nike or victory on the orb (a symbol of sovereignty which survives in the English regalia to this day). Certain Christian emblems, particularly sacred monograms in Greek characters, were in common use ; though often these Christian devices were in the strange company of Venus and her nereids, or other frankly pagan motifs.

The emblem of the Pagan Goddess Hecate, the moon, was adopted into Christian iconography by Constantine, and in later Gothic sculpture is very often found associated with the Virgin. Strangely enough, it was re-adopted from Christian Byzantine art and became the national symbol of the Mohammedan Turks.

The article on sculpture in Encyclopedia Britannica (fourteenth Ed.) boldly states that the fourth century A.D. marks " the lowest point of degradation " in the art of sculpture. The world of Europe was engaged in other affairs. The head of the Christian church, the Pope, was challenging the authority of the Emperors. The great edifice of the church, both im-materially and materially, now stood for the peace of the church instead of the peace of Rome. The church stood between conqueror and conquered and told all—Roman, Barbarian, slave and citizen—that there was one God, one equal soul, one common judgment, one common life hereafter, and she was gathering to herself all the knowledge of the time, conserving it and subordinating it to the religious life, and in due time passed it on to the modern world. A new literature was arising, and though Augustine deleted from his works a treatise *On the Arts* as " trash ", yet art was neither extirpated nor degraded. It was merely reduced to very simple terms and from the confused Pagan and Christian devices, emblems and attitudes there gradually emerged a noble and splendid art in the service of the Church for teaching didactic truth, and in the service of church architecture as decoration. This was the art of mosaic. There was little sculpture, but there are many ivory reliefs which show superb skill. The famous St. Michael in the British Museum is among the finest ; the date is uncertain. Mr. O. Dalton, the writer of the *Guide to Early Christian Antiquities*, dates it " probably fourth century ", while Labarte dates it to the time of Justinian in the sixth century.

By the middle of the fifth century, the great school of Christian mosaic had arisen. The tomb of Galla Placida at Ravenna is a notable example of its work. For the next five hundred years the mosaic workers produced some of the most splendid and enduring monuments of Christian art in the world, in almost every church built from the time of the building of St. Sophia to that of St. Mark's, Venice, just before 1000 A.D.

The sculpture of this age was almost wholly decorative, and orna-mental emblems and symbols were always used rather than representation. It was allusive art and seldom in any sense pictorial. The Peacock repre-sented the soul ; the Vine symbolized the church ; the Phœnix was an emblem of the resurrection. The consuming passion of the age was not for representation but for subtle theological speculation and discussion. Gibbon quotes a comment on this characteristic aspect of fourth century life in Byzantium in a contemporary letter from Gregory of Nyssa : " People swarm everywhere, talking of incomprehensible matters, in hovels, streets and squares ; when I ask how many obols I have to pay, they answer with philosophemisms about the born and the unborn. If I inquire the price of bread I am told ' The Father is greater than the Son '. I call the servant to tell me whether my bath is ready and he rejoins that the Son was created out of nothing." It is clear that to this generation emblematic expression would be more natural than representation. The church of St. Sophia at Byzantium is one of the noblest buildings in Christendom. In the sixth century, Justinian depleted the treasury and left the Empire bankrupt, to build it. " Glory be to God who hath thought me worthy to accomplish so great a work. I have vanquished thee, O Solomon," said Justinian at the consecration of this vast and beautiful building. There were columns, candelabra, and ornaments of silver to the extent of forty tons in the sanctuary, and the altar was of enamelled gold ; so that, as Gibbon in his ironic way remarks, " One might be tempted to suppose it to be the residence or even the workmanship of the Deity ". The building was designed by Greek architects and perhaps it is not fanciful to see in this work, as March Phillips does, the supreme expression of the later Greek spirit. Greek philosophic thought, Greek science, and all the subtle speculation of the Greek mind is here embodied. It is noteworthy that in all this vast building there is no sculptured statue or even a relief of the human figure. The decoration is almost wholly mosaic and the effect must have been stupendous. It remains today perhaps the only building in the whole world which fitly embodies the spiritual aspirations of man. The vast dome, the smaller domes and semi-domes, the great arches which have to bear this tremendous burden and which are, themselves, only a part of an elaborate system of burden and thrust bearing—all this affects one as the architecture of ecstasy, and appropriately enough seems to have required Divine Wisdom to conceive and build it. And it is strangely significant, that very soon after it was built, it was with a new and officially secret explosive known as Greek fire that Leo the Isaurian repelled the Arab invaders, and saved the city and the Eastern Empire from the menace of Islam and the Saracen. Though Justinian suppressed the Platonic school of Athens as inimical to Christian thought, yet Christian theology, Christian art and ritual were formed out of a Greek matrix.

Byzantium remained Christian for more than seven hundred years. But no sooner had the menace to the Church from outside been repelled than the whole Christian world was rent by a controversy over the use of images. This was an age in which theological subtleties, such as finding a formula for expressing the idea of the Godhead and Manhood of the Second Person in the Trinity, exercised the acutest intellects ; it was also an age of unreasoning credulity, in which miraculous legends were accepted as history, and power was even believed to reside, not only in the Saints, but also in carved and painted representations of them. The Mohammedans scornfully pointed to the many gods of the Christian idolaters. So, in 726, the Emperor, Leo the Isaurian, proscribed all images, and ordered the removal from every church of all sacred statues and pictorial representations of saints or people. He ordered plaster to be spread over all the gigantic mosaic pictures in St. Sophia (incidentally thus helping to preserve them. Today St. Sophia is a national monument, and the plaster is being gradually removed). He allowed the Cross to be used as a symbol, but banned the crucifix bearing the image of Christ. He ruled that " All

59

visible symbols of Christ except the Eucharist were blasphemous and heretical and that Image Worship was a corruption of Christianity and a revival of Paganism ". Here again the Church made no abatement of its claim to spiritual pre-eminence ; the Pope vigorously defended the use of images and excommunicated the Emperor, whose authority in such matters he refused to recognize. The Emperor replied by sending a fleet and army to attack Rome, but a providential storm thwarted this intention. The quarrel dragged its unseemly length for more than a century with no finality, and left as its legacy only the knowledge that many beautiful works of art had been destroyed, and the useful word " iconoclast ". A beautiful defence of the use of images is found in St. John of Damascus, eighth century : " I am too poor to possess books, I have no leisure for reading ; I enter the church choked with the cares of the world ; the glowing colours attract my sight like a flowering meadow, and the glory of God steals imperceptibly into my soul. I gaze on the fortitude of the martyr and the crown with which he is rewarded, and the fire of holy emulation is kindled within me. I fall down and worship God through the martyr, and I receive salvation." But one unforeseen result was that during and after the Iconoclastic quarrel many sculptors and artists were starved and ex-tirpated while others wandered all over Europe to places which were less affected by the proscription. These wandering artists conveyed and spread all over Europe from Russia to Ireland, and from Norway to Spain, a strangely similar artistic style, so homogeneous as to be unique and to correspond with the dogmatic unity of the Roman Church.

The rise of the Carolingian school of art, which, under the fostering care of Charlemagne, produced notable work in miniatures and ivory reliefs, was perhaps much aided by these exiled Byzantine artists, whose influence may also be seen in the great and flourishing art of Ireland during the eighth and ninth centuries.

During the European chaos of the fifth, sixth and seventh centuries—that welter of bloody invasions of which almost the only record is destruc-tion and the synonyms Hun and Vandal (an echo of the Vandals is em-bedded in the name of their last stronghold, Andalusia), Ireland was remote and free from invasion, providing a quiet haven for scholars and saints. In these centuries she built up a native culture, orally transmitted, especi-ally of literature and law ; and she also received and preserved the learning of the Ancient World. It is only in relatively late years that sufficient attention has been given to the influence on European mediæval culture and art of this Celtic civilization. The whole period from the fifth to the tenth centuries was apt to be dismissed by earlier historians as the Dark Ages. Yet the term Dark Ages seems a strange misnomer when one thinks that this was the age of Byzantium, Rome, Ravenna, Ireland and Iona in the Western world. Clonmacnoise was founded just before the dedication of St. Sophia, and Columba founded Iona just before the death of Justinian. Ireland, lying on the outer rim of the vast Roman Empire, was yet never Romanized. In the sixth century the Vandals blotted out the last remains of Roman culture in Gaul but Latin and Greek were still studied and taught in Ireland. Indeed, Mrs. J. R. Green says : " Probably in the seventh and eighth centuries no one in Western Europe spoke Greek who was not Irish or taught by an Irishman. St. Columba ruled Iona for thirty-four years and by the free association of men through the power of human brotherhood, learning, religion and the arts were saved to Europe."[1] " The history of Latin," says W. P. Ker, " is the history of Education, and follows the great schools. There is a line from Ireland to Iona, from Iona to Jarrow and York, and from there to the court of Charlemagne. If studies failed in Gaul or Italy, they flourished in Ireland. Latin literature was all one."[2] When all learning was kept within the compass of the Church, it was almost impossible to distinguish between secular and sacred knowledge. To quote from Ker again : " They (the churchmen) taught the liberal arts, they collected material for natural and civil history and expounded it, they preserved the classical forms of verse and prose, their rhyming hymns are the original Latin poetry of the dark ages." And it is characteristic that Gibbon, though admitting that Iona had a " classic " library, dismissed all this intellectual activity with its implications and potentialities in one sentence : " And Iona, one of the Hebrides which was planted by Irish monks, diffused over the Northern regions a doubtful ray of Science and superstition."

Ireland had close relations with the Continent. There were Irish scholars and teachers at Luxeuil, Bobbio, St. Gall, Cologne, Metz and Mainz, most of which were Irish foundations. The Library of the Monastery at Bobbio was catalogued in the tenth century and it then had seven hundred volumes including Horace, Virgil, Juvenal, Ovid, Cicero, Livy, Terence, Demosthenes and Aristotle, besides the writings of the fathers and all the sacred books. Bobbio survived till 1803, when it was suppressed by the French government. Irish scholars taught Charlemagne and from the eighth to the tenth century they wandered over Europe, teaching, bringing manuscripts, writing new manuscripts, and founding monasteries. They were the possessors and bearers of a higher culture than was then known anywhere else in Northern Europe. The art of illumination was developed in unique excellence. The Books of Kells and Durrow are the most astonishing books in the world, and they have had an immense influence, not only on calligraphy, but on sculpture and all the decorative arts, for all these artists reacted on each other. In the century between 700 and 800 there were forty known scribes in Ireland alone, and these artists put into current circulation a vast range of decorative designs which were copied into many and varied media. The beautiful stone crosses of Ruthwell and Bewcastle seem to owe something to the missal writers and perhaps too some influence from Byzantine or other ivory relief carvings. Irish scholars travelled as far as the Holy Land ; and, about the time of Charlemagne, Brother Fidelis of Clonmacnoise sailed up Trajan's canal to the Nile, measured the base of the great pyramid, and found it to be 400 feet. Irish monks at the same time reached Iceland and left there a

[1] " Irish Nationality."   [2] S. Gwynn, " Ireland's Culture."

61

foundation which long survived. Again, Ferghail of Aghaboe, in the middle of the eighth century, while the iconoclastic dispute raged, taught that the world was a sphere and that there were people living in the Antipodes. Moengal, instructor of St. Gall and sometime Abbot of Bangor, taught the seven liberal arts of Grammar, Rhetoric, Dialectic, Arithmetic, Music, Geometry and Astronomy, and was especially concerned to impart the Greek language. Moengal was an artist as well as a scholar ; at Basle there is a psalter written and illuminated by him, in Greek text with a Latin translation. The Celtic artists who wrote the Books of Kells and Durrow, who made the Ardagh chalice and the Cross of Cong and the shrine for St. Patrick's bell, who carved the hundreds of crosses and gravestones scattered over Ireland, Scotland and northern England, certainly made a notable contribution to the arts of the world. It is to be noted that the word Irish denoted not so much the country as the fact that these people all spoke the Irish language. They came from both Ireland and Scotland and both these countries still show a rich heritage of their work. This inheritance of design probably survived longer in Scotland than in Ireland.

Yet during these centuries Ireland contributed little to the parent art of architecture. One hundred and fifty years after the founding of Iona and Clonmacnoise those busy and important abbeys consisted only of groups of wattled huts, gathered around tiny oratories ; while on the continent the Benedictine abbey of St. Gall had grown into a stately stone building. " Thus," as Stephen Gwynn says, " while in one sense the Irish were the founders of mediæval Christendom in the Europe north of the Alps, in another sense northern Europe had to break away from the asceticism of Irish teachers to reach that mediæval Christian culture of which Gothic architecture is the splendid expression."

The Iconoclastic Edict of 726 is a sort of midway point between the founding of Constantinople and that intellectual flowering time of the twelfth century, in which Arnold of Brescia and Peter Abelard were conspicuous for far-reaching thought and profound philosophical analysis. In the hundred years that lie between the crowning of Charlemagne and the death of Alfred the Great, France, Germany and England were welded into nations. Meanwhile the Northmen came into France, and these Vikings gradually became Normans, whose power and influence on France and England became so important in the next two centuries. Charlemagne's great Eastern contemporary, Haroun-al-Raschid, remains vivid to us today by the immortal stories associated with his name. But great as was the organizing power of Charlemagne, life under him in northern Europe was barbarous and insecure as compared to life at Byzantium. During the eighth, ninth and tenth centuries that great capital of the Roman Empire was still the seat of the most stable and cultured power in the world, and on its existence depended the future of civilization. From the time of Justinian to the Crusades, wealth, organization, knowledge and art were safeguarded there, and the flickering torch of Greek culture and art was through them handed on to the pioneers of the great age of the mediæval Christian builders. Yet this epoch was dismissed by Voltaire as " a worthless repertory of declamation and miracles—disgraceful to the human mind ". And the Rationalist historians of the nineteenth century used the word Byzantine as synonymous with any elaborate and effete ceremonial —an absurdity comparable to the Renaissance use of the word Gothic as meaning barbarous.

In the ninth century the Church was finally and irrevocably divided over the doctrines of the Procession of the Holy Ghost from the Father and the Son, and of clerical celibacy. The Eastern Church denounced these as damnable heresies, while the Roman Church regarded them as fundamental. The struggle for supremacy between the Emperors and the Popes was ever recurrent and never finally resolved. The great and powerful Pope Hildebrand claimed that the temporal was subordinate to the spiritual power; the Emperor to the Pope. He thus claimed, as Sovereign Pontiff, a universal and absolute authority over all Christians in the world. He excommunicated the German King Henry IV and absolved his subjects from their allegiance. He forced a bitter abasement from the king at Canossa ; and, although Hildebrand died twenty years before the king, the Church was so strong that, when Henry died in 1106, he was denied absolution to the last. Fifty years later, the Emperor Barbarossa, claiming to be the head of United Christendom, was yet forced by the Pope (the only English Pope, and appropriately called Breakspeare) to alight from his horse and hold the reins of that of His Holiness. Another fifty years, and Innocent III, claiming to be God's vicegerent and above all temporal princes, forced the English King John to surrender his crown to the Pontiff and receive it back again from His Holiness' hands ; thus acknowledging the King's vassalage to the Pope. This sense of immense and despotic power and authority is fitly expressed in Romanesque and Norman architecture. Durham cathedral is the expression in stone of the Church Militant. And in France, in the noble group of Romanesque churches at Poitiers, for instance, the sense of the majesty and strength of the Church is almost overwhelming. This religious power and fervour had in an earlier age led to the founding and development of the religious orders, bound to an ideal rule of life (notably the Benedictines and the Cistercians) ; now to this same impulse was due the foundation of the military orders of Knights Templar and Knights Hospitaller. Together these groups and Rome inspired the Crusades—that last great clash between the East and the West, and one which did irreparable damage to Byzantium.

In all the Romanesque and Norman architecture of this age, sculpture has a very subordinate place. Figure sculpture is scarce before the beginning of the twelfth century. Norman and Romanesque sculpture is generally rich and effective as decoration, but it is noteworthy that the rich effect is achieved more by the repetition of simple forms than by the use of forms which are in themselves beautiful or subtle or natural. The famous west doorway of Iffley Church is very elaborate and rich in decorative effect, but the units of which it is composed are all simple. In the twelfth century, sculptors seem to have found themselves able to do beautiful decorative work, including figure work—the figures being often small and subordinate to the ornament. The twelfth century remains at Malmesbury (an Irish foundation—and in earlier ages the greatest seat of learning in England) show sculpture which clearly derives from the missal painters' decorations, but the small figures which are half hidden in the elaborate ornaments are delicately carved and the whole design of the sculpture is beautiful and skilful. The rich ornamental work, deeply undercut and carved with great delicacy, does not seem to be based—even remotely—on natural forms. In this it resembles the miniature painter's work. Indeed, in all this art, especially in the Western Empire and in Ireland, there was little reference to Nature : it was concerned almost wholly with symbols and formulæ. When natural forms, either animal or human, were represented they were reduced to an almost abstract simplicity. They were used for their decorative value and natural representation was as foreign to the Byzantine artist as it was to the Celt ; yet both produced work of enduring beauty and interest. Last century a painter's handbook (perhaps of the eleventh century) was found in the Monastery of Mount Athos. This gave the motifs of hundreds of designs for compositions representing almost every incident in sacred story. The scheme there used as traditional for the Last Supper is essentially that adopted by Leonardo, and that of the Last Judgment resembles Michelangelo's fresco. The elaborate practical rules for the painter are probably based on traditions much older than the book. Study of Nature had little or no part in a painter's life. What was studied was the formula, not the natural concept from which the formula derived. " In the Eastern Empire," says Roger Fry,[1] " an art was cultivated which followed the . . . direction of a reversion of elementary symbolism, but which followed it not from indifference or incapacity, but with self-conscious zest and fervour. The artists of Byzantium accepted this de-naturalized and schematic art as the formula most capable of conveying that perfervid and speculative dogmatism and that love of elaborate ceremonial which were salient characteristics of their civilization. They, too, like Western artists, neglected Nature ; but the history of Byzantine art is one of the many proofs that the love of Nature, and curiosity about natural forms, are not the only things, are not even necessary things, to keep an art alive."

Art is kept alive despite proscriptions, war and bloodshed, because the sense of æsthetic needs seems to be permanent and ineradicable in mankind. But great changes were at hand. In the twelfth and thirteenth centuries, the Crusades brought an infiltration of Eastern details and forms. The growing dissatisfaction with the formulæ and rigidity of the Byzantine tradition, the intellectual awakening, the dawning consciousness of the beauty of the natural world—these diverse but related factors and elements led to the growth of a civic-religious culture such as had not appeared on earth before.

[1] " Art before Giotto."

62. RUTHWELL CROSS : RED SANDSTONE :
SEVENTH OR EIGHTH CENTURY

63. PAGE FROM THE BOOK OF KELLS: TRINITY COLLEGE, DUBLIN

The Books of Kells and Durrow are the most astonishing books in the world, and they have had an immense influence, not only on calligraphy but on sculpture and all the decorative arts. In the century between 700 and 800 there were forty known scribes in Ireland alone, and these artists put into current circulation a vast range of decorative designs which were copied into many and varied media. The beautiful stone crosses of Ruthwell and Bewcastle seem to owe something to the missal writers and perhaps to some influence from Byzantine or other ivory relief carvings.

SEA · MARIA

64. CROSS AT KILBRIDE, ARGYLLSHIRE: CELTIC STONE WORK: EARLY SIXTEENTH CENTURY showing a strangely primitive type of figure for its late date. The hair is in fact very similar to the hair of the Kells MS. There is an I.H.S. monogram at the top—very rare in Celtic work.

65. MADONNA AND CHILD: STONE RELIEF: TENTH OR ELEVENTH CENTURY: YORK MINSTER

66. IFFLEY (OXON): HEAD OF WEST DOORWAY: *c.* 1160

The doorway of Iffley Church is very elaborate and rich in decorative effect but the units of which it is composed are all simple. Tools were probably few and simple and even this lovely doorway might have been carved with only two or three chisels— the stone being an easy one to work.

The well-known relief sculpture at Chichester is among the earliest figure sculpture in England (excepting the Celtic work at Bewcastle, etc.). It is very primitive and has evidently been carved by one unskilled in figure sculpture, and probably hampered by his few simple tools. The drill holes in the eyes (for the drill seems to have been known in all ages) are so wildly large that it has been suggested that glass eyes were inset, but this is unlikely ; the whole relief was coloured and set high up on the wall.

68. THE RAISING OF LAZARUS :
STONE PANEL : *c.* ELEVENTH CENTURY :
CHICHESTER CATHEDRAL

67. IVORY PANELS FROM A CASKET :
EARLY CHRISTIAN, FIFTH CENTURY
BRITISH MUSEUM

69. NOTRE DAME DE CHARTRES : STONE

Several of these Queens of the Royal House of David bear a remarkable resemblance
to the Attic Kore of the sixth century B.C.   See plate 25.   The similarity extends even
to the technique of the drapery carving, with its thin zigzag folds, the faces with sweet
impersonal smile and flattened, simple modelling.   All this is like a Greek echo, yet

70. S. GILLES DU GARD, PROVENCE : STONE TWELFTH CENTURY

by no possibility could the Chartres carvers have seen any examples of archaic Greek work. But it is worth noting that it was exactly at this time that Chartres was the centre of a school of philosophy inspired by Greek, and especially Platonic, thought. The drapery of the S. Gilles figures is reminiscent of Roman classical drapery.

72

71. STONE FIGURE
TWELFTH CENTURY
SOUILLAC

In spite of its fantastic
elongation and
distortion, this is
expressive sculpture
united with technical skill
with complete success
in conveying the
message of the Church.

73   74   75

72. CHARTRES : STONE :
TWELFTH CENTURY

73. RHEIMS : STONE :
THIRTEENTH CENTURY

74. CHARTRES : STONE :
THIRTEENTH CENTURY

75. TROYES : STONE :
FIFTEENTH CENTURY

Four treatments of the same
subject showing the
development from the crude
but touching figures of the
twelfth century Visitation.
The later versions show
marked classical qualities in
folds and arrangement of
draperies.
In later centuries carvers had
considerable latitude in their
use of draperies and the two
rich, gossiping burghers'
wives wear elaborate
contemporary clothes.

76. CHARTRES : STONE
FIGURES : ELEVENTH
CENTURY

77. CRUCIFIX FIGURE : PROBABLY FRENCH : IVORY THIRTEENTH CENTURY :
VICTORIA AND ALBERT MUSEUM, LONDON

78. GROUP IN STONE:
FOURTEENTH OR
FIFTEENTH CENTURY: WORCESTER

79. CRUCIFIX FROM SOUTH
TRANSEPT OF ROMSEY ABBEY:
ELEVENTH CENTURY:
STONE

80. CELLINI, (1500–1572)
NUDE CHRIST
MARBLE: PRADO, MADRID

The long drapery was reduced
gradually until it became only a loin
cloth, which, especially in Italy,
shrunk to a narrow ribbon, until
finally both Michelangelo and
Cellini made a wholly nude Christ.

81. BRONZE TABLET
IN LOW RELIEF :
EARLY THIRTEENTH
CENTURY : AMIENS

Portrait sculpture was rare in the earlier middle ages. Earliest memorials were engraved stone or bronze slabs and only gradually, through low and high relief, was the effigy evolved into a portrait representation.

These are upright statues laid horizontally. The drapery falls as if the figure stood, and it was only later that the portrait effigy took on the aspect of a dead and recumbent figure, with drapery falling as if it were on a bier. Indeed, later effigies were often simply the bier and the dressed body rendered in a permanent material.

82. DEAN AQUABLANCA : HEREFORD

3. WILLIAM DE VALENCE, EARL OF PEMBROKE : THIRTEENTH CENTURY : WESTMINSTER ABBE

84. DEPOSITION GROUP: IVORY: LATE THIRTEENTH
CENTURY : THE LOUVRE

85. A MASON'S LODGE : THIRTEENTH CENTURY : CHARTRES

86. WILLIAM TOREL, (1272-1291): HENRY III : BRONZE
WESTMINSTER ABBEY

87. FIGURE OF QUEEN
STONE
THIRTEENTH CENTURY
LINCOLN CATHEDRAL
A beautiful fusion
of realism with spirituality
and great technical skill of carving

THE FLOWERING OF MEDIAEVAL
SCULPTURE

"$\mathbf{F}$ROM the fourth to the thirteenth centuries it is the Church which
always marches in the front rank of civilization. . . . It is just at the
moment when the Roman Empire is breaking up and disappearing that
the Christian Church gathers itself up and takes its definite form—political
unity perishes—religious unity emerges. . . .

At this moment the Christian Church proclaims most loudly the
unity of its teaching, the universality of its law, and from the bosom of the
most frightful disorder the world has ever seen has arisen the largest and
purest idea which ever drew men together—the idea of a Spiritual Society."
Guizot's *European History*.

This claim of the orthodox historian is one which it is difficult to
challenge. The Church was the most powerful force in shaping the course
of this civilization, though it is right to remember that society, and even
laymen and artists, helped to shape the church. The same thousand years
which Guizot saw as lighted by the glow of a great spiritual concept,
Professor Bury saw only as " A millenium in which reason was enchained,
thought was enslaved, and knowledge made no progress " !

Yet during that time there arose men of wide ranging intellect, as
Abelard, Duns Scotus, Roger Bacon, Aquinas ; and is it not strange that
it was men whose " reason was enchained " and with whom " knowledge
made no progress " who reared those vast cathedrals which soar towards
heaven, as at Chartres, Westminster, Amiens and Lincoln ? These buildings
were the expression of a living faith, and to raise them involved the solving
of entirely new problems in the science of building and engineering—
problems which they solved with triumphant success. They evolved a
system of subtle and intricate theology to which their carvers gave visible
and tangible expression in thousands of figures of extraordinary beauty
which still challengingly grace those buildings. In every conceivable craft
or art allied to architecture they created masterpieces ; silver and gold
work, magnificent vestments, service books, illuminations, sculpture, wall
paintings, drama, ordered ritual, noble music ; everything that was
required for their great ceremonies of praise to God reached its highest
point of achievement in that millenium that lay between the fall of Rome
and the opening of the fifteenth century. The eleventh century is the turning
point of this great renaissance.

It has been propounded by March Phillips (*Form and Colour*) that
colour is an emotional apprehension while form is an intellectual perception. It would follow, therefore, that sculpture should flourish in times

of intellectual ferment and among peoples of quick and vital thought, and it is significant that two epochs in which sculpture reached unique heights are the classical age of the fifth century B.C., and the three centuries of Gothic art. Both these periods are times of wide intellectual pioneering when the horizon of man's experience was greatly widened, and the sculpture of both periods has much in common. Until the later phase of Greek art, sculpture kept a serene intellectual detachment. Greek thought was lucid ; therefore Greek art was clear and final, with an entire absence of perplexity or mental agitation ; those permanent types and images are " like a statue solid set and moulded in colossal calm ". So mediæval thought and mediæval art during the first half of these three centuries have a notable clarity and serenity.

But mediæval thought, in contrast with the theories and life of antiquity, held tenaciously to two great ideas : the belief in a great corporate organization, and the idea of the imperishable value of each individual soul. The two strands in mediæval life were a passion for unity, and an equally constant assertion of the individual soul. In their art, therefore, there is this persistent duality ; it attempts to express both matter and spirit and it seeks at once the particular and the universal, using the finite to express the infinite. Indeed, Renan says somewhere that the great gift of the middle ages to the world was the idea of infinity. The Church and mediæval thought borrowed much from antiquity ; a " reverent dependence on the ancients " was part of scholastic studies at Chartres. Virgil was held to unfold the story of human life from infancy to old age. Ovid was allegorized to point a moral ; religious ritual was largely adapted from ancient pagan altar rites ; festivals were re-named and adapted to Christian ideas ; philosophy, symbols, and even ancient images were all absorbed, and by the power of mediæval thought were fused into one living flame of intellectual life. The Church dreamed of a world in which Catholic faith was supreme, encompassing within its bosom every living soul yet recognizing that each individual had an absolute value. This gospel, like St. Paul's words to the Athenians : " He hath made all men of one blood for to dwell upon the earth ", was in marked contrast to the Roman State, which with great prescience had seen that the claim to complete spiritual independence of the Christians was incompatible with the authority of the State. The same is true today and the authoritarian states see it. The mediæval church sought to embrace all and to impose its authority on all, and mediæval sculpture expresses in stone the lessons and dogma which make the faith of the church. The subject matter for all this mediæval art is almost wholly confined to sacred stories, biblical and patristic ; yet within the bounds of entire obedience to church doctrine, and the further important restriction that all sculpture had to be subservient to architecture, these mediæval sculptures show a passionate assertion of individuality, and are charged with a spiritual exaltation such as cannot be found in any other sculpture in history.

This sense of ecstasy is well conveyed in the insecure and floating poise of much French sculpture of the twelfth century, especially in that at Moissac, Autun and Vezelay. These figures are usually in high relief; very seldom are they statues in the round. The sharp definition of contours and the crisp edges to draperies show a beautiful sense of stone chiselling.

The curious poised motion of the attitudes and the swirling lines and intricately patterned edges of the draperies may be, in part, a reminiscence of manuscript paintings; such manuscripts were a sort of art currency and the carvers were peripatetic, so actions and details were copied from one medium to another; but whether copied from manuscript painting, or whether the strange action arose out of the sculptor's desire to convey a sense of spiritual exaltation, it is supremely successful as art. Figures floating between earth and heaven seem a natural mode of expression to men who thought of life as a journey between earth and heaven, and used " the way " as a description of man's mortal life. In the next century Dante cast the great epic poem of the middle ages into the form of a journey and it shows the potency of classical thought that the guide was Virgil— " courteous soul of Mantua whose fame shall last as long as the world endures."

The intellectual revival of the twelfth century is epitomized in the life of Peter Abelard, who, as Helen Waddell remarks, " had a vocation for letters as some men might have for religion ". He was unique in his age in making a claim for reason against mere weight of authority, and though he was broken by St. Bernard and died in 1142, he had vindicated his claim and his life, and the sculptors followed the scholar in breaking with the rigidity of authority, and almost as Abelard died those touching and beautiful kings and queens of Chartres were being carved, and the sculptors there achieved the triumph of statues in the round almost for the first time since the proscription of images in the iconoclastic quarrel. The delight in new knowledge, so characteristic of the time, is well noted by Dean Church[1] in a description of a mediæval scholar, which echoes the spirit of that age with its intellectual and artistic pioneering. " Struggling painfully against difficulties, eager and hot after knowledge, wasting eyesight and stinting sleep, subtle, inquisitive, active minded and sanguine, loose in premise, and ostentatiously rigid in syllogism, filled with the passion of universal knowledge and with the desire to communicate it." Something of this eager pursuit of new knowledge and new beauty pervades the twelfth century sculpture, and it is supreme at Chartres. In the kings and queens who represent the ancestors of Christ the figures are so perfect in technique, so exquisite in expression, so fused with the architecture that no further development of sculpture allied to architecture seems possible.

This Chartres sculpture is remarkable not only for its beauty, but also for its tender and loving craftsmanship which can be readily seen even in the plaster casts of the Musée Trocadero; but it is also sculpture, not added to architecture, but a part of it. Even more than a Greek temple, a twelfth century church shows a perfect fusion, the full beauty of which can only be realized by studying it as both architecture and sculpture. As

---

[1] F. C. Church " Dante."

W. R. Lethaby says of this early Gothic art, " It is impossible to explain in words the content of perfect Gothic art ; it is frank, clear, gay ; it is passionately mystical and tender ; it is energetic, clear, sharp, strong and healthy. It would be a mistake to try to define it in terms of form alone ; it embodied a spirit, an aspiration, an age."[1] It is surely wrong to think of mediæval culture as being wholly cloistered ; its roots were in Nature and in labour and through those they transformed the Roman inheritance of which Latin literature, language, and art were but a part.

A living culture must draw its power from a living source and this the mediæval artist found in Nature and in that faith to the spectacular expression of which he devoted his life. The artist was one of a group, lay or clerical, and as there was a stupendous amount of building being done there was developed a co-operative and communal spirit, a splendid sodality of men engaged in the great enterprise of building houses to God. A letter written by Abbot Haimon to the religious at Tutbury, England, describes a scene at the building of S. Pierre-sur-Dives in 1115.

" Who has ever heard or seen the like ? Princes, powerful and wealthy men, men of noble birth, proud and beautiful women, bent their necks to the yoke of the carts which carried the stones, wood, wine, corn, oil, lime, everything necessary for the building of the church and the support of those working at it. One saw as many as a thousand people, men and women, attach·ᵤ to the reins drawing a wagon so heavy was its burden, and a profound silence reigned among the crowd, pressing forward with difficulty, in the emotion which filled their hearts. . . . Nothing proved an obstacle. The ruggedness of the mountains, the depth of the streams . . . could not delay the march. When they had arrived near the foundations of the church the carts were drawn up round it as on the borders of a camp. From dusk to dawn the sound of hymns arose."

That may seem mere romanticism to some, and superstition to others, but it expresses an essential aspect of mediæval life and no real understanding of mediæval life or art is possible till this sense of community is realized.

In a strange way perhaps, this is one reason why the Middle Ages seem curiously remote to many people today and the mediæval mind seems more strange than that of a Greek or a Roman. Today we rather dread that unity of belief which bound men together across all Europe, a unity which garnered the subtle wisdom of Plato, the logic and acute observation of Aristotle, the spiritual intensity of the fathers, and which nourished and revealed to mankind his soul and took cognizance of all sides of man's nature. In its material manifestation those great churches which were the visible house of God are the greatest examples in the world's history of co-operative skill, raised by the workers under the widest conditions of human liberty in their crafts, yet unified and ennobled by a great sustaining central idea.

Apart from the figure sculpture the decorative sculpture of this time is very subordinate. It is most rich in southern France where a certain classicism persisted as at S. Trophime, Arles. In northern France and in

[1] W. R. Lethaby " Architecture "

England the decorative sculpture, though often rich in effect, is composed of simple elements intricately designed and varied in section, but requiring few tools and not more than average mason's skill.

The twelfth century doorway at Lincoln could be carved by any stonemason, yet the effect is rich and impressive. The next development of decorative sculpture based on natural forms must have tended to make a special class of carvers, for work like the famous Vintage capital at Rheims or that on the chapter house at Southwell must have required delicate and fine grained stone, good tools, and a high degree of technical skill and training[1]. For it must be remembered that these myriads of carved capitals and bands of decorative sculpture were not " designed " for the carvers by some superior artist or architect or " designer "—indeed, the mediæval carver would not have known what the words " architect " or " designer " meant—they were carved as required by men who ranked with the stonemasons and who in all probability could not have " designed " or drawn these beautiful natural forms on paper, but could carve them from what must have been very slight drawings. The thirteenth century sketch book of Villars de Honnecourt shows the kind of drawings which a mediæval architect or master builder made in his studies, and though this architect (but the term was not known) could plan and assist in building a beautiful and vast cathedral, he was really only a master mason ; his sketches were such as would not today pass a freshman architecture student. With a living building tradition, drawings were of little value, paper was unknown, and just as the drawings of the architecture were relatively slight, so with the sculpture.

The statues which peopled those buildings (and any great cathedral might have four or five thousand figures, some very large, many of life size or a little larger, and vast numbers of smaller figures) were not " designed " by a superior sculptor in the quiet of his " studio " ; rather, they were carved by those of the stonemasons who had special gifts or training, and they were carved as simply and as freely as the other masons shaped mouldings or calculated a thrust and built accordingly. These mason sculptors knew what work was being done in their own field ; occasionally there are records of payments made to masons to visit such and such a church to see what the carvers there had done ; they were allowed travelling expenses and some wages, and it would be very interesting if one could see what sort of sketches, if any, they brought back. Probably, like those of the master builder, they were slight enough. Certainly none of these sculptured statues was first of all modelled in clay, then cast in plaster and the plaster cast handed over to the carver for him to copy, as is the usual practice today. That would have seemed an interminably long process to the mediæval carver who probably could carve in the fine French or English free stones almost as quickly as the modeller of today could model in clay ; and as I have elsewhere said, to *copy* the model is slower than to create the form.

[1] See N. Pevsner " Stones of Southwell "

The study of mediæval sculpture must also involve some study of the architecture of which the sculptor's work was an integral part ; and the architecture of the Middle Ages was in a peculiar degree the expression of mediæval thought. The vast and all-pervading power of the mediæval Church is completely expressed in its buildings and it was natural that the intellectual expansion of the twelfth century should find its expression in stone and that they should then achieve the triumph of building—the stone vaulted roof.

In the thirteenth century this Gothic construction reached its highest point ; and at Amiens, Rheims, Westminster and Lincoln, for instance, the spirit of the age is made visible and imperishable. Great creative forces shaped the art, the philosophy and the poetry of this age, and these are all related. That unique outburst of natural beauty which began as the century opened was a part of the expanding movement of thought and of poetry, and precisely as the poets (incidentally, how significant that they were called trouveurs—or finders !) then began to borrow associations and use images from every phase of Nature, so the sculptors turned with delight towards the representation of every aspect of natural beauty which could be fitly expressed in stone, and they showed that even in the most faithful rendering of natural forms these forms did not lose their significance or beauty, because of the living tradition of design which governed the artists.

This living tradition was a vital part of the artist's life, and it gave him an unequalled power to express the liturgic truths and teachings of that faith which was the organic principle and the cohesive force of all mediæval life. The thought of the twelfth century had been patristic and Platonic, but after the twelfth century Plato's influence faded before that of Aristotle, " the master of those who know ", and the re-discovery of Aristotle with his all-powerful observation of nature and of life coincides with this sudden outburst of the study of natural beauty, and it also coincides with the rise and spread of the Franciscans and the Dominicans. Monasticism had been all-powerful in holding the Church together during the earlier ages ; and at the height of monastic power the Abbot of the Cluniac order was second only to the Pope in ecclesiastical position ; but now the Church overflowed into the world. This fresh, free spirit of St. Francis gave life and brought a zest for beauty, a wide and eager desire for a life that should flower in art and song. Of course the great and splendid ecclesiastics frowned on the movement, and indeed had they only known, this new challenging mysticism and naturalism was to lead inevitably to free enquiry and the denial of authority.

As Benedetto Croce says, " It was not that the convents and hermitages became nests of singing birds. Rather, the essential poetry in the minorite attitude to life was doing its natural work, showing the beauty of the world, calling to the new service which knew no serfs, uttering the needs of the heart of man, giving glimpses of the soul of things. These were flashed not merely on lonely, lofty souls but on the senses and imagination of pilgrims on the common roads of life. This for a time did St. Francis and his brothers."

They spread also certain democratic principles. The great ecclesiastical system of the Church was maintained by collective wealth, though individuals were poor. Gradually the endowments gave the Church immense wealth and power ; it was " rudimentary capitalism ", as Dr. Coulton points out, and indeed it formed a state with laws, lawyers, law courts and gaols of its own ; it levied tithes and taxes. All this power given by wealth was cast aside by St. Francis. Other teachers, both Christian and pagan, had shown the insignificance of riches. St. Francis preached and lived to show the deep significance of poverty : through poverty man obtained freedom. It was revolutionary doctrine, as was the artist's study of Nature, for they, like the friars and the trouveurs, were " finders ", or " makers ". And it was in the thirteenth century that craft guilds began to be organized. They protected the craft or trade ; they established and maintained a standard of quality in work, and gradually they became benefit or insurance societies ; and their existence is an evidence of the power of the group.

All this intellectual ardour is characteristic, and it invades the whole period of the development of Gothic art and architecture. It is expressed in the aspiring " verticality " of any typical Gothic building.

The development of architecture was a long progression towards enclosing great space. The forest of fat pillars at Karnak or Thebes enclosed probably less space in plan than their own area. In a Greek temple like the Parthenon a new relation between the stone and the enclosed space was reached. Their empirical and intellectual vitality enabled them to achieve this new and more perfect relation, and as far as human logic and the science of trabeated building went this was the final adaptation of means to ends. There is a finality about a Greek plan which will allow of no irregularity or alternative, but a Gothic building, based not on the logic of the lintel but on the arch principle, with its far greater potentialities, is something totally different.

The arch allowed imagination and immeasurably extended the possibilities of building and of lighting, and when these Gothic builders after a century or two of experiment had mastered the science of holding all the various thrusts and pressures in abeyance, they achieved in buildings like the Lincoln Cathedral and the " Sainte Chapelle " in Paris superb examples of the logical development of inside and outside building, and the technical skill, great though it was, was less important and less evident than the beauty and spirit which controlled it. The certitudes of paganism were fitly enclosed within the rectangle of the Greek plan ; with the inspiration of the new religion and the boundless enthusiasm which that religion inspired, these Gothic buildings not only carried men's thoughts up the sinewy lines of the piers and groined vaults to heaven, but the plans spread out laterally into strange and symbolic shapes, opening into cloisters and chapels with a sense of abounding life : which was truly, building in being. This was " functional " architecture seven centuries ago ; and it was charged with emotion and saturated with the spirit of worship. In France alone in the hundred years between 1170 and 1270 there were built eighty great cathedrals and nearly five hundred churches. This great outburst of building was a living school of all the arts, providing training and experience in every branch of architecture, sculpture and all the allied arts to thousands of craftsmen.

The intellectual awakening of the twelfth century synchronized with the growing skill of builders and sculptors, and it is closely connected with an awakening consciousness to the fact of natural beauty, a fact which was secondary and indeed almost ignored, by Celtic and Byzantine artists. By the time of St. Francis, whose forty years of life, 1186-1226, marked the very apogee of Christian art and achievement, this love of natural beauty had become a marked characteristic of art, in missal painting, in sculpture, and in fresco painting.

The relation between the widening thought of the time and the realization of the beauty of the visible world is too obvious to be a mere accident of date. St. Francis himself was so saturated with the love of Nature that to him the evil thing was the pride of human reason, and it is strange to think that his distrust of scholastic logic, and his belief that wealth had corrupted the church (and therefore the friars must have no possessions, either individually or collectively in the order) marked the beginning of a movement which was to prove subversive of the authority of the Church. That God was everywhere, and that " He hath made everything beautiful in His time, and He hath set the world in their heart ", was a simple pantheism and left little room for the great organization of the Church. But a vital and abounding life was spreading. The troubadours with their love songs, the scholars with their courts of love, had a real relation to the humanization that was pervading the arts. The Church was slow to adopt the new attitude towards women involved in this—women represented the vices in sculpture—but it was far from intolerant, and it is noteworthy that in many monasteries from the twelfth to the fifteenth centuries there were written songs, plays and poems dealing very frankly with human love and passion ; often, indeed, they approach near blasphemy and grossness, yet the Church preserved the poems and acted the plays. This tolerance came from the sense of security ; the Church was so clearly the dominant power that she could afford to be laughed at, and to laugh at the failings of her people.

Manuscript illustrations of the thirteenth century began to show beautiful naturalistic details, easily identifiable flowers replace the ornament of the earlier painters who worked under the influence of the Byzantine and Celtic missals, and birds and butterflies and fauna appear delicately drawn and painted with minute accuracy. The Chapter House of Westminster Abbey has in its decoration a great outcrop of roses, often very naturalistic in treatment. They are found in both painting and sculpture, and Lethaby in his book on the Abbey and its craftsmen[1] records that it is to be noted that there was in the middle of the thirteenth century a great burst of rose cultivation in Europe. The roses were originally said to have been brought

[1] W. R. Lethaby " Westminster Abbey and the Kings Craftsmen "

from Syria, and it is noteworthy that it was then that the great rose windows began to appear, and the *Romaunt of the Rose* was written, and the central point of Dante's Paradiso was in the form of a great white rose. This newly realized natural beauty, the rapidly increasing skill due to constant occupation and living traditions of the crafts, and probably with an increased range of tools, especially for the wood and stone carvers, produced great numbers of versatile and inquiring artists who created those buildings which are yet unrivalled in the history of Christian art.

On a thirteenth century window at Chartres there is shown a picture of sculptors at work, and it is noteworthy that they are represented as carving a stone statue which is not in situ or even standing upright but lies on the mason's bench or banker. In practice I have found this convenient only at two stages, in rough hewing, and when undercutting and doing final finishing. I think the Chartres window shows the final stages of the work, before the statue was painted. Painting certainly would be easier and more conveniently done before erection.

It is certain that all this sculpture was coloured, with gilded or silvered enrichments of such parts as mitres, croziers and fringes to vestments. Draperies were often diapered with repeating patterns. The whole effect of a cathedral front must have been inconceivably rich and beautiful. Certain conventions are generally found in the treatment of figure sculpture. In statues of the Apostles there is often a reminiscence of classical garments, while with less important personages the garments are often more nearly contemporary, but that the carvers had considerable latitude in their use of draperies and costume is evident when one looks at any great group of mediæval sculpture. One man makes the figures elongated ; another had a peculiar treatment of hair which can be traced over many figures. There is great diversity and yet a certain unity. Changes appeared gradually. The earliest sculptured representations of Christ crucified show an upright figure clothed in long drapery, crowned and with outstretched arms ; the legs were not crossed, and if nails were shown there was one in each foot. By the thirteenth century innovators were changing this. The long drapery was gradually shortened and there are records of protests made by the clergy against any change in what had become accepted as the " true representation ". A Bishop of Tuy, in Spain in the thirteenth century wrote with horror against " the heretics who in derision and scorn of Christ's cross carve images of Our Lord with one foot laid over the other so that both are pierced by a single nail, thus striving either to annul or to render doubtful men's faith in the Holy Cross and the traditions of the sainted Fathers by superinducing these diversities and novelties."[1] Yet it is this " heretical " type of crucifix which has become orthodox and even stereotyped. Later, we shall note what happened to the Crucifix at the Renaissance.

The practice of making portrait statues as commemorative art may date back to Roman work, but portrait sculpture was rare in the earlier

[1] G. G. Coulton, " Art and the Reformation."

middle ages. The earliest ones are engraved stone or bronze slabs, and only gradually was memorial portrait sculpture evolved. By the end of the thirteenth century, however, portrait statues were being made. In the last decade of the century William Torel of London made the gilt bronze effigies of Henry III and Alainor of Castile, wife of Edward I, at Westminster, which must rank among the most beautiful examples of such art in Europe. It is interesting to note certain technical beauties ; the exquisite finish of these works, the engraved hair and beard, the beautiful simplicity of contours and the metallic quality ; all combine to make these figures among the most superb examples of bronze portraiture in history.

Both French and English masons contributed nobly to the science of building (the more pretentious word " architecture " was first used, it is stated, in 1510). Building, to the enquiring and versatile Villars de Honnecourt, was *bonne maconnerie*, and this certainly was produced in great quantities in both countries, and as E. S. Prior says, " The two countries were as sisters succeeding as co-heiresses to the same estate, but taking no wealth one from the other." That many French masons were employed in England is evident from the recorded names in the ancient rolls, particularly those of Westminster, and in French words like " quoin " for angle stones, " voussoirs " ; " asselars " for squared stone, axe-faced, has only altered in spelling to " ashlar " ; while today any Cotswold mason using a bar of wood as a bearer for two men to carry a block of stone, calls it a " porter stick." Masons in the thirteenth century were divided almost exactly as they are today in England into hewers, setters, (now called fixers) and wallers. The rights and privileges of each group were jealously guarded by the guilds and with the increasing power of these craft organizations there was achieved a gradual change from a clerically-controlled monastic art to a lay art very largely controlled by the craft guilds. The central period of this change was in the thirteenth century, a period well described by Frederic Harrison : " This thirteenth century was the last in history of mankind in Europe when a high and complex civilization has been saturated with a uniform and unquestioned creed. It was an era equally poetic, political, industrial, artistic, practical, intellectual and devotional. And these qualities acted in harmony on a uniform conception of life, with a real symmetry of purpose. There was one common creed, one ritual, one worship, one sacred language, one Church, a single code of manners, a uniform scheme of society, a common system of education, an accepted type of beauty, a universal art, and something like a recognized standard of the Good, the Beautiful and the True. Men as utterly different as were Stephen Langton, St. Francis, Aquinas, Roger Bacon, Dante, Giotto, St. Louis, Edward I, all profoundly accepted one common order of ideas, equally applying to things of the intellect, of moral duty, of action, and of the soul, and they could all feel they were together working out the same task. It may be doubted if that has ever happened in Europe since."[1]

[1] F. Harrison " The Meaning of History "

> " There are but two strong conquerors of the forgetfulness of men—Poetry and
> Architecture—and the latter in some sort includes the former, and is mightier
> in its reality. It is well to have, not only what men have thought and felt, but
> what their hands have handled and their strength wrought, and their eyes
> beheld, all the days of their life."
> " The strongest, proudest, most orderly, most enduring of the arts of men."
>
> J. RUSKIN

GOTHIC SCULPTURE
FOURTEENTH TO SIXTEENTH CENTURIES

OF course, below the surface of mediæval life there were darker aspects, and contradictions, mingled humanity and cruelty, rapture and sense, incredible poverty and hardships among the poor, dirt, plagues, and superstitions in the lives of all classes. The spiritual exaltation which produced the conscious art and thought of the thirteenth century was one aspect of mediæval life—another aspect is to be found in the gross but very popular fifteenth century " Cent Nouvelles Nouvelles."

The period of equilibrium ended. Almost as the fourteenth century opened the unity and cohesion which had characterized mediæval life, with the church supreme, was broken, and the disaster was plain to the world. There was a great rift within the church, and presently this rift widened and produced a second Pope ; and men had to choose, not between loyalty and disloyalty to the faith, but between loyalty to one or other of the rival claimants to the headship of the Church. The long struggle of the church to assert and maintain her authority over the kingly, feudal, and secular powers—a struggle which fluctuated as the Popes like Hildebrand and Innocent were powerful and dominating—took a new phase when, owing to the power of the Italian nobles, a pope was elected who was supposed to support Edward I of England. This newly elected Pope, Clement V, took up his residence in 1309 at Avignon, then a part of Provence belonging to the Angevin house of Naples. It was seventy years before the Popes returned to Rome, and this enforced exile was called the " Babylonish Captivity."

Edward I of England challenged the claims of the Papacy. He gave England her parliamentary system, which saved the country from feudal anarchy, and despotism ; but plain to the whole of Europe there was the spectacle of the Church of Christ torn by internal dissension, with two claimants to headship, challenged from without by new heresies and from within by friars and minorites holding and preaching doctrines which the popes and cardinals despised and disliked ; all this was bound to lower the credit of the Church as the spiritual leader of the world. The great schism still further exposed the weakness of the church and these divisions and disunities stimulated the growth of a free and widely critical judgment upon authority. Presently Wycliff challenged the Church doctrine

75

of the supreme importance of the mass ; and by translating the Bible into English he appealed to the authority of that book as rivalling or exceeding that of the Pope. It was not Luther who first attacked the authority of the Church—it was the friars and persons like Wycliff within the church who first began undermining the Rock of St. Peter two hundred years before Luther. The movement was hastened when towards the end of the fourteenth century the outward prestige of the Church was restored by the return of the Popes to Rome, and to signalize this, the great church of St. Peter's was begun as the outward sign and visible symbol of the greatness and power of the church ; but decay had already set in beneath the throne, and that great basilica became the visible manifestation of the Church's spiritual decline ; even artistically the pompous and rhetorical style of its architecture is in marked contrast to the spiritual quality pervading the earlier great cathedrals—an entirely new spirit had arisen.

In 1312 Philip " the fair " of France showed his power over Papal authority by disbanding the Order of the Knights Templar, and appropriating the accumulated wealth of the Order ; and in the middle of the century the whole of Europe was devastated by The Black Death—the plague—which entirely altered the structure of mediæval life. It is estimated that a third of the population of England perished, and perhaps over most of Europe the ratio was similar. The Black Death altered all the conceptions on which mediæval life was based, especially in its economic, religious, and artistic aspects. It broke down the system of feudal serfdom, for labour became so scarce that the workmen could bargain for their services ; the rise of a new class of artisans called *journee* or day-men is significant.

William Morris, whose understanding of mediæval life was profound and instinctive, says in his *Lectures on Architecture and History*: " By the beginning of the fourteenth century the Guilds were supreme—their constitution was thoroughly democratic. As towns grew bigger and population flowed to them from the enfranchised field serfs and other sources, the old craftsmen began to form a separate and privileged class within the guilds ; they had their privileged apprentices and the " journeyman " made his appearance. After a time these journeymen attempted to form guilds under the master craftsmen. When workmen became mere journeymen, their collection under one master, in a big workshop, gave economy of space, rent, fire, lighting, etc., and the division of labour began, and led to that division into workmen who were not artists, and artists who were not workmen." In London alone there were 30 guilds embracing almost every craft and the control they exercised over craftsmen was very thorough.

As the clergy had been active, often especially active, in nursing and tending the plague-stricken, thousands of their number perished, and their places were often taken by others quite untrained and wholly unfitted for clerical duties ; this deterioration in the quality of incumbents probably hastened the decay and corruption of the church. The plague left all Europe impoverished, and people began to look enviously at the rich abbots and clergy who owned so much of the land, that great source of mediæval wealth, for though the monasteries had been founded as places where work was to be done, yet as their corporate wealth increased, the monks often passed on the heavy manual labour to outside serfs or workers, and became, as it were, rich employers.

Froissart has left us in his *Chronicles* a spirited and convincing picture of the wars and pageantry of his time, and, though belonging to the nobility, he saw the changes implicit in the rise of a new spirit of challenge to a feudal authority, owing to the scarcity of labourers, after the many plagues, and the consequent growth of a strong feeling that ultimately power lay with the people and not with the rulers. " These unhappy people began to stir ; because they said they were kept in serfage ; and, in the beginning of the world, they said, there were no bondmen. They were men formed in the similitude of their lords—why should they be kept under like beasts ? the which, they said they would no longer suffer, for they would all be one, and if they laboured or did anything for their lords, they would have wages therefor as well as others." Froissart thus clearly states the spirit which produced the Jacquerie in France ; and, in England, the uprisings under John Ball and Wat Tyler, those characteristic expressions of the new spirit of independence and challenge.

In religious art, it was after the culminating plague of the Black Death, that a new emphasis began to be laid on death and mortality, until gradually the theme became one of the obsessions of the later mediæval mind ; the walls of the earlier churches had been decorated—as a contemporary describes, " as a vision of God's paradise bright with flowers of every hue, fresh green of grass and leaves, even as a mantle embroidered with flowers "—now they were often decorated with rivers and fountains of blood. Faustus was but recalling some such painted church fresco, when at his doom he exclaims : " See, See ! where Christ's blood streams in the firmament. One drop would save my soul ! half a drop ! Ah—my Christ ! " There were pageants and plays on the theme of the Doings of Death, and in the middle of the fifteenth century a great Dance of Death was performed at Bruges. This morbid, but understandable preoccupation with mortality can be readily traced in mediæval sculpture. From the beginning of the thirteenth century the tomb effigy had been a common subject for sculpture. These were usually serene and placid representations of death, hardly differing from sleep, and it is characteristic that they were merely standing statues laid down, either on a slab or, as in the long series at Fontevrault, on a draped bier. The drapery of the figure differed in no way from a standing statue but in the later effigies this is entirely changed, and the drapery was designed as on a recumbent figure, falling away from the body ; the statue took on the appearance of death and became a replica of the bier in a permanent material. These effigies in earlier work were hardly to be considered as portraits but almost as symbolic representations. As late as 1380, the will directing the making of the effigy of the Black Prince at Canterbury, merely orders " a Knight fully armed " but certainly in some of the fourteenth century effigies the sculptors endeavoured and succeeded in making sensitive and moving portrait representations.

77

The John of Eltham in Westminster Abbey and the Edward II at Gloucester, with its strange and uncanny beauty, are stamped with authentic individual character recorded with consummate power. (Prof. Lethaby thinks that both these statues were made by the same carver). And the statue of Charles V of France, (perhaps the work of John of Liége) is an obvious attempt at close portraiture based on a study of facial and psychological characteristics. Already, too, it is to be noted that as the individual portrait develops so does the individual artist emerge, and new technical experiments begin to be made, effects of polychromy being obtained, as the long forgotten Romans had done, by the use of different coloured stone or marble. A Prioress of Passy who died in 1401 is represented in two different marbles ; black for the outer cloak, and white for the alb or under-robe and the face is tinted. And a statue of Beatrice of Bourbon has an exquisitely finished and polished alabaster face, fitted into a stone figure.

A little later in the fifteenth century, the emphasis on the terrors of death was increased by the custom of representing two effigies ; the upper one showing the dead clothed in the robes or vestments of life, with every detail of fur, jewellery and trappings worked out elaborately in the marble or alabaster, while below was carved a naked and emaciated figure, some-times even represented as almost a decayed and putrescent corpse with worms emerging from cavities in the body and efts or newts feeding on the entrails. Both these effigies were commonly canopied over with tracery work of a strange and intricate beauty, mouldings and cuspings endlessly interlacing and even interpenetrating each other, as if in wanton defiance of all the qualities of stone ; all the decorative and naturalistic elements of earlier decoration were now discomposed and grew rankly luxuriant. The small angels which decorated the sides of the earlier tomb slab and which were often, as in the Aymer de Valence tomb at Westminster, of unique beauty, were now replaced by weeping figures, On occasion, as in some of the Burgundian tombs, these weepers are no longer small subsidiary figures, but are almost life sized ; the realism of grouping, the tears and agonised expressions are so vivid that the whole effect is of a great funeral cortège suddenly halted and then petrified.

This sculpture, designed as if it were a tableau, is sometimes of extraordinary power. The Entombment groups at the Church of the Holy Blood, at Bruges, and at Troyes are so violently emotional that all the horrors of death are rendered with unflinching realism and this was per-haps the most popular subject at that time. Certainly the Flemings and Germans of the fifteenth century revelled in blood and horror—one notes the fierce energy with which, in pictures or sculptures of the Passion the long nails are being hammered ! The executioner in Hans Bruggeman's sculptured Stations of the Cross has no pity, nothing but cruel scorn for the stumbling and bleeding Christ. This apotheosis of death and blood was the last grim jest of the expiring middle ages. The theme haunted the mind of that strange child of the fifteenth century—Villon—who though using the language of his age is essentially modern. The tolling bells of

Notre Dame recall to the vagrant poet only the indubitable truth that " Death seizes all without exception."

Meanwhile changes were taking place in other aspects of mediæval life. Commercial development was making a new middle class and the people were no longer divided into the two simple divisions of nobles and serfs. Individuals grew richer, not nobles but tradespeople, wool merchants and traders. The rise and growth of Trade Halls and of secular universities was an evidence that knowledge was no longer confined to the church, that it was being widespread, and was widely desired. The ardour, which, in a previous age, had produced the Crusades, which were at once religious, commercial and colonising, and which had introduced new and vital ideas, and widened the mind of mediæval life now turned towards the spread of knowledge, both sacred and secular, and men of the new orders of friars like the Franciscans and Dominicans as well as scholars without the church, now spent their energies and sacrificed their lives as missionaries and teachers to spread the new knowledge.

The fourteenth century in England is the time of the three Edwards— and, strangely enough, though it is a time of incessant war and recurring plagues it is marked in architecture by a consistent style known as Decorated, and characterized by certain new and beautiful features, perhaps the most marked being the great skill, beauty and richness of the naturalistic decorative sculpture. At the opening of the fourteenth century, Dante still looked to France as the centre of culture, but in the course of the century the intellectual and artistic leadership of France, which dominated Europe in the thirteenth century, was largely modified. The language of the English Court was French. The first Royal Speech spoken in English was by the Lord Chief Justice in 1362 just when Wycliff was translating the Bible into English. French influence is evident in much English architecture, but in characteristic buildings like Lincoln Cathedral or Westminster Abbey the borrowings are transmuted into something essentially and triumphantly English.

There was a marked development of local schools and greater expression of individuality. This involved loss as well as gain ; the loss of a certain universal and timeless quality in art of the older tradition, and the gain in a vivid sense of contemporary life with its costumes and appurtenances. This is seen in the sculptured representations of apostles and sacred characters who were now often represented in contemporary costume and thus, in a very real sense, " came down to earth."

But, just as the humanization of the gods of Greece had hastened the decline of belief in them, so now the representation in contemporary costume of sacred persons and events led inevitably to the loss of any clear distinction between sacred and secular, and in artistic representations the biblical story passed insensibly into classic myth, and into allegory, and the clear distinction, so dear to the earlier middle ages was merged into a wider unity. The Schoolmen had said of debate, "never admit— seldom deny, *always* distinguish," and the mediæval carver had learned to tell his story, or record the features with exquisite definition and distinction. Some of this was lost in the development of sculpture and art towards greater verisimilitude to life. In the two most characteristic ecclesiastical subjects for the sculptors, the Madonna and Child and the representation of Christ crucified, there were marked and important changes.

In the thirteenth century, the Madonna was usually represented seated—crowned—holding the Holy Child for the world's adoration. There was a certain impersonal quality evident and consequently a feeling of remoteness and detachment from life. The next century substituted for this conception a very human mother holding in her arms, and for her own delectation rather than as an object for adoration, a very human baby, the whole group pervaded by a winsome and gracious spirit, the very embodiment of happy motherhood. These sculptors were not always—or even often—successful in reproducing the proportions of infancy ; this failure is the more strange in that the theme of the Holy Child is a constantly recurring one all through the middle ages, and babies must have been studied by the artists. Yet it is to be remembered that this same failure characterized the sculpture of the Greeks who even at the height of their powers in portraying adolescents and men and women, seemed quite unable or unwilling to record the strangely different proportions of infancy. That was not achieved till the Hellenistic age when artistic power in general had decayed ; so with the mediæval artist it was not until the end of the fifteenth, or even well into the sixteenth century, when the great creative urge of mediæval life had declined, that the Gothic sculptors achieved a perfect understanding of the contours and proportions of babyhood. In both epochs it seems impossible to determine whether the failure was due to a deliberate convention, or to ignorance and lack of skill ; in so many matters the mediæval sculptor was, like St. Benedict " wisely ignorant and knowingly unlearned." It is certain that in north Europe generally in the fourteenth and fifteenth centuries the child is represented as about six heads tall. Now the normal baby's length, from birth for about a year, is about four heads, and the proportion of six heads is that of a child between four and six years old.

An interesting study might be made of this aspect of mediæval sculpture. It is characteristic that very rarely in France, Germany or England is the child represented nude, while in the warmer climate of Italy the nude Child is more often found. In French, German, and English sculpture, the Child is usually quite heavily clothed, and these draperies gave the sculptors the opportunity to devise some lovely and harmonius line compositions between the Mother's head and headdress and the action of the Child. Traces of this interesting action are readily seen in the fourteenth century French Madonna statue reproduced in plate 98.

The early Christian Church shrank from the representation of Christ crucified, and expressed the doctrine of His sacrifice symbolically by a lamb at the intersection of the cross, and sometimes, as at St. Mark's, Venice, the apostles were symbolically represented by twelve sheep ! In the seventh century the Quinisext Council held at Constantinople decreed that " the form of Him who taketh away the sins of the world, the Lamb

Christ our Lord, be set up in human shape on images henceforth, instead of the Lamb formerly used." The early representations of this human Christ show Him clothed, generally to the feet, and standing in the attitude of a cross, sometimes crowned. The third stage began in the twelfth century, when, as was noted in the last chapter, innovations began to be introduced, and in later centuries the representation became more and more realistic. The long drapery was reduced gradually until it became only a loin cloth, which, especially in Italy, shrunk to a narrow ribbon, till finally both Michelangelo and Cellini made a wholly nude Christ.

The typical Christ on the cross in mediæval sculpture of Northern Europe shows the head hanging towards His right shoulder but in Spain and Italy especially many examples show the head thrown back and up, as in Guido Reni's painting " Ecce Homo " ; a favourite subject for the later middle ages. The church authorities often protested against any changes in the disposition, not only of the limbs of the figure but even of the arms of the cross itself. A case is cited by Dr. Coulton, quoted from the register of Ralph Baldock, Bishop of London, 1306 : " We have heard on trustworthy authority that one Tidemann of Germany hath sold, to Geoffrey, Rector of St. Mildred's in the Poultry, a certain carved crucifix with a cross beam which doth not represent the true form of the Cross ; which crucifix the said Rector had placed in his church, and whereunto the indiscreet populace flocked in crowds as to a true image of the Cross (whereas it was no such image), when as we foresaw it might chance that their souls should be imperilled. . . . We caused the said Tidemann and Geoffrey to be summoned to Our presence, and having made diligent inquisition from both we have ordained as here ensueth, lest by continuance of this error, worse things should befall : That the aforesaid Tidemann should take (and he hath indeed so taken) his oath on the Gospels that he will never henceforth make, nor suffer to be exposed for sale, within Our city or diocese of London, such crucifix as this, or crosses with arms contrary to the accustomed fashion, under pain of excommunication for disobedience. And because the said Tidemann claimeth to be an alien and a simple man, who might probably and innocently have ignored the accustomed mysteries of the Crucifix and the Image thereunto attached, therefore : We have graciously granted to him as here ensueth :—That he, having first restored to us the letter of obligation for twenty-three pounds sterling which he hath from the Rector aforesaid, shall obtain restitution of this crucifix which hath been sequestrated and deposited in keeping for the avoidance of peril to men's souls, by the discreet Master Richard, of Newport, who was then our Vicar and official. Wherefore we enjoin and command you that, having received from this Tidemann the image aforesaid ; provided always that it be borne forth from your Monastery to some place without our Diocese, either at early dawn, or late in the evening, when it can be done most secretely and with the least scandal, and that you shall set a watch to assure the execution of this command, and to intimate the same to Us . . . . Given at our Palace of Fulham. August 2, 1306."

81

This document is interesting in many ways : it shows the absolute authority of the church in maintaining a definite tradition, and the cost of £23 is remarkable, as in money values it is a very high price indeed. One would like to know in what way this cross and figure was so offensive as to invoke such a heavy penalty.

A century or so later there is a record noted by Jusserand, from a Cistercian monastery in Yorkshire, of a monk being engaged in carving a stone Christ on the Cross, and of his getting a brother to pose naked for him, and of his working at this only on fast days so that the flesh is more mortified. This search for realism would have been quite foreign, and perhaps even shocking, to an earlier carver, who was content to repeat the drooping pose and the usual drapery arrangement, and whose knowledge of anatomy, though not very great, was still adequate for expressiveness. In their humble ignorance, the thirteenth century carvers, in spite of a lack of complete power of expression, could always convey the spiritual meaning. It is a sign of the expanding knowledge of the fourteenth and fifteenth centuries that the artists were growing more daring and experimental, not only in the mechanics of building but also in such details as these.

All this new knowledge was, as knowledge often is, dangerous. Just as scholastic thought had been clear and definite, limiting the field of man's intellectual probing (but within that field it was searching and acute, and lucidly expressed), so also the contemporary artists had been limited and circumscribed by the authority of the Church and by the forced subservience to the parent art of architecture. Yet they reached a height of spiritual expression and technical skill never excelled in any age. But scholastic thought gradually degenerated till by the time of Erasmus— (who hated war, pestilence and schoolmen equally) it was described by him as " mere logomachy and hair-splitting " ; so in art all this new knowledge of anatomy and perspective and science generally, changed the power of artistic expression, and gradually, for the deep feeling, disciplined design, and precise technique, they substituted more complete verisimilitude, more realistic draperies, more drama, heightened emotion, and yet emptied their work of spiritual content so that it is seldom emotionally satisfying. It was characteristic that the later church substituted the study of rhetoric, for the earlier scholastic study of logic. Herein is study something analogous to the artist's study of effects, rather than that of form itself.

So in sculpture the search for pictorial effects led to such innovations as the representation of landscape and architectural backgrounds worked skilfully into a diminishing perspective, the very elaborate costumes were rendered with such variety of texture and meticulous detail, that though there was often a gain in vividness, and contemporaneity, yet there was a distinct loss in beauty and in universality. A dual quality is visible in much of this later mediæval sculpture ; it is still religious narrative art, telling its story with skill and power, but one is often repelled by the strangely materialistic mode of expression. The appeal is almost wholly to the eye, and to the sense of touch—the emphasis is laid on the external world, and the spiritual world is overlooked. All this suggests a pre-occupation with the sense of sight, a delight in complexity and manner-isms, and a consequent atrophy of thought. Yet the spectacular effect is often very impressive, and in sculptured reliefs, like those in Amiens of the legend of St. Firmin, and of John the Baptist, the pictorial effect is as of some great stage setting, which has become fixed and made permanent in stone.

Indeed, Emile Male suggests that much of the pictorial sculpture of the fifteenth century was actually derived from dramatic representations of religious " mystery " plays. As has been noted, the sense of individuality which led to exact portraiture, and is so characteristic of later mediæval art, led also to the individual artist, and this in turn led to a certain specialism. Workshops, as those at London and Gloucester, became known for a particular kind of figure, or for working in a special medium.

The alabaster carvers of the English midlands sent their retables and altar reliefs all over England and the Continent, and even to Iceland, an indication that religious sculpture in the fifteenth century was still suffi-ciently similar and coherent in style over the Catholic world, for work to convey its message intelligibly to the people of widely separated countries.

This trading in works of art, must have influenced and modified sculptured stylisms. When Robert Bruce, King of Scotland, died in 1329 his tomb was made in Paris, an indication of the close relation between France and Scotland which persisted for three hundred years and which has left indelible traces on Scottish architecture, sculpture, language and culture.

The centre of the alabaster industry (for this is almost commercial art), whose retables and altar panels were so popular in the fourteenth and fifteenth centuries, was the town of Nottingham. Alabaster is a lime deposit found in pockets or " balls " in the Keuper marls of Staffordshire, Nottingham and Derbyshire. It was therefore natural that the big work-shops should be near the places where the material was quarried. Many of these reliefs are clearly workshop pieces carved quickly and almost to a formula, but some of the recumbent statues or effigies are works of great beauty and feeling. The material lends itself to rapid handling yet it can be worked to a delicate finish and is capable of the most elaborate detail. The colouring of these alabaster figures differed somewhat from that of stone (and it should not be forgotten that *all* mediæval sculpture was coloured). The alabaster workers used a great deal of gilding, and often concentrated their rich colour on borders, veils, and diapered patterns or vestments or drapery, adding brilliant spots of colour represen-ting jewels on such details as morses, crosses, mitres, etc. Hair was often painted over gilding, and faces were often just polished, with lips and eyes tinted. Alabaster lends itself to a wide variety of surface treatments ; polished, it has a semi-transparency which gives a strange elusiveness to the shadows, so that deeply recessed folds show less rather than more shadow ; it can be half polished to a sort of egg-shell surface, which is effective, and it can be roughened into a very white texture by the use of a "comb" or by "rasping," which gives a curious realism to white draperies. This has been done with striking effect on the effigy of the Duchess of Clarence at Canterbury, where the linen kerchief and the angels' robes are so finished, while the rest of the statue is polished.

It is a soft and easy medium to carve, and wood carving or carpenter's gouges can be readily used without blunting ; care has to be taken with the lines of the deposit, where it is always liable to fracture. It can be rendered quite opaque by being immersed for a short time in boiling water. It then looks like the whitest and most sugary carrara marble. All these treatments and devices were known to the mediæval carvers who exploited every possibility to achieve their rich and pictorial effects. At times, alabaster was used in conjunction with different coloured marbles, thus obtaining an effective polychromy.

England is peculiarly rich in tomb effigies. They represent persons in almost every walk of life and are fashioned in many different materials : bronze, often gilded ; gilding metal, generally known as latten. The stones used range from chalk, and the fine Beerstone of Devonshire, all the oolites and sandstones, alabaster, and many kinds of marble, (and some English marbles are of great beauty and fineness) including the very dark, hard, Purbeck marble. Wood also was commonly used for effigies. Of these a large number still survive—mostly oak of a fine quality. These oak figures were coated with gesso (a creamy paste made of glue and plaster). For the finest surfacing, the glue was made from boiled parchment cuttings, which gilders still use (or did a few years ago !). This gesso filled up the grain, making a smooth surface for painting, so that the material was almost obscured. Accessories on ecclesiastical figures, like croziers, mitres, morses, were added in silver or gilt metal, and set with glass and semi-precious stones. These oak statues were hollowed out behind, so that they were relatively light. This reduced the chances of wood splitting owing to changes of temperature, and most of the surviving statues are almost intact today, thanks to this careful hollowing, no sign of which was visible when the statue was attached to the slab on which it rested. It is possible that the origin of the portrait effigy was the wood and leather " image " carried or wheeled in the funeral procession, though apparently the " image " was sometimes personated by a living friend of the deceased. A contemporary account of the funeral of Henry V, 1422, records : " The body was embalmed and cired (waxed) and laid on a Royal carriage, an image like to him was laid upon the corpse, open. Afterwards was laid on his tomb a royal image like to himself of silver and gilt, made at the cost of Queen Katherine." Obviously, there was here first a funeral image, then " afterwards " the permanent statue.

Professor Lethaby whose knowledge of mediæval craftsmanship was unequalled has given a splendid record of this in his book on *Westminster Abbey and the King's Craftsmen*. The Abbey, being the Chapel of the Royal Palace, the building accounts are all preserved with those of the Royal Household and they give very valuable and interesting data. For instance John of Gloucester who came to work at Westminster in 1250, in addition to a substantial salary, received " a furred robe of office twice a year—in 1256-57," an indication of the high status of a master craftsman. These carvers, or makers of statues, were variously called imaginator, image maker, imagere and carver. Not until the time of the Henry VII Chapel, c. 1500, is one John Hudd called sculptor.

In 1506, " L. Imber, imagere, contracts for making the patrones in timber, for images to be cast by Nicholas Gwen "—" the imagere saith that the two images which be lying on the tombe, and the King's image kneeling upon the tombe, the workmanship perfectly done, with four Lords and twelve small images (presumably the small " weepers ") will cost sixty-four pounds." This price is only for the patrones (patterns) from which the final statues were to be made. These patrones were evidently made of wood, probably some soft and easily worked wood with little or no grain showing, and capable of taking a high finish, such as would cast well and show no traces of wood in the metal cast. In my own wood carving apprenticeship in the 'nineties, the finest grained pine was always used for pattern making, as all metal castings required a " pattern " from which the sand mould was made. Pattern making was a specific and highly skilled craft, requiring both carving and cabinet-making skill, as well as a knowledge of the whole process of metal casting so that the models might be reproducible in metal. Today, such bronze effigies are usually made from plaster models, which are cast from modelled clay. Detail, being difficult to model in soft clay, is often carved in the plaster cast. It seems probable from a contract such as that of Lawrence Imber, that gilt latten images, such as those of Queen Alainor and Henry III, made by William Torel, and also the John of Eltham, made by Alexander of Abingdon " de imaginator," were cast from wooden models. If so, they are essentially carver's work and distinguished as such by their firm contours and hard metallic surfaces, so different from most modern bronzes which too often reproduce the claylike surfaces of the original models. cf. page 10 et seq.

The unique and beautiful bronze effigy of Richard Beauchamp at Warwick is, I believe, not a cast bronze except for the head and the hands, the armour being forged and so beautifully jointed that the leg can be bent back to the head. Certainly the maker of that statue in 1454, William Austen, of London, had mastered all the technical problems of forging, casting and finishing bronze, and it is only necessary to step from the Beauchamp to the Leicester chapel to see in the monument to that great Elizabethan the degradation to which the art of sculpture fell by the collapse and abandonment of mediæval traditions during the sixteenth century. England has three great examples of the last phase of Gothic architecture and sculpture in the Henry VII Chapel, at Westminster, St. George's, Windsor, and King's College Chapel, Cambridge. In these one sees that the pursuit of light and height in building has reached so far that nothing farther on these lines could be achieved. The groined fan vaulting of Henry VII Chapel and of King's Chapel is superb, while the roof of

St. George's Windsor is even more elaborate with its richly carved pendentives. Every one of the thousands of stones required for this roof is cut to a bevel and is held in place only by slight wedge shaping. This mastery of technical skill could only be achieved by long generations of training. The Chapel of Henry VII contains almost the last great monument of Gothic sculpture in England—the tomb and grill of Henry VII. This was the work—or at least the design—of an Italian, Pietro Torregiano—in English documents often called Peter Torresany. Henry VIII having called the sculptor from Italy, the contract was made in 1512 " To make and work, or to do to be made and wrought, well, surely, cleanly, workmanly, curiously and substantially, for the sum of £1500 sterling, a tomb or sepulture of white marble and black touchstone, with images, figures, beasts, and other things of copper gilt, together with other diverse images, epitaphs and other things." The work was carried through under many difficulties and vicissitudes, and was finished in 1518. After the work was begun, Torregiano returned to Italy to get assistants. He got Benedetto da Rovezzano, who made the marble sarcophagus (which was not used) and he tried to persuade Cellini to come back to England with him. Cellini, however, refused to assist a man who had broken Michelangelo's nose ! For it was Torregiano who, in a quarrel, in Michelangelo's youth, had thrown a mallet and broken the bone. Michelangelo was now busy on the Moses statue for the tomb of Julius. The effigy of Henry VII is probably Torregiano's own work and is a consummate piece of portraiture. Lethaby thinks that Holbein used this sculptured portrait as the basis for the beautiful drawing of the King which is at Chatsworth. The splendid terracotta bust of Bishop Fisher in the Metropolitan Museum is probably by Torregiano.

During the fifteenth century, the vitality of mediæval life, with the church predominant, was steadily sinking. Many great churches begun on a vast scale could not be proceeded with for lack of both funds and interest, and splendid and ornate as late Gothic art is, it was often financed by specious means ; like the Tour de Beurre at Rouen built by the sale of indulgences. It is significant that it was the sale of such indulgences to raise money for the building of St. Peter's at Rome that roused the anger of Luther and led to the convulsion of the Reformation, just while Torregiano was making his memorial to Henry VII. In northern Europe, particularly in France, Germany and England, the development of art at the beginning of the sixteenth century was still on recognized mediæval lines though new details were creeping in, but socially and politically life was changing rapidly. As Froude says of England in 1529, " Parliament presided over a people from whom the forms and habits by which they had moved for centuries were falling like the shell of a chrysalis."

The invention of printing from moveable type and of wood engraving as a means of multiplying copies of books and drawings had an immense influence on the development of art, particularly in the field of wood sculpture. A Dürer woodcut might be brought to England by Erasmus, or sent to Bellini in Italy and thus carried its message far and wide. These woodcuts were often used as the basis for relief sculptures especially in reredoses and retables.

Just at the time when Luther was publicly defying the authority of the Pope as the corporate voice of the church, there was in England, France, Germany and the Netherlands a great outburst of rich and elaborate wood sculpture. Wood had always been used for sculpture, but towards the end of the fifteenth and early in the sixteenth centuries these carvers achieved work of extraordinary beauty and surpassing skill.

In England there is the stallwork of Chester Cathedral and of New College Chapel, Oxford, and the beautiful work in the Henry VII Chapel, but nothing in England can compare with the stallwork at Amiens, which, for rich inventiveness of design and technical mastery of craftsmanship stands absolutely unique in the whole range of wood sculpture.

Begun in 1508, it was finished in about ten years. The 120 stalls are carved into a pictorial Bible, old and new Testament scenes, endless subjects drawn from history, allegory and moralities. Every phase of mediæval life may be traced here. As Ruskin says in the Bible of Amiens : " Aisles and porches, lancet windows and roses you can see elsewhere but such carpenter's work you cannot. Wood carving was the Picard's joy, from his youth up, and, so far as I know, there is nothing else so beautiful cut out of the goodly trees of the wood. Under the carver's hand it seems to cut like clay, to fold like silk, to grow like living branches, to leap like living flame. Canopy crowning canopy, pinnacle piercing pinnacle, it shoots and wreaths itself into an enchanged glade, inextricable, imperishable, fuller of leafage than any forest, and fuller of story than any book." In the hundreds of small figures there is hardly an undistinguished one and many, like the dreaming Pharaoh, are unsurpassable.

In this same period, Germany also produced a group of wood sculptors whose work is unique and distinctive. Veit Stoss, Michel Pacher, Hans Bruggemann, Tilman Riemenschneider and Conrad Meit all worked in wood and, though the work is almost wholly ecclesiastical and the scale varies from minute and exquisite reliefs, figures and portrait heads in boxwood, to over-life-sized statues in oak like Veit Stoss' Angelical Salutation in Nuremburg, yet seldom is the work less than superb in craftsmanship, and powerful and moving in expression. Of these carvers, Riemenschneider was perhaps the most varied and accomplished.

Two small heads in the Victoria and Albert Museum, London, which used to be attributed to Dürer, are now usually credited to Riemen-schneider, and they are works of consummate mastery. The high degree of finish and the exquisite nervous beauty of the man's head is something quite unique in the art of wood sculpture. Another beautiful group is the St. Anne and St. Joseph in the same museum and this group with its sensitive and distinctive handling and feeling may reasonably also be attributed to Riemenschneider. In Gotha Museum are two small boxwood statuettes by Conrad Meit, which are interesting examples of late Gothic treatment of the nude figure. Based as they obviously are on a close study of living models, yet they lack the grace of French or Italian work, and

87

fail to achieve that real distinction which comes from a sense of style. These figures show some kinship with Dürer engravings. This Conrad Meit was one of the sculptors of the tomb of Philibert of Savoy and his wife, at Brou. Dürer spoke of Meit as " that excellent carver whose equal I have never met." That tomb was completed in 1526 and it must have taken some years to produce. It is interesting to find that Riemenschneider and Meit, though known chiefly for their work in wood, both worked in stone, and Meit may have done some of the alabaster figures on the tomb at Brou. Perhaps also he carved the two recumbent figures of the Duke and Duchess. The whole tomb is impressive and beautiful and 300 years later it suggested the theme of a noble poem to Matthew Arnold. This last phase of Gothic art was of exceeding richness and intricacy. In France, it is fitly called *flambouyant*, and, like the last flare-up of an expiring light, it was of extraordinary brilliance and intensity.

Another work of the same period is the Puits de Moïse at Dijon by Claus Sluter, a sculptured group of which only a part survives, but it is a work of great force and originality.

The dramatic and theatrical power of this work may be due, as E. Male suggests, to the fact that the figures of the six prophets seem to be based on characters in a then popular mystery play called *Judgement de Jesu* ; the texts painted on the scrolls which the statues hold, are quotations from the play, a clear indication of a close connection. Another result of this collaboration is seen in the passion for rich and elaborate clothes in sculpture, and perhaps, too, these dramatic representations suggested the use in sculpture of contemporary dress (then at its most fantastic) for sacred figures, and so carried further the passion for new and ever more vivid realism. Figures like the bronze King Arthur and Theodoric, by Peter Vischer, on the tomb of Emperor Maximilian are almost like casts from living models dressed in elaborate armour. And the miracle plays also influenced the development of the Drama. As J. A. Symonds says, " Comedy found its germ in the lighter scenes conceded to the popular appetite for entertainment. Realistic drama emerged from stories like that of the woman taken in adultery and the biography of the Magdalen. The history play had its origin in subsidiary pieces adopted from the Apocrypha of which the story of Esther may serve as an example."

There was a considerable infiltration of Italian craftsmen into England at the end of the fifteenth and early in the sixteenth century. Torregiano was only one of a great number though he was the most important, and these foreigners left their mark on English art. In a late Gothic building like King's College Chapel, Cambridge, there are details which show clearly the influence of Italian sculptors. In France, the same influence may be readily seen in many churches, for instance the rich and lovely stone screen in the ambulatory of Chartres has many details, not only in ornament, but even in a statue of the Virgin with a Mona Lisa smile, which could only come from the study of Italian work. There were, of course, many Italian artists called to France by Francois I, of whom the greatest were Leonardo, Andrea del Sarto, and Cellini, but besides

88. TOMB OF
AYMER DE VALENCE
STONE
WESTMINSTER ABBEY

89, 90. TOMB OF
PRINCE JOHN OF ELTHAM
STONE
WESTMINSTER ABBEY

DETAIL OF FIGURES
FROM NORTH SIDE

91, 92.   RICHARD BEAUCHAMP, EARL OF WARWICK :
BRONZE : BEAUCHAMP CHAPEL, ST. MARY'S WARWICK

Complete tomb showing small figures and canopy
work : fourteenth century stone.

Elaborate and intricate canopy work
only possible with fine oolitic stones.
The recumbent figure of the King is
of alabaster, slightly coloured.

93, 94.   TOMB OF EDWARD II : GLOUCESTER CATHEDRAL

GOTHIC SCULPTURE

95. MADONNA AND CHILD : STONE : FRENCH :
LATE THIRTEENTH CENTURY

96. MADONNA AND CHILD : IVORY : FRENCH :
THIRTEENTH CENTURY

The early type of Madonna holds forth the Child for
adoration

97. MADONNA AND CHILD : FRENCH :
FOURTEENTH TO FIFTEENTH CENTURY: THE LOUVRE

The human Mother and playful Child

98. VIRGIN AND CHILD:
SANDSTONE:
FRENCH:
EARLY FOURTEENTH
CENTURY:
VICTORIA AND ALBERT
MUSEUM, LONDON

100. BISHOP CHICHELE'S TOMB
ALABASTER, COLOURED
CANTERBURY CATHEDRAL

'It is interesting to find that Riemenschneider and Meit, though known chiefly for their work in wood, both worked in stone, and Meit may have done some of the alabaster figures on the tomb of Philibert of Savoy and his wife at Brou. Perhaps also he carved the two recumbent figures of the Duke and Duchess. Durer spoke of " that excellent carver whose equal I have never met."

'The tomb must have taken some years to produce and was completed in 1526. The whole work is impressive and beautiful and some 300 years later it suggested the theme of a noble poem to Matthew Arnold.'

1. TOMB OF PHILIBERT LE BEAU: STONE, ALABASTER, MARBLE: SIXTEENTH CENTURY: BROU

One of a series of very high relief carvings of
the life of St. Firmin.   Painted and parti-gilt.

102. WALL DECORATION : STONE : AMIENS CATHEDRAL

these great men there were many lesser craftsmen, bringing new and fertilizing ideas to French sculptors and artists and so exercising a great influence on French art. In England the passion for Italian things affected the development not only of art but of the Drama, and the leaders in this humanist movement from Henry VII and Henry VIII in youth, to More, Colet and Linacre, were all steeped in Italian culture. The rich bankers and merchants were often Italians, Echoes of their power may be seen in the curious fact that England still uses Italian contractions for its monies, L.S.D. standing originally for Lire, Soldi, Denari, and the street of the bankers is still Lombard Street !

After Henry VIII had broken with Rome and Papal authority there was a rush of craftsmen from Protestant Flanders, and they too left their mark on English architecture and sculpture, particularly on the houses of the new Elizabethan noblemen ; houses often built from the stolen funds of the despoiled religious houses. The majestic central tower of Canterbury had only lately been finished in the most elaborate Perpendicular style when Henry VIII plundered its great shrine, the tomb of Becket, the richest of all the shrines, and these spoils were used to make some of Henry's friends the new aristocracy of England. The art and architecture of these great new houses became eclectic and confused, no longer autochthonous and coherent in style.

The closing of the great religious houses and the consequent stopping of all ecclesiastical building and craftsmanship broke finally the long tradition of design and workmanship on which Gothic art was based and with which it had functioned for four hundred years. During all that time, in spite of great and growing changes in life and in architecture and all the subsidiary crafts there had developed a system of building in which stone was held in equipoise. As Walter Pater says, " Like the age which projected it, like the impulsive communal movement which is here its motive, the pointed style at Amiens is full of excitement—go for repose to classic work—the sustained equilibrium of oblique pressure on all sides is the essence of the hazardous Gothic construction." This sense of vitality pervades all good Gothic sculpture throughout its whole course.

This very quality of vitality in building has been held as a fault by Dr. W. Worringer for whom, because of its inherent weight and stability, the natural use of stone is in the posts and lintel of classic construction. " In the Gothic cathedral there is a movement to the vertical in which all the laws of weight seem abrogated. Vainly do we seek what our natural feeling demands, some suggestion of the relation between burden and strength to bear : one would say that no burden any longer existed, only freely acting forces that with a mighty impulse are striving upward. It is clear that stone has here given up its character and in a word has become dematerialized . . . it is in its innermost being irrational, supernatural, transcendental." But this transcending of the material is precisely the mark of the greatest art, which annihilates material to express spirit—who thinks of plaster walls and pigment in the Sistine Chapel ? Who seeing the superb sweep of the cheek of the Sphinx thinks of sandstone ? The artist's task is always to transmute the material and it is characteristic that at the end of the middle ages when the so-called scientists were absorbed in magic, necromancy, and the transmutation of base metals into gold, the workmen in building and sculpture had achieved this transmutation of base material and had so filled their stone with spirit that it moves us with its beauty today.

It is to be noted too that these builders and craftsmen had such living pride in their work that they had little regard for the work of their predecessors. When called on to continue a building after perhaps a century of delay, they never made the smallest attempt to continue building or to carve figures in the manner or stylism of any previous age. Yet there is a living thread of tradition running through a cathedral which may have been built at intervals over two or three hundred years, so that it became and remains still, a coherent unity. The clearness of thought and feeling characteristic of mediæval art, the disciplined activity under which it was produced, gave it a harmony obtainable only by moderation and tradition, and the sense of effort gave it an intensity of life that can be matched in no other art. Like the Greeks the mediæval sculptor conceived of form not as an appearance, but as the tangible expression of Reality.

As the middle ages expired, there was developed an intense consciousness of personality, and there arose an entirely new attitude to established authority and to the visible world. The discovery of new continents, both physical and of the mind, heralded a change which was to destroy the last props of mediæval life and thought. " That free and roving thing," as Montaigne called the human soul, was to seek and find many strange things in the world suddenly so widened ; and again " ' Tis not a soul, 'tis not a body, we are training up—but a man—and we ought not to divide him. Of all the infirmities we have, the most savage is to despise our being." Montaigne here speaks with the voice of the Renaissance.

THE RENAISSANCE

MONTAIGNE'S note of self-realization is characteristic of the new movement which came to be called the Renaissance. It gradually destroyed by undermining them, the ideas on which mediæval life was based ; ideas which were an amalgam of the natural, the unnatural and the supernatural. Yet the comparative rapidity with which the new ideas spread was partly due to the long seed-time of mediæval discipline and faith. The roots of the Renaissance may be traced to many causes, among others to the intellectual probing of the thinkers, who, in the twelfth century made anew the discovery that reason too was a gift of God. Yet the movement ended, not in the enthronement of reason in human affairs, but in the absolutism of Machiavelli's " Prince " ; in the detached and inhuman indifference of Leonardo, and in the substitution of the authority of the ancients, for the authority of tradition.

It was in Italy, from the thirteenth to the sixteenth century, that this new movement arose and flourished, influencing the course of art and culture over the whole of Europe. The later phases of Gothic art in England, France and Germany were all altered and modified by Italian ideas and influence. Perhaps Vasari, a Florentine, who in the sixteenth century wrote a series of *Lives of the Painters*, was the first person to use the word " Rinascita " to denote this artistic movement of which he was the great contemporary historian. The very word is a recognition of the sense of a long period of decay and death, and Vasari's attitude towards earlier art and architecture may be seen in his tribute to Brunelleschi, who, he says, " was given to us by heaven for the purpose of imparting a new spirit to architecture, which for hundreds of years had been lost, for men in these times had badly expended great treasures in the erection of buildings without order, constructed in a wretched manner after deplorable designs, with fantastic inventions, laboured graces and worse decorations." Seldom has Gothic architecture been so travestied or attacked with such complacent self-confidence. This proud consciousness of a new spirit and life is echoed in the decree made by the commonwealth of Florence as early as 1294.

" Whereas it is the highest interest of a people of illustrious origin so to proceed in their affairs that men may perceive from their external works that their doings are at once wise and magnanimous, it is therefore ordered that Arnulf, architect of our commune, prepare the model or design for the rebuilding of S. Reparata with such supreme and lavish magnificence that neither the industry nor the capacity of man shall be able to devise anything more grand or more beautiful : inasmuch as the most judicious in this city have pronounced the opinion in public and private conferences, that no work of the commune should be undertaken unless the design be such as to make it correspondent with a heart which is of the greatest nature, because composed of the spirit of many citizens united together in one single will."

This decree unites in a striking way the mediæval sense of solidarity with the proud self-consciousness of the Renaissance. This movement was national as well as artistic. The word Gothic used by Raphael to convey the impression of " barbarous " implied also that such art was foreign and alien. Surviving buildings and monuments from " the grandeur that was Rome " were daily impressed on these Italian artists and it was natural and inevitable that Roman rather than Greek classicism should linger on in Italy and in Gaul. " They worked," as Symonds says, " with half their attention always on the past."

In a sculpture like the Cenacola relief at Modena the drapery arrangements are entirely classical Roman, though the date of the work is twelfth century. As in Roman art, there is found in this early Italian art a constant use of inscriptions in Latin and, at times, in Greek, and these are so obviously done as it were, freehand, that they often overflow their spaces and are contracted and fitted into the design with difficulty. Such miscalculations are an evidence of a way of working similar to that of the mediæval mason in France and England. These carvers were only workmen and they may even have been less well paid than the masons or the painters. As in northern European Gothic building in the twelfth and early thirteenth centuries, much of the decoration was sculpture in relief, and secondary to the architecture. In Italy in some churches, great bronze doors (themselves a reminder of the age of rapine and of their defensive necessity) were the main decorative elements in the scheme of the building. The bronze doors of the Cathedral of Pisa are notable examples of the more elaborate relief work, superbly designed and marvellously cast in bronze. Other doors are much simpler and at times they are hardly in relief, but deeply engraved like mediæval brasses.

Niccolo Pisano (sometimes called Niccolo d'Apulia) was at once the last fruit of the Roman classical tradition and the first sculptor of the new Renaissance : this duality is characteristic of so many great artists. In his work are united both elements, the classical and the newer and more naturalistic mode of his own day. From this fusion of the study of the past and the study of nature there was born a new spirit in sculpture which altered the whole course of the art and breathed a new life into its forms. The rapid changes in life and outlook in the latter half of the thirteenth century may be traced in Niccolo's own work. In one panel of the Pisan pulpit (1260) a composite relief of the Annunciation and the Nativity, the virgin is shown receiving the angel's message with a haughty Juno-like gesture ; there is no trace here of Christian humility. The architectural background is a pagan temple, with pediment and dentils. The draperies are classical in feeling and the whole is suffused with a pagan

Roman spirit, though nobly so. In another panel in the Siena pulpit, of only six years later, the whole conception of his art is changed. Again the subject is the Nativity, but, for the joint episode, instead of the Annunciation, there is a touching and tender visitation ; the architecture is changed to pointed Gothic, the relative scale of the various figures is changed, Juno is dethroned and in her place is a sweet-faced Christian Madonna. As Roger Fry expresses it : " a whole new world of spritual experiences has here found expression . . . instead of the serene and indifferent self-possession of the earlier work, this expresses a sentiment of tender and introspective humility." Was this change the result of some contact with contemporary northern European sculpture ? Chartres, Amiens, Lincoln were being built and carvers were there achieving statues which in their own way remain unrivalled as the expression of spiritual loveliness. Perhaps it is reasonable to assume that the passion for pilgrimages and the steady stream of pilgrims always going on " the path to Rome" brought drawings, missals, and portable works of Gothic art which were absorbed, studied and echoed by the quick and sensitive artists of northern Italy ; for native Italian art is Tuscan (Etruscan) in origin and Niccolo Pisano was the most powerful influence in giving it power and direction. Lord Lindsay has summed up our debt thus :

" Neither Dante nor Shakespeare can boast such extent and durability of influence. Whatever of highest excellence has been achieved in sculpture and painting throughout Europe has been in obedience to the impulse he primarily gave, and in following up the principle which he finally struck out."

In this immense influence Niccolo resembles his great successor Giotto who though not a sculptor is yet a significant figure for sculptors ; his paintings have the clarity and directness of relief sculpture ; they are superbly designed and movingly expressive.

Through the study of Pisan sculpture the school of Giotto received inspiration from the example of antiquity. With his counterpart, St. Francis, Giotto turned men's eyes towards the loving observation of natural beauty and by their blitheness of soul, and vivifying and cleansing spirit they ennobled their age. They humanised the mysteries of faith and made art a living and vital force in the minds of men. Petrarch, a little later, grasped something of the significance of his age and of its importance in world history. " I see myself standing at the borderline of two peoples whence I survey at once the past and the coming race, and the plaint which our fathers did not utter I shall, at least, sound in the ears of our children."

This sense of the unity and continuity of life is one of the gifts of the Renaissance, and it is characteristic that Petrarch urged Simone Martini to depict ancient Romans, as dressed in different costumes from those of contemporary Italians ; a great innovation, and one which had immense influence on the development of art and archæology. Mediæval art had developed and worked on a basis of tradition and authority. At the Renaissance men turned towards nature, and in their art they showed that the representation of nature was not so simple as it had appeared to earlier artists. The science of perspective brought new relative planes into pictorial representation. The study of chiaroscuro revealed the possibilities of a third dimension. The study of anatomy put new powers at the command of artists and this influenced powerfully the development of sculpture. Donatello, working on the traditions of the Pisani, gradually extended the boundaries of his art and achieved new triumphs of realistic power. The marble figure of the slim and nervous St. George is a work within the older traditions of the craft, and has a certain Gothic or mediæval quality, while later works like the Zuccone, and the terra-cotta portrait bust of Niccolo d'Uzzano, are entirely new in conception and in style. Their vivid life-likeness had no previous parallel (except in Græco-Roman portraiture), and even their broad simplifications were new, for Donatello had discovered that " distance consumes diligence ", and the bold and violent modelling of the Zuccone, though grotesquely exaggerated in a detail photograph, is entirely successful and convincing when seen in its position. This powerful realism is probably the quality which Rodin so admired in Donatello, and which made the great modern realist sculptor place Donatello above Michelangelo, a judgment which reveals to us a greater sense of Rodin's limitations than of Donatello's skill.

The exquisite stone relief of the Annunciation shows Donatello as a sensitive and consummate craftsman ; the carving of this macigno stone, as of the marble St. George, is masterly and beautiful. Both works are essentially carvings and not modellings translated into other materials. The long shield of the St. George, which almost covers the legs, acts as the main support of the figure, for the ankles of a standing marble statue are almost always too weak to support the weight of the figure. In the Annunciation, the necessary compactness is gained by the device of placing each figure against the pilaster sides of the panel. For some unknown reason, the cherubs which surmount the panel are of wood. Both the St. George and the Annunciation have a certain architectural quality which marks them as designed for a specific place and purpose. The Zuccone, however, is as plastically conceived as a figure by Rodin, and here Donatello, though the work was to be placed in a niche in the Campanile, made no concession to the architecture. Zuccone demands and achieves a separate existence ; this is sculpture added to architecture, not integrated with it. This refusal of the sculpture to be subordinated to the parent art of architecture is part of the demand of the Renaissance for individual expression. It culminated, for instance, in a building like the Certosa at Pavia, which is more a work of sculpture than of architecture.

Everywhere authority was challenged, and power succeeded to power. When a great usurper established his position, he aroused such envy that others determinedly challenged his authority, and this led to that excessive individualism which permeated all life and which, as Burckhardt believed, proved to be the great disruptive force of the Renaissance. The results of this were sometimes incalculable; for instance Burckhardt implies that the moral and political survival and salvation of the Papacy was due to the relentless challenge of its mortal enemies and he suggests that but for the

Reformation, which forced the Popes to initiate great reforms, their own corruption and degradation would have brought the whole ecclesiastical state to an end. It was of this corrupt Roman organization that Michelangelo said sadly and bitterly, " No one should laugh when the whole world is in tears." Savonarola and " the bonfire of vanities " gave the answer to the corrosive and pagan unbelief, and the almost entire loss of Christian values. Symonds saw the Renaissance as the coming of dawn after the mediæval darkness, but the new light and life had to bought at a price. That price was the destruction of the corporate and cohesive life of the Middle Ages when thought ran closely along a single line.

There is a symbolical significance in the exquisite beauty of the myriad statues shaped by nameless mediæval carvers. There is a like symbolical significance in great statues like Gattamelata, and Colleone, who ride forever, the superb embodiment in history and art of individual power, as distinct from the corporate and spiritual enthusiasm of mediæval life. The driving force of the Renaissance was individual energy. Men rose to power, and held it by war, like the Sforzas ; or by money, like the Medici. This led to the economic assertion of the individual, to the gradual decay and destruction of the more democratic guilds, and so to the rise of capitalism and the financier.

The expansion of life and thought in so many directions in the fourteenth and fifteenth centuries in Italy was great, and in the field of art the conquests were stupendous. Symonds suggests that art is the thread of Ariadne to which one must cling to comprehend the labyrinthine windings of the Renaissance mind and character, but he himself has to trace its expression in many other fields in order to interpret its meaning and power. The spiritual corruption, and the loss of moral standards was part of the price paid for intellectual freedom. It was not in the wickedness and corruption of popes and cardinals and of countless men and women that death and degradation lay, but in the universal toleration of this ; in the fact that the age did not see them as iniquitous, except for great souls like Dante, Savonarola and Michelangelo, in whom thought transcended their age. How significant that Dante is shown in Raphael's frescoes among the Muses, and also in the Disputa! In the mind of Raphael and his age, Dante belonged both to the ancient and the Christian world. In the disinterested pursuit of knowledge for its own sake, the problems and responsibilities of social living were often forgotten, and one of the anomalies of this age of intellectual activity is that there was also a strange survival, and development even, of witchcraft, sorcery, alchemy, necromancy and astrology. There was much pseudo-knowledge. Even the Church sanctioned the use of magic and in 1462, Pope Pius II (the great humanist Aneas Sylvius) ordered Sigismondo Malatesta to be burned in wax effigy as a heretic in front of St. Peter's. Yet the same Pope issued a bill for the protection and conservation of all the monuments of antiquity and complained somewhat peevishly in his Roman palace that " so many church bells were disturbing to a man of letters ".

The newly widened boundaries of art brought into both painting and sculpture a sense of wonder and mystery, and the re-discovery of antiquity led to an immensely widened conception of natural and human beauty. In the characteristic great works of art of this age one has a consciousness of beauty achieved effortlessly and inevitably. The aura of tranced peace which surrounds the figures of Perugino's Crucifixion, or the still beauty of Quercia's Saint Ilario, with its hushed and reverential repose, which yet conveys an impression of expectant renewal—these are qualities which had not appeared in art before. The persistent, unwearied, but loving study of nature, of new science, and ancient art and philosophy led to an assured expressive and intellectual power which is everywhere evident and which culminated in the art of such great masters as Quercia, Donatello, Verrocchio, Leonardo and Michelangelo.

Jacopo della Quercia was a virile and accomplished sculptor, as the Ilario tomb shows. He was also a great master in the art of wood sculpture (as his name implies). A series of prophets carved in limewood are at Siena, and the Louvre has a superb life-sized oak Madonna and Child which has something of the grandeur of the sibyls of Michelangelo (painted 100 years later). In competition with others he submitted a panel for the Florentine Baptistry doors, but his work was rejected as " lacking delicacy of finish " and the more suave and gentle Ghiberti was entrusted with the work and produced the doors so well known, and so accomplished in technique. In these doors sculpture rivals painting in the perspective and aerial treatment ; and perhaps the pictorial beauty is achieved at some loss of sculptural dignity, yet the triumphant assurance and graceful vitality, especially of all the figures, witness to the power and mastery of the artist. After Quercia made the superb fountain at Siena, his contemporaries changed his name to Jacopo della Fonte. Vasari has some interesting notes on Quercia's technique : " The models used by sculptors in our own day are prepared in a manner invented by Quercia. Over a wood armature, with hay, hemp-tow, well bound clay is mixed with cement, paste, glue, shearings of woollen cloth, etc. This gesso is not liable to crack." This would imply that statue models were wrought in this plaster and tow, etc., rather than modelled in clay and then cast in plaster. This method of work is convenient for it can be used over a long period of time. It saves casting and the substance—gesso duro—can be carved away if too much is applied, and it can be added to if required. (Watts in the nineteenth century made the model for his great equestrian statue Physical Energy in this way with a gesso of plaster and tow.) Vasari also describes the use of horsehair or coarse cloth, and pressed tow, or hay to lessen the weight and the shrinkage of the clay and thus make it less liable to crack. All this is for the nude model, and he then proceeds, " if the statue is to have thin drapery he takes fine cloth, if with heavy (drapery) he takes coarse cloth and wets it and covers it with clay of the consistency of thick mud, and arranges it round the figure in such folds and creases as the mind suggests." The drapery of Donatello's Zuccone looks as if it had been based on some such realistic study, though in the carving some of the realism is modified and adapted to the chisel. But there is something unrelenting in

96

Donatello's realism in spite of his Christian sentiment and his distinction of style. Yet, at times, he achieves, as in the David, not a portrait of a youth but a transcending of the physical type by an all-powerful animating impulse, which raises the figure to a height of spiritual power. Yet Vasari says this statue was refused by the Church when first shown. The sculptor, however, persuaded the authorities to erect it, and leave it for two weeks, after which it was " universally admired ". Of Donatello's St. Mark, Michelangelo said, " If the Apostle looked like this we may safely believe what he has written." It is this living quality animating his figures which stamps Donatello as a great artist—the union of strength and delicacy— of searching realism allied with a sense of style, an extension of the boundaries of art without a break with craft traditions.

Many Italian artists were painters, sculptors, architects, and craftsmen in various media. The number of artists apprenticed to goldsmiths is remarkable, and this rigorous and exacting training in craftsmanship produced artists for whom no purely technical problem offered any serious difficulty. The glimpses of artist and apprentice workshop life given throughout Vasari's *Lives* show how rigorous was the training, how constant was the labour of the working artist. It began early when their minds and bodies were young and receptive ; usually about the age of 12 or 13, occasionally, as with Mantegna, as young as 10, and they learned by assisting in every branch of art practised in the workshop of the master. Almost all artists had a retinue of assistants and apprentices, and this life of constant artistic activity proved to be a superb training for artists. What they learned was not only craft skill and the technique of art, but in the intellectual activity expressed in the constant workshop rivalries, dis- cussions of problems of art and philosophy, the pleasantries of workshop life, there was a potent means of acquiring a richly cultivated mind and spirit for only from such could art like that of the Renaissance have been produced. Architects and sculptors alike were associated in the same guild with masons and " stonecutters "—as even Niccolo Pisano was described. They lived simply, as Vasari's story of Donatello and Brunelleschi shows, buying eggs and cheese for lunch at the Mercato Vecchio and carrying it to the studio in their aprons. At their art they laboured unremittingly and in many fields. Donatello designed a great stained glass window for the Cathedral of Florence. His friend Brunelleschi, architect of the Duomo, carved a most moving crucified Christ in wood, which Donatello said was " a miracle ". Every artist developed a distinct personality and stamped it on his work.

Mina da Fiesole lives on in his dimpled babies and slender, gracious Madonnas showing some kinship with the lyrical art of Botticelli. In the monument to Cardinal di Portugallo, Rosselino achieved a triumph of exquisite beauty, and truly Christian feeling, while his little kneeling Virgin in the Metropolitan Museum has an idyllic and poetic grace which is all his own. Verrocchio, though primarily a painter, yet did some beautiful and vigorous sculpture, including, in collaboration with Leopardi, the great statue of Colleone, that most triumphant fusion of the real and the ideal in the history of equestrian sculpture, which Symonds calls " a masterpiece of Florentine science and Venetian fervour."

Though neither Fra Angelico nor Mantegna were sculptors, they have their own significance in plastic art. Angelico, by his resolute disregard of the prevailing study of antiquity and by his fervent contemplation, produced art which was a sort of mystical recreation, rather than representation. His saints are martyred but do not suffer ; placid, beatic, embodied ecstasies they stand in their flower-strewn paradise ; while Mantegna, absorbed in the study of antiquity produced an art, born out of pagan sculpture, in which he turns his men and women into stone, thus reversing the legend of Pygmalion. Signorelli, with his scientific and anatomical naturalism, and Orcagna, with his strong simplicity and stern presentation of death and resurrection, also both powerfully influenced sculpture, especially that of Michelangelo.

All these newly discovered powers and possibilities in art led to a deeper understanding, not only of the facts and aspects of nature, and of representation, but also to the relation and deeper meaning of these facts. Donatello reproached Uccello for his study of perspective, " exchanging the certain for the uncertain ", but this new science made figures detach themselves from the walls, or merge themselves with the painted architecture as do the brooding titans on the Sistine ceiling, or move, bathed in heavenly light, as in the dome of Correggio. A priest, refusing to accept a picture painted by Titian, complained, " Your scandalous figures stand quite out from the canvas ; they are as bad as a group of statues " !

All these developments were pursued sedulously and tenaciously by the individual artists. The study of anatomy overflowed into studies of symmetry and proportion, to the mystic significance of numbers, and to an attitude of almost insatiate curiosity. They learned from the study of reality to understand and appreciate the beauty of the antique ; and to the realization that the physical beauty of classic art was the result of generations of living athletes and a high regard for bodily beauty. Barriers were broken down ; symbols developed into allegory, and thence to paraphrase. Minerva and Apollo might be renamed as Judith and Christ, and Diana with her quiver of arrows made to represent Theology. New life and new art developed as ancient life and ancient art were exhumed and studied, but there were significant changes.

The Greek sculptor had sought a concrete and actual beauty ; the Renaissance artist sought a deeper kind of beauty. Even the decadent Venus de Medici, for instance, has a certain exquisiteness of body, but when Botticelli retranslated her into the Venus of the sea she becomes strangely exotic and her beauty is almost incorporeal. She passes from the sphere of artistic representation into that of mystical and lyric poetry. Before those strange figures of Botticelli, poised or moving with willowy bodies and insecure tread over the flowered earth, one is reminded of Keats' profound saying, " Poetry should be great and unobtrusive, a thing which enters into one's soul and does not startle it, or amaze it with itself, but with its subject. How beautiful are the retired flowers." So

Botticelli's art steals upon one and its plastic beauty is only slowly realized.

All these great developments and changes in art were achieved by disciplined activity and a constant and intense study of the beauty of the visible world. Art was pursued, not only for its own sake, but also for the sake of wider life, and as one of the harmonious functions of existence. In great artists like Raphael, Leonardo and Michelangelo, who mark the final phase of the Renaissance, there is no distinction between art and life. In their art they embarked on emotional experiences as other men embarked on great adventures. The baffling eyes and faintly smiling lips of Leonardo's women are an index of his own remote and amoral soul, viewing and recording all things, finding nothing dull but unreality, challenging authority. "Anyone who in a discussion relies on authority uses not his intellect but his memory." He moved in his impersonal way, unrelated to his contemporaries or to his age, beautiful in person, serenely epicurean, courting mystery, unhurried, unwearied and unsatisfied ; he dreamed his life away in an atmosphere of war, murder, and intrigue, not a humanist or religious, but yet spiritual, and always an artist ; subtle, and elaborate, sensitive and imaginative, yet inhumanly detached, Leonardo is the epitome of all the varied energies of the Renaissance. Believing that " Wisdom is the child of Experience ", he is contemptuous of all activities except the search for perfection ; particularly is he scornful of lesser artists. " If the sculptor says he cannot restore the superabundant substance which has once been removed from his work, I answer that he who removes too much has but little understanding, and is no master. Because if he has mastered the proportions, he will not remove anything unnecessarily ; therefore we will say that this disadvantage is inherent in the artist and not in the material. But I will not speak of such men—they are spoilers of marble, and not artists."

In strange contrast was his contemporary Michelangelo who, amid the corruptions and licentiousness of the Roman court and ecclesiastical life, sought, like Socrates, for that beauty in the inward soul, that congruity between the inner and the outward man, which is the secret of the Platonist, seeking an affinity between beauty and human worthiness. " Because the beauty of the world is fragile, I seek to attain the eternal and universal beauty." How strange would these words sound from Leonardo ! How characteristic they are of Michelangelo. And so, as Helen Waddell says, Platonism brought to the sixteenth as to the twelfth century, " the beauty and the abiding value of the sensible appearance of things." His passion was always for the plastic beauty of the human body. " Nor hath God deigned to show Himself elsewhere more clearly than in human form sublime, which, since they image Him, alone I love." In that lies the secret of Michelangelo. He was apprenticed at the age of 13 to Ghirlandaio and worked with his master for three years ; when about 18, he began the study of anatomy, and, because the Prior of San Spirito gave him a room in which to study, he carved a life-sized wooden Christ for the church. There seems to be no trace of this today. He admired and studied the virile and powerful work of Quercia ("Art, vehement and towering, tragic as

Æschylus," says Faure), but very early asserted his own individuality in masterly works. Surely never in the history of sculpture was such a work of emotional power, deep feeling and consummate technical skill as the Pieta which Michelangelo carved in Rome in his twenty-fourth year. Already in this work are to be found the distinct and essential qualities which characterize all his work ; the power to transcend the personal and the specific, and to seize on the universal type forms ; the intellectual power which called forth his heroic concepts ; above all the technical mastery beyond that of any other sculptor. It is a strange and pathetic fact that this Pieta is the last work he ever quite finished, even to his signature !

Before he returned to Florence in 1501, he had carved the two splendid reliefs in the Bargello and in London, the Madonna and Child at Bruges, and perhaps also painted the unfinished Deposition picture in the National Gallery, London, in which the features of the dead Christ strongly resemble those of the Christ in the Pieta sculpture. The unfinished relief in London gives a good opportunity to study his carving technique. One can trace the use of the point, various claw tools, and chisels, and these are used with great strength and precision, and both right and left handedly. There is no sign of hesitation. One notes the certainty with which the forms are revealed. This technical mastery must be recognized and noted, for it shows that his power to conceive forms and carve them directly was a skill which he acquired in his youth. In the sculpture of Michelangelo the technique must be specially studied, for the carving of the marble is entirely his own work, and the impressive emotional power of his sculpture is, in a peculiar degree, related to his method of working. In 1504, in his twenty-ninth year, he carved the great David, 14 feet high, from a block of marble which had been put aside for 30 years as spoiled. This was an immense physical achievement, for he carved it in about 20 months ; even apart from the art, this would show his titanic strength and skill, and it is a work of splendid and assured power, alike in conception and execution. This would seem to have been carved from small scale wax models, several of which are in London. The scale is perhaps a linear tenth, i.e. one inch in the model represents ten inches in the statue. One of these, of the thigh, is *écorché*, showing the anatomical structure without skin or subcutaneous tissue. He had a profound knowledge of anatomy and it was this exact scientific knowledge which, aided by his clear visual sense of form, enabled him to carve directly in the marble, using only the simplest of measuring devices. The article on " Carving " under the general heading of *Sculpture* in Encyclopædia Britannica, fourteenth edition, referring to Michelangelo's David : " A sketch was made smaller by one tenth, finished in all the minutest anatomical details." But the model in the Casa Buonarotti is in no sense " finished in the minutest anatomical details ", and Vasari explicitly says that this was the wax model from which Michelangelo carved the David. " Smaller by one tenth ", is surely an error. No one would make a nine foot model for a ten foot statue. Evidently the scale is meant to be one tenth, that is, one foot equals ten feet. There is in the British Museum a small wax model of about this scale, apparently a preliminary study for one of the Medici tomb reclining figures. This study much more nearly approximates to the proportions of a normally developed man and shows that in the carving of the final figure Michelangelo made no attempt to " copy " the wax model, but filled out the forms with ennobling stylism as he carved. This is the true use of models.

Vasari describes the simple means of measuring : " using a carpenter's square vertically and horizontally put against the model and against the block of marble . . . so that measuring the model and the marble, in proportion, he gradually chisels away the stone till the figure thus measured time after time, issues forth from the marble, in the same manner that one would lift a wax figure out of a pail of water evenly and in a horizontal position." The last part of this sentence has misled some writers into assuming that a model was actually submerged, the water representing the interstices being gradually withdrawn, revealing the shapes of the background to be cut away. This was in no sense what Vasari meant. It happens, however, that Michelangelo, judging by some very unfinished works, does appear to have worked largely from the front, chiselling away the background, rather than working from all sides and " picking up " the forms of the limbs, as the background was pushed further and further back, till the figure was free. " The Giant ", as the David was called, established his reputation firmly, and there was a great popular demonstration when it was drawn through the streets of Florence to its site, chosen by a vote of the artists of the city, on the terrace of the Signory.

In 1505 he was called to Rome again by the Pope and ordered to make a great tomb for Pope Julius II. This was meant to be the greatest sculptured monument in the world, and he laboured intermittently on it for many years, but, of the many statues designed for the tomb, only one was ever finished. This was the great figure of Moses as the Lawgiver, a majestic and awe-inspiring statue. Perhaps it is a dramatized portrait of Julius. This tomb haunted his life. After years of wasted work, he wrote pathetically, " Every day I am stoned as though I had crucified Christ. My youth is lost. I am bound hand and foot to this tomb."

In 1508, he was ordered by the Pope to paint the ceiling of the Sistine Chapel ; protesting that he was a sculptor and not a painter, he nevertheless set to work and is said to have prepared the design of the whole scheme, erected the scaffolding, and begun painting, within six weeks of his arrival in Rome. Vasari and Condivi both assert that he painted the whole work entirely unaided—without even an assistant to grind and mix colours—in about two years, but it seems that the final dedication of the chapel was in 1512, so it may have occupied about four years. Here again is revealed a stupendous and even terrifying sense of power ; the types are incredibly grand and heroic, and on a great scale, and painted with the same certainty as his sculptured figures were hewn, and with far greater rapidity. It seems clear (for his day-by-day work can be traced by the junctions of the plaster) that the Adam, a figure eight feet long, was painted in three days, and the Sibyls and Prophets, 18 feet high if they stood up, were painted each in four or five days. The whole is a vast and splendid

achievement, such as no other man ever conceived and carried out.

Released from painting, he returned to Florence to make the figures commemorating the Medici family in the Sacristy of San Lorenzo. Again the scheme is incomplete. The two seated figures of Lorenzo and Guliano di Medici, are in no sense portraits. They have no trace of contemporary trappings, or clothes, nor is there the slightest attempt at portraiture. They are generic types ; one alert and poised, the other meditative and contemplative. Below on curved pediments over sarcophagi, are two pairs of reclining figures, male and female ; usually called Night and Day, and Dawn and Evening, but again no titles can explain their import nor are names needed to discern the tremendous power which surges in those brooding and titanic shapes. Probably they reflect the sculptor's own thoughts about life and death, the Medici and the times. To fix their meaning precisely is of no importance ; they are charged with emotion in a way that has no parallel in plastic art. " Nature made him, then broke the mould ", said Ariosto of Michelangelo. So, with these troubled marble forms of exquisite and moving beauty, yet filled with repressed energy, with something of the resistless power of the ocean, not quiet but quiescent, they had no progenitors, and they have had no descendants. Something enigmatic and frustrate in them recalls a phrase of Lorenzo di Medici himself : " The beginning of the true life is the end of the life that is not true."

In the statue of the Madonna and Child, also in San Lorenzo, there are summed up all the qualities of his art. To my mind this is the noblest Madonna and Child in plastic art, though perhaps not the most beautiful. The qualities which give the work such a sense of nobility are technical as well as emotional and artistic ; indeed, there can be no separation of all its beauties and excellencies, for all are fused into a stupendous and moving whole. It is so compact that there are no piercings in the composition, the rectangle of the block of marble is still visible as the enclosing shape of the figure. It is true the work is not " finished ", in the sense that every detail is expressed, but it is entirely finished in the sense that it completely conveys to us the emotion which filled the sculptor as he freed the figure from the enclosing marble. There is here an amplitude of form, strangely different from any mediæval work, or indeed from any other work of sculpture. The peculiar majesty of type is not only in the head, but breathes through the whole figure. The mouth is strangely asymmetrical, giving an elusive and enigmatical expression to a face which is otherwise impersonal and remote but essentially and nobly Madonna-like. The marks of his impetuous and powerful technique can readily be traced on this figure (even in a plaster cast) : the heavy point used with great force and strength, a smaller point used very skilfully and over large areas. Sometimes so evenly and parallel are the marks of this tool that it seems unlike the fierce and arrogant hewing with which he is usually credited. Over most of the draped body of the Madonna and the nude Child the forms have been revealed largely by claw tools, apparently of at least two sizes, one about half an inch wide with only two or three teeth, and one about an inch wide with five or six teeth. This corresponds to a statement made in Vasari. " Sculptors are accustomed, in working their marble statues to begin by roughing out the figures with a kind of tool they call ' subbia ', which is pointed and heavy ; it is used to block out their stone in the large—and then with other tools called ' calcagnuoli ', which have a notch in the middle (two teeth) they proceed to round it till they come to use a flat tool more slender than the calcagnuolo, which has two notches and is called ' gradina ' (this would give three teeth) with which they go over all the figure, gently chiselling it to keep the proportion of the muscles, and the folds, and treating it in such a manner that the notches or teeth give the stone a wonderful grace. This done, they remove the tooth-marks with a smooth chisel, and in order to perfect the figure, wishing to add sweetness, softness and finish, they work off with curved files all traces of the gradina. They proceed in the same way with slender files and straight rasps to complete the smoothing process, and lastly with points of pumice-stone they rub all over the figure to give that flesh-like appearance that is seen in the marvellous works of sculpture. Tripoli earth is also used to make it lustrous and polished."[1]

Every one of these tools and methods can be traced in the work of Michelangelo, even to the exquisitely highly polished limbs of the Dawn, than which no higher finish is conceivable. There are small wax models for the Medici tomb figures of Gulio and Lorenzo and of the Madonna in the Scottish National Gallery, Edinburgh. These models certainly convey a vivid sense of Michelangelo's power and force but neither the models nor the marbles are in any accurate sense realistic ; they are conceived in a heroic mould and they convey to us still a sense of weary, titanic shapes, brooding and dreaming.

The question of how Michelangelo worked, whether only from small models (as in the case of the David), or even at times only from drawings, is important, but cannot finally be resolved. For work like the two relief tondi there would be little need for any models at all. There exists a beautiful pen drawing by the artist for the S. Lorenzo Madonna and Child group and that is handled exactly as a sculptor would, using the pen strokes almost as if chiselling ; the forms are clearly defined in planes and every touch of the pen speaks of the sculptor's sense of form, conceived clearly, and expressed with the greatest mastery. *Vasari on Technique* quotes Cellini as saying that most sculptors preferred to work from full sized models but that Michelangelo was impatient of such. W. W. Story, a sculptor and a scholar, quotes from Vigenero who thus describes the sculptor at work : " I have seen Michelangelo, although sixty years of age . . . smite down more scales from a hard block of marble in a quarter of an hour than three young marble cutters would in three or four times that space of time. He flung himself upon the marble with such impetuosity and fervour as to induce me to believe he would break the work into fragments. With a single blow he brought down scales of marble three or

[1] " Vasari on Technique," L. Maclehose

four fingers in breadth, and with such precision to the line marked on the marble that if he had broken away a very little more he risked the ruin of the work." But, entirely ignoring the admitted " precision " with which the sculptor worked to his line, Mr. Story comments only that " it is pitiable to find him so engaged . . . while he should have been creating and designing, he was doing the rough work of a stone cutter."

This comment seems to me to be " pitiable ", for here is that confusion which results from the separation of " creating and designing " from the very process of creation ! The only way in which Michelangelo could " create " his sculpture was to carve it. He must have regarded the studies he made towards this end, whether drawings or small models, as means towards the clarifying of his own vision, rather than as models to copy or to work from. Herein lay the secret of his power over the material ; it is never other than marble and used with a beautiful regard for the inherent qualities of that material. Yet one does not think first of material, but rather of the emotion and the beauty with which he has filled and yet transcended the material. Yet let no one too readily think marble carving is easy, or that it is a soft and tractable material. Even Ruskin, usually so careful in his technical distinctions, refers to " softness " as being the characteristic quality of marble—and Vernon Lee, an acute and suggestive interpreter of Italian Art, makes a similar misstatement : " Granulated like a living fibre, susceptible of delicate polish—it can imitate the actual substance of human flesh . . . it is so docile, so soft, yet so resistant that the iron can cut it like butter or engrave it like agate." A little experimental study with chisels and marble would have been a revelation to both these writers. Marble is of course " softer " than granite or the igneous stones, but no one who has ever tried to chisel it would call it soft, or docile ; its softness is very relative. To understand fully the greatness of Michelangelo's art, it is essential to give consideration to his unique method of working. Even if it were possible to separate the qualities of his art from the technical expression, it would be fatal to do so ; yet if one could look at any work of his hand, and try to see it *only* as carving it would still be memorable and unlike any other sculpture.

Of course this initial creation in stone was a " dangerous " method of working, and it is possible to find unfinished parts where it seems difficult to see how he could achieve the desired form. In one of the Slave statues, for instance, there is a foot which is deeply sunk into the plinth, yet even so it is flat and the bony structure is uncertain, but discrepancies like these are trifles compared with the gain in filling the marble with his own sense of power.

He said of Dante, that great spirit, kindred to his own soul, " No man like unto him was ever born " and the words stand for the sculptor as well as for the poet. In both there was that strange amalgam of terrible power and great tenderness.

Dante—" who loved well, because he hated,
        Hated wickedness that hinders loving "—
and in the drawings of Michelangelo both qualities are apparent. In many

103. PART OF THE STALLWORK AT AMIENS : OAK

104. HANS TILMAN RIEMENSCHNEIDER (1460–1531) : A YOUNG MAN : LIMEWOOD
VICTORIA AND ALBERT MUSEUM, LONDON

GOTHIC SCULPTURE

105. PROBABLY by PIETRO TORREGIANO
(1474–1522) : BISHOP FISHER :
TERRA-COTTA :
THE METROPOLITAN MUSEUM OF ART,
NEW YORK

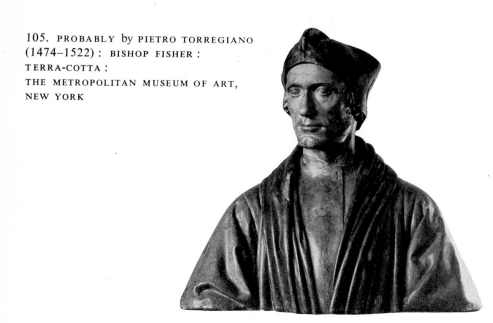

106. HANS TILMAN
RIEMENSCHNEIDER
(1460-1531)
DETAIL OF A HEAD
WALNUT

107. PIETRO TORREGIANO :
HENRY VII :
ELECTROTYPE FROM THE
BRONZE EFFIGY
IN WESTMINSTER ABBEY :
NATIONAL PORTRAIT GALLERY,
LONDON

108. TWO HEADS
(ONE PROBABLY MARGARET OF
MALINES) : BOXWOOD :
SIXTEENTH CENTURY :
BRITISH MUSEUM

109. PROBABLY by VEIT
STOSS (1447-1542):
VIRGIN AND CHILD:
BOXWOOD STATUETTE:
VICTORIA AND ALBERT
MUSEUM, LONDON

110. VIRGIN AND CHILD: FIFTEENTH CENTURY: STONE:
FROM THE CHARTREUSE DE CHAMPOL, NEAR DIJON

111. DONATELLO
(1386–1466)
ST GEORGE
MARBLE
FIFTEENTH
CENTURY
BARGELLO,
FLORENCE

2. JACOPO DELLA
QUERCIA (1367–
438) : MADONNA
AND CHILD
OAK
THE LOUVRE

The majestic and
noble type
ticipating the sybils
of Michelangelo

113. NICCOLO PISANO (active 1484—1538): PANEL OF PULPIT, PISA (1260): MARBLE
114. NICCOLO PISANO: PANEL OF PULPIT, THE CATHEDRAL, SIENA (1266): MARBLE

Note the change of spirit and feeling

of the pen drawings one sees the fierce strokes of the pen defining planes and marking contours with an arrogant and defiant certainty, while in other chalk studies he seems to have handled his crayon loosely, tenderly and delicately, feeling gently for the form he seeks, then, with the very slightest of emphasis giving it definition. Even Leonardo cannot surpass him in this quality.

His whole life and nature was dual, and superficially contradictory. Angry, truculent, and defiant towards Popes and authority ; tender, loving and endlessly forgiving with his family ; haughty, imperious and contemptuous, yet living frugally to send money to his family, he was gentle and affectionate to those whom he loved. Even when in his art the subject is pagan and sensual, as in the hypothetical Leda picture in London, the nobility of treatment (even at second hand as this may be) shows that there are no themes which a great artist cannot ennoble. His art shows neither the intellectual curiosity nor the serene repose of Leonardo but always it is the art of a great contemplative poet. Great poetry and moving religious art filled his later years : writing poems and hewing marble : as he himself expressed it, " the hand obedient to the brain." He dreamed of a religious revival that should arise renascent and triumphant, and in that age of spiritual corruption and neo-paganism is it not strange to find this old, lonely man a soul athirst for God—" So near to death, so far away from God ", seeking with profound and patient interrogation of the realities of form, for that universal beauty first sought out by Plato. " Because the beauty of the world is fragile I seek to attain the Eternal and universal beauty." And yet saturated as he was with Platonism, his art had nothing of the serene, archetypal quality of Greek art ; it was wholly individual and yet strangely august ; the search for universal beauty led him towards the unity of faith. " Neither painting, nor sculpture, can any longer bring peace to the soul that seeks the Divine Love which opened its arms on the Cross to receive us ", and again : " It is needful for an artist to be very good in his mode of life, even if possible a Saint, so that the Holy Spirit may inspire his intellect." So, seeking always for a reconciliation between the soul and the sense, between art and faith, beauty and religion, he turned, as 50 years later did Spenser, towards

> " That soveraine light
> From whose pure beam all perfect beauty springs
> Even the Love of God."

When Michelangelo died in 1564, the Italian Renaissance was a spent force, Yet it had exerted a powerful influence over the whole of Europe, not only in art, but also in philosophy, religion and literature. Germany was torn by dissension and religious wars, the fierce Biblical fervour of Luther was entirely uninfluenced by the humanism of the Renaissance. Luther and his friend Albert Dürer both belonged to the Middle Ages, though Dürer's versatility of mind had some affinity to that of Leonardo. Yet his art, intensely and consciously individual as it is, reflects the simple piety and the humility before nature, characteristic of a mediæval artist. Erasmus, almost alone in that generation, had the Renaissance disinterested pursuit of knowledge and with his scholarship and serious satire he anticipated the independent and sceptical attitude of Montaigne, and like Montaigne, he aroused the suspicion that such disinterestedness must imply a lack of conviction.

Dürer wrote sadly :

" Erasmus where wilt thou tarry ?
Hear, Christian Knight—
Ride forth with the Lord Jesus
Defend the right and obtain a martyr's crown."

In the beautiful engraving called " Melancholia ", Dürer offered a sort of allegory of the futility of all intellectual and scientific knowledge and therein he seems to sum up the dying spirit of his age, for the Renaissance was a climax—the end of an epoch, as well as a new beginning. It is characteristic that not only Dürer's art but German art generally developed without any influence from the study of the classical antique. In France the presence of Italian artists, particularly those at the court of Francis I at Fontainbleau, led to the growth of a French Renaissance school, and the work of Jean Goujon and Germain Pilon shows a refinement and lyrical elegance akin to Italian art, yet remaining indubitably French and somewhat cynically lacking in any deep feeling. Goujon, who carved the great wooden doors of S. Maclou, Rouen, is described in the accounts as a " stone cutter and mason ", an evidence of his status and his versatility. Later, as a " sculptor of great ability ", he made the impressive monument to the Duc de Brézé, with its strange variations of scale and style, but impressive dignity. Beside this, Pilon's " Graces " seem decadent and " stylish ". In the tomb of Henry II and his wife he achieved an impressive monument, the nude figures below in their relentless realism offering a violent contrast to the richly apparelled kneeling figures above. This represents a late phase of the monumental effigy ; the next stage was to exploit all the horrors of bones and skulls. Pilon also carved a superb series of medallions of the Valois kings.

Spain in the sixteenth century was absorbed in the Jesuit revival or, as Vernon Lee calls it, " The Quixotic Catholicism of Loyola ", so that country never came fully into the fertilizing contact with the great art of the Italian Renaissance. Torregiano, it is true, went there, and introduced his own vivid work by making a terra-cotta St. Jerome of astonishing anatomical realism, but Spanish art as a whole kept to its own course, pursuing an ideal of a realism almost beyond the pale of art.

In England the influence of the Italian Renaissance was mainly on literature and on costume and the trappings of life. Torregiano and his fellow craftsmen who made the tomb of Henry VII left but a temporary impression on the course of English art ; but by the middle of the sixteenth century Italy was overrun by English students, noblemen, scholars—eager to learn, greedy for intellectual gain, gathering ideas and material for drama, and much of this ore and dross was later fused into precious metal by the heat of English genius, and, borrowing from the Platonism and Epicureanism of Italy, they achieved the splendid serene humanism of

Shakespeare and Beaumont and Fletcher, and so created the great age of English culture. Both Henry VII and Henry VIII fostered Italian culture and Sir Thomas More's ideal in scholarship was the versatile Pico della Mirandola, while he hated equally the scholasticism of Aquinas and the authoritarian tyranny of Machiavelli—" this poison sent out of Italy ". At the Reformation, England became a home for religious refugees from Italy ; there was an Italian protestant church in London, and there is a poem by an Italian in England on the death of the Scottish King at the battle of Flodden.

Later there was a reaction against the Italianate Englishman and by the beginning of the seventeenth century, though learning was a necessary part of the education of a gentleman (even in the eighteenth century Dr. Johnson regarded Castiglione's *Courtier* as " the best work on good breeding ever written ") it was no longer sought only in Italy, and the sense of nationality had become powerful ; in this lay the seeds of the great revival —when imagination flamed and the vast drama of English life was played not on a stage but over the whole known world. This same sense of nationality was also working powerfully in France and in the mid-sixteenth century Joachim du Bellay was urging the use only of French, the abandon- ment of all the so-called " barbarous " forms of the Middle Ages, and the following of classical or antique forms. This classical obsession became first a fashion—and then a superstition.

The architecture and sculpture of Tudor England had little of this cohesion and nationality. Italian, Flemish, and German artizans and crafts- men came in great numbers, bringing diverse elements and new forms which mixed as best they could with the remains of late Gothic perpen- dicular architecture. The results were sometimes interesting as at Hampton Court and Montacute. It is characteristic that architecture should now be concerned almost wholly with great houses and that ecclesiastical building should have ceased with the dissolution of the monasteries, until the destruction of eighty-nine London churches in the Great Fire (1666) gave Wren his opportunity.

These new great houses were often on a vast scale and they mark the final extinction of feudal and mediæval life. No longer does the lord live among his people ; the common dining hall for lord and retainers is gone, the desire for privacy is apparent, and social life has completely changed. It was a time of ferment and vast expansion when, with the spirit of adventure and exploration, men first circumnavigated the world ; in the glowing words of a sailor in the reign of Henry VIII : " There is no land uninhabitable, no sea innavigable." That spirit produced immensely expanded life but strangely enough it produced eclectic and incoherent sculpture and architecture. The sculpture on these elaborate new buildings was a strange medley of classical and Italian and Flemish forms confusedly mixed with the dreary criss-crossing of late Perpendicular Gothic.

Tuscan columns are used as chimneys, the lower parts of men and women terminate in balusters. The results are sometimes skilfully blended into harmony but seldom into an organic unity. And from this chaos there gradually emerges a desire for unity and the first elements of pedantry creep in, and the poetry and vitality of Gothic architecture is levelled down into the formulæ of rules.

Even a great and original artist like Rubens wrote in 1622 : " In our country we see the style of Architecture called barbarous or ' Gothic ' becoming obsolete, and gradually disappearing. We see men of taste introducing, to the great ornament of the country, that style of Architecture that is possessed of true symmetry, and which conforms to the rules established by the ancient Greeks and Romans." The passion for following only classical standards led to the destruction of the communal guilds and provincial institutions of the Middle Ages, and so, for the " obscure and empirical mechanics " of mediæval building, there was substituted the scientific architect—the " designer " who planned and designed a whole building, including sculptured details. Vitruvius was first translated in the sixteenth century and his formula of the classic " Orders " became a fixed standard, and so for the free and exuberant work of the Gothic carver there was substituted only a disciplined exactness. The " Orders " had to be observed, and thus the past laid a tyrannous dead hand on the work of a living age.

As William Morris sadly reviewed the results of the Renaissance :[1] " When the brightness of the Renaissance faded—and it faded very suddenly—a deadly chill fell upon the arts ; that new birth mostly meant looking back to past time wherein men of these days thought they saw a perfection of art ; this perfection they were ambitious to imitate—this alone seemed to be art to them ; so wonderful was their energy, their success so great, that perfection seemed to be gained—and, being gained, what are you to do ? You must aim at standing still, which you cannot do."

This view, though admittedly partial, contains a profound and neglected truth, and it must be set against the more usual view which sees the enormous expansion of the physical and the intellectual world at the Renaissance, as positive good and as leading towards the enlightening dawn of modern science. The change from the mediæval worship of the relics of saints to the Renaissance worship of the relics of antiquity was merely the substitution of one superstition for another, and is one more evidence of the strange moral and intellectual confusion of the time. To naturalize the supernatural, to humanize and extend all the modes of man's expression, architecture, sculpture, painting, music, literature, was a great achievement, yet the paradox of the Renaissance was that the conquest of these new intellectual worlds brought also corruption and decay. And one has to set against all these splendid attainments in art and culture a spiritual corruption and corrosive scepticism which led to moral decadence.

So there is a strange and symbolic significance in the dying words of that great Renaissance figure " The Duchess of Malfi " :—

" My laurel is all withered."

[1] " Lectures on Architecture."

—" *Past noon, her toil began to irk*
And Art sought talismans, and turned in vain
To soulless self reflections of man's skill."

D. G. ROSSETTI : THE HOUSE OF LIFE

BAROQUE

THE knowledge and learning of antiquity were not lost during the Middle Ages, as is often suggested. The Benedictine and Celtic monasteries preserved a great deal of them, but at the Renaissance, and with the help of printing, there was an immense recovery of classical literature, a wide extension of knowledge of classical art and science, the study of which became an obsession. This was one of the factors which made possible that strange amalgam of neo-paganism and Christianity so characteristic of the Renaissance age. For instance Verrocchio's Medici monument in St. Peter's has no sign of a Christian emblem, or symbol of Christian teaching. The art was an end sufficient in itself. And Leonardo painted a Bacchus and a St. John Baptist from the same model and infused with the same spirit, and made no effort to disguise his so doing. This dualism, which could at will be called a spiritualizing of earthly things, or a humanizing of spiritual things, led almost imperceptibly to a new relation between man and nature, and to a greatly increased range and understanding of sensuous perception. Yet there remains the anomaly of spiritual corruption in an age of widely extended physical and intellectual boundaries, and a high standard of culture ; and the outward splendour and refinement of life, though it veiled, yet could not hide the deep and mortal evil of the time.

Characteristic works of late Renaissance art like Cellini's " Nymph " and Gian Bologna's " Rape of the Sabines " (though this was hailed by a spate of epigrams of praise) are entirely devoid of any spiritual or even intellectual beauty or power ; such qualities as they have are sensuous and dramatic, often allied with great and even unique technical skill. To such a depth of corruption did life and art descend that J. A. Symonds records that on the great sculptured monument to Pope Paul III, there is a nude figure, symbolically representing Truth, which is a portrait of the Pope's sister, Giulia Bella, who was a mistress of Pope Alexander VI. This decay was part of the price paid for the freedom of temperament in art, the freedom of intellect in culture, which led to the development and dominance of great personalities. But it was a time of great anarchies, and from the moral and religious confusion and corruption of the sixteenth century, the Society of Jesus, with its rigid military discipline, arose and exercised an immense influence.

Baroque art, so far as it is ecclesiastical, is inseparably connected with this religious revival, which was meant to counter both Italian neo-paganism and the Protestantism which had separated a vast area of northern Europe from Papal authority and the rule of the Church. It was at the Renaissance too that the arts also separated themselves at once from the control of the Church, and from the parent art of architecture and from each other—though paradoxically enough it was only to mingle and coalesce again—and in the next generation painting influenced sculpture, and sculpture influenced both architecture and painting. " Baroque " sculpture (the word, like the word Gothic, was originally an abusive term) often dominated architecture unduly, and the sculptors borrowed from paintings the use of clouds and rays of light, entirely inappropriate to solid representation.

Mr. Roger Fry refers to the " vigorous and declamatory gestures " of Michelangelo's sculpture as having " created the Baroque style ". But " declamatory " seems a strangely wrong epithet to describe those quiet titanic figures, however appropriate to Baroque sculpture, which exploited every art and artifice to achieve sensational and rhetorical effects. Indeed " effects ", rather than form, were what the sculptors aimed at, and with their extraordinary skill they often did achieve unparalleled " effects ".

The lavish admiration bestowed on Baroque sculpture in our own day is perhaps partly due to a better appreciation of its technical accomplishment, and partly perhaps due to a reaction from the undue disparagement of all such art in the eighteenth century and into the nineteenth century as long as the classical revival fixed the canons of taste. As late as 1893, Claude Phillips wrote of " Bernini, whose very name is now anathema ".

Lorenzo Bernini, born just as the sixteenth century ended, exercised immense influence on the sculpture of the seventeenth century, not only in his own country of Italy but over most of Europe. He was the son of Pietro Bernini, a Florentine sculptor. There is in Naples a Madonna and Child of the elder Bernini's which, though too obviously influenced by the S. Lorenzo Madonna of Michelangelo, yet has grace and charm, and is remarkable for a treatment of drapery which resembles strangely the broken and crinkled folds of Dürer and the German sculptors. Although the son very quickly showed himself as much the greater artist, yet he must have learned at least some technical skill in his father's workshop.

The first great work of the son to attract attention was the Apollo and Daphne now in the Borghese Palace at Rome, and this work quite deservedly made him instantly famous, not only in Rome but in Europe. In this group may be seen already, as in the youthful work of Michelangelo, evidence of great technical ability and unmistakable sculptural power. There is not a sign of immaturity, nor of any tentative or rudimentary sense of form ; everything is masterly and indeed not since late Hellenistic and Græco-Roman art had marble been chiselled into movement with such audacious skill. Even Gian Bologna's group had not caught the fleeting moment and fixed it as Bernini has here done. The powerful quiescence of his great forerunner Michelangelo is completely and deliberately abandoned. Bernini defies the nature of marble in a way that differs entirely from that sculptor's transcending of his material ; nor has Bernini any trace of the grandeur, the nobility and the universality of the Florentine, but the beauty of the design and composition of the group and the skill of carving leave one breathless with admiration. His contemporaries at once called him the Rubens of sculpture, and that was meant as the final word in praise ; he had neither the robust exuberance nor the inventive fecundity in design of the painter, but he did have a similar technical virtuosity, and he was able, like Rubens, to fill his figures with a sense of vigorous movement which was unique in sculpture. Like Rubens, Bernini was an adventurer in the field of technique, and both achieved in their art an unprecedented freedom and vigour of movement. His success was stupendous ; his workshops must have been on a great scale and his workers must have included every artistic craft : carving stone and marble of every colour and texture and degree of hardness ; bronze, silver and metal casting, sometimes on a great scale ; modelling in stucco and gesso-duro, mosaic working, gilding, enamelling and chasing in gold and silver. Every technical skill is pressed into service and charged with something of his own great creative energy and power and used to produce effects which were meant to enthrall and impress the world with the passion and rhetorical fervour of the new Catholic reaction, which was to regain the world for the Church and to make Rome, and St. Peter's especially, the abiding monument of the triumph of the true Church.

Of the artistic expression of this movement, Bernini was the recognized leader and master. He was architect, sculptor, painter and stage designer, and all his work is stamped with his own versatility, his love of sensation and declamation. As Corrado Ricci says,[1] " Bernini was the supreme master of ' effects '. He moved mountains of marble, lakes of molten metal, and the streams of rivers, and transformed them all into works of art full of seduction and vigour—thanks to him marble took on a melting and pictorial splendour." The inter-relation of the arts of architecture, sculpture, and painting, already noted, now appeared fully developed, and in many of the painted vaults of the churches it is almost impossible to tell where the real architecture ends and simulated architecture begins ; so with the angels and cherubs in marble or stucco, they mingle imperceptibly with painted mouldings and cornices, clouds and curtains, a confusion of spectacular effects unparalleled in any previous architectural decoration. Bernini's marble group Noli me Tangere has even a painted background with a landscape and palm trees and a cyclopean tomb or archway from which the marble figure of Christ is supposed to have emerged.

In the Gesu church the sculptured figures, which in a mediæval building would have been a part of the architecture, seem now to have come alive, and in immensely fluttering and agitated draperies they pause momentarily in niches which hardly hold them, or float around doorways and windows in a sort of riotous ecstasy of movement.

The wealth of the Jesuit order enabled them to build on a vast and splendid scale, and the result, as in the Gesu church, is an impressive and tremendous sense as of a vision of opening heavens, tumults of angels and cherubs, every action and detail charged with fervour and leading on to a kind of ecstasy where religion, art, emotion, propaganda and rhetoric are

[1] " Bernini and Baroque Sculpture."

all dramatically and seductively presented, so that the exuberant vitality seems almost to justify it artistically. There is evident everywhere a great love of display, yet behind must have been power and enthusiasm, for all the work is charged with a certain fullblooded sense, as of great creative energy. Repose, reflection, or contemplation are totally absent ; instead there is a rhetorical fervour, sensational and violent gestures, restlessness and eccentricity, allied to an amazing technical dexterity such as had never been achieved in sculpture before—tons of marble curtains, pierced lace frills and fringed draperies, faces contorted with dread of death or in an ecstasy of religious fervour ; all this turgid declamation is used to embody resounding and empty platitudes, and to represent in marble, visions, martyrdoms and miracles, attempting to achieve a foolish and delusive realism, as if angels really were sitting in odd attitudes on cornices, and cherubs really were pulling back curtains, and skeletons with hour-glasses or scythes were actually emerging from vaults shrouded with black marble curtains, among tons of artificial rocks. There is even a bronze oak tree of great size, a skull with luminous eyes which revolves, and a shrouded and grinning skeleton behind a grille.

The great altar-piece in S. Maria della Vittoria of the Ecstasy of S. Theresa is a characteristic work of Bernini's middle period. The lingering traces of classicism as in the Apollo and Daphne are now completely absent, and this altar-piece and the great Tabernacle and Baldachino in St. Peter's are entirely representative and typical of Baroque ecclesiastical sculpture. The spiralled pillars of the Baldichino were not invented by Bernini but they spread over Europe like a disease (owing to the tradition that the Pillar of the Scourging was of this kind), for about the same time Nicholas Stone and some Oxford masons added a porch with spiralled columns and floating angels, and so made a beautiful but strangely inappropriate addition to the noble Gothic church of St. Mary the Virgin.

Bernini's St. Theresa group is set in a great double curved architectural altar-piece, with gilded Corinthian capitals and broken pediments fantastically curved ; within this framework, illusively and theatrically lighted from above from a hidden source, descend gilded rays of light on to the figure of St. Theresa, who is swooning on a marble cloud in a transport of ecstatic bliss, while over her hovers a dreadful smirking angel, smiling lasciviously, and preparing to stab the Saint to the heart with a real arrow. The whole group is a strange and yet typical compound of eroticism and religiosity, and illustrates well the truth *Amor spiritualis facile labitur in nudum carnalem amorem.* Yet this close relation between sensual and super-sensual—or ecstatic exaltation—is here marvellously observed and forever fixed in marble. The draperies are wonderfully and realistically designed and superbly carved, and on the angel's wings the feathers are ruffled and displayed in an entirely new manner, for neither in classical nor in mediæval sculpture had wings been represented with this sense of fluffy lightness. Other artists of the late Renaissance had achieved a triumphant fusion, alike in art and in humanism, of the carnal and the spiritual, the pagan and the Christian worlds.

115. PORTRAIT BUST
FIFTEENTH CENTURY
WOOD
THE LOUVRE
typical
of the gracious spirit
of the Renaissance
and showing some kinship
with the lyrical art of
Botticelli

116.   ANTONIO ROSSELINO (1427-1479) :
MONUMENT TO A CARDINAL (1461) :
BASILICA DE S. MINIATO AL MONTE, FLORENCE
the beautiful repose of death

119. MICHELANGELO : EVENING (DETAIL) : MARBLE (See plates 120-123)
showing the use of point and claw tools—vivid and expressive ' roughing-in '

117. MICHELANGELO : UNFINISHED
FIGURE CALLED ST. MATTHEW
MARBLE : ACCADEMIA, FLORENCE

The form is being achieved by pushing the
background further and further in,
working entirely from the front.
The *Cupid* is an early work of beautifully
chiselled forms

118. MICHELANGELO : CUPID (1497) :
MARBLE : VICTORIA AND ALBERT
MUSEUM, LONDON

THE RENAISSANCE

The action of the wax models, particularly the heads, closely resembles but is not exactly similar to that of the finished marbles. This increases rather than lessens the likelihood that they are models made as studies for the figures ; exactness as to attitude and close resemblance in detail would rather suggest that the models were made later, from the finished work. Undoubtedly works so renowned and so admired as these figures would be studied and copied by students and artists, but the handling of these models is no students' work ; in largeness of conception and nobility of style they take rank with the original sculptures.

120. MICHELANGELO: DAWN : MARBLE: TOMB OF LORENZO DE' MEDICI, FLORENCE

121. WAX MODEL OF DAY

MICHELANGELO: DAY (1523-1533): MARBLE: TOMB OF GIULIANO DE' MEDICI, FLORENCE

123. WAX MODEL OF DAWN

124. MICHELANGELO:
MADONNA AND CHILD
WITH THE YOUNG
ST. JOHN (c. 1500):
MARBLE:
BARGELLO, FLORENCE

Relief
showing the use of
point
and claw tools
and chisels

125. MICHELANGELO: PIETA (1498): MARBLE: ST. PETER'S, ROME
The limpness of death contrasts with the splendid living beauty of the Mother

126. PIETA (DETAIL)

127. MICHELANGELO : HEAD OF DAVID (1504) : MARBLE : ACCADEMIA, FLORENCE

e the drillholes and deep recesses in hair. A powerful type with a wonderful anatomical structure

A wonderful
compactness
and quiet majesty
of type.

128. MICHELANGELO : THE VIRGIN AND CHILD JESUS (*c.* 1530) :
MARBLE : MEDICI CHAPEL, FLORENCE

129. MICHELANGELO : BRUTUS (c. 1540) : MARBLE : BARGELLO, FLORENCE

The *Brutus* is almost certainly direct carving. Note the extraordinary power and force, the traces of the ' point ' in the hair, of claw tools—coarse in the neck, fine in the face.

130. MICHEL-ANGELO : SLAVE (UNFINISHED 1514–1522): ACCADEMIA, FLORENCE

31. BERNINI (1598–1680): APOLLO AND DAPHNE : MARBLE : GALLERIA BORGHESE, ROME

Both these works
show an extraordinary freedom of movement
and openness of composition
held together by flying drapery.
Neptune and Glaucus, like the *Apollo and
Daphne* is a triumphant achievement, for
behind its appearance of pictorial freedom lies
a complete understanding of the limits of
brittle marble, and the disposition of all the
separate parts required to sustain it in
equilibrium.

133. PULPIT
SEVENTEENTH CENTURY
OAK
ST. ANDREW'S, ANTWERP
the structure of the pulpit
is quite hidden.

132. BERNINI: NEPTUNE AND
GLAUCUS: MARBLE: COLLECTION,
THE EARL OF YARBOROUGH

BAROQUE

134. BERNINI (1598–1680) : THE ECSTATIC VISION OF ST. TERESA : MARBLE

THE ECSTATIC VISION OF ST. TERESA (DETAIL OF ANGEL) S. MARIA DELLA VITTORIA, ROME

136. ROUBILIAC (1703–1762): DEATH, FROM LADY ELIZA-
BETH NIGHTINGALE'S TOMB: MARBLE: WESTMINSTER ABBEY

This grisly type is characteristic of the
violence and emphasis of the Catholic reaction.

137. PORTION OF MONUMENT TO GISLENI:
MARBLE: S. MARIA DEL POPOLO, ROME

Even in England, almost contemporary with Bernini a certain Dean of St. Paul's, John Donne, that strange " mystic of the senses ", wrote poetry in which erotic and gross elements are fused into mystical and religious art ; but in Bernini, and the Baroque sculptors generally, there is no mystical element whatsoever, nor any intellectual power. Their work is saturated with an emotional force which, if not openly sensual, is seldom free from sensuality ; it bludgeons the senses and one gets a vivid and ineffaceable impression of art embodying in characteristic forms the violent revivalist fervour of the Catholic reaction.

Indeed Mrs. Arthur Strong says : " The period between Michelangelo's ceiling and the death of Bernini (1680) was the last time in European history that art appears as an essential movement of the life of the spirit, at once the powerful ally of the Church, and the faithful interpreter of religious thought." But this art was also the too-faithful evidence of an age of spiritual decline. What Bernini and his followers and pupils did was to force their message on the world with the crusading ardour of the Jesuits, and they did this by exploiting new methods of representation, and with widely increased and enlarged technical skill.

The fusion of sacred and profane things and thoughts had been achieved in art before ; indeed in the naive and sometimes childish details of mediæval art there was this same fusion, and any French or German village might represent Jerusalem or Bethlehem, but the result was that to the simple piety of the Middle Ages everything might be sacred or holy, while to the cultured and corrupt artists of the seventeenth century there was little or no distinction between temporal and spiritual things because everything was only subject matter for the display of their unprecedented skill ; and cardinals and prelates owned and enjoyed pictures like Titian's " Venus " and other licentious and erotic paintings by contemporary artists, and nothing was sacred.

Yet the very fidelity with which their art reflects the corrupt and sensual life of the time is an evidence of its vitality and power, and when they turned their quick perceptions and enlarged skill to portraiture, they achieved some astounding works of psychological understanding and technical mastery. The marble bust of a Cardinal, by Bernini, is a triumphant piece of portraiture in its ruthless delineation of a face in which worldliness, sensuality and power are all strikingly evident, yet subtly presented. This portrait is in sculpture a sort of parallel to the exactly contemporary portrait by Velazquez of Pope Innocent X with its mingled cruelty, craftiness and power. Bernini's success as a portrait sculptor was so great that King Charles I of England sent for him to make a portrait bust, but Bernini was too much occupied to make the long journey, so Van Dyck was commissioned to paint a picture, giving three views of the King's head, and from this Bernini—still in Rome—made a superb bust. The Baroque sculptors both in Italy and France produced a long succession of spirited sculptured portraits. These are mostly carved in marble but occasionally they used bronze or silver and other metals, sometimes used together with coloured marbles. In the treatment of all the varied " stuffs " represented, the broad folds of heavy drapery, the crinkled fineness of silk and satin, the elaborate armour, the curled hair and wigs, the sculptors discovered and invented new methods and new devices to produce a greater verisimilitude and a more impressive " style ".

For instance, Michelangelo in the David had treated the hair in a manner which, though based on the classical and Græco-Roman " tufts " was yet original and powerful. But Bernini and his followers brought a new pictorial realism to the treatment of hair ; this was not a plastic or modelled treatment, for with all their freedom of movement and pictorial licence they yet preserved an admirable sense of marble. Probably this was because the marble carving was still regarded as the sculptor's job, and mechanism had hardly, if at all, invaded the craft. It would be interesting to know from what sort of models these works were done. The scarcity of replicas, and the absence of such models of either Renaissance or Baroque sculpture, suggests that these works were still largely the original works of the artist, and that there was little in the way of the atelier of copyists so active in Græco-Roman art. In the treatment of the eye in sculpture, both Bernini in Italy and Coysevox and Coustou in France found new and successful devices for its representation and achieved very striking results. This was almost entirely a new field, for classical sculpture had painted the eye till relatively late Roman times, and mediæval carvers had also relied on painting to give the eye its true effect. Even Donatello and Michelangelo, when they represented the iris of the eye, had done it very simply, but the Baroque sculptors found means not only to show the great variations in the types of eye represented but they even discovered how to leave up a small point of marble to catch the light and so to give the effect of shine as well as the deeply recessed iris to represent the colour. The use of such devices to get " effects " is considered wrong by many purists in sculpture, and it is true that this device is using form to represent an effect of colour, but every innovation in art is justified only by its success and although Baroque figures by the use of such devices lost something of the static repose and dignity of earlier sculpture, they gained thereby a liveliness and vitality entirely their own. The mediæval sculptor had never sought to achieve this sense of movement, nor had he sought this complete realism, for that was beyond the range of his art.

But the Baroque sculptor revelled in this new-found freedom, and used it sometimes licentiously and with no regard for tradition, exploiting every new technical device, and exploring new paths in order to express himself and to display his skill to the world. Bernini, for instance, found entirely new dynamics for his sculptured groups. Even in an early work—the Apollo and Daphne—he achieved a freedom and balance greater than Gian Bologna, whose work had aroused such admiration in the previous generation. The cloudlike form which supports and partly clothes the fleeting Daphne, her flying hair which ties and supports the two figures into what looks a precarious, but is a successful static balance, the free right arm and left leg of Apollo, all these show his power and mastery over the intricate dynamics of representing in sculpture two figures in rapid movement. The well-used classical devices of a tree stump, or a vase with drapery to achieve the support of a marble figure, seem childish and inadequate compared with this wonderful scientific understanding of balance.

It is true that Bernini carried this freedom of movement to its last limit, and in the group of Neptune and Glaucus one has to admire the ingenuity with which the floating drapery of Neptune, a necessary support to keep the balance of the group, is yet made as if it were really floating ; and the free end of the drapery is carved to an almost unbelievable thinness, such as, I believe, no modern sculptor would dare to attempt, though today, with abrasive grinding and electrical power, there would be far less risk of breakage than with the hammer and chisel of Bernini.

Stucco, being a plastic medium easily and freely handled, and lending itself readily to the frenzied actions and movements so much in vogue, was a medium much used by the Baroque sculptors, especially in decorative work where it often merges imperceptibly with both the architecture and the painted decoration. This was a true and fine use of a plastic medium ; a medium which had been developed and used by the Romans, as combining rapidity of handling with lightness and permanence, and it has seldom been used so effectively as by the seventeenth century modellers.

Fountains, too, became important and common in cities and gardens. This was almost a new field for sculpture, and allied to architecture offered wide scope for the display of sculptural skill, and allegorical representations ; nude figures symbolising the great rivers, naiads and tritons engaged in dividing endless cascades of water over vast and theatrical grottoes artificially shaped into great rockeries. Sometimes these fountains were on a gigantic scale and they offered great opportunities for sculpture in every material—bronze, lead, marble, stone and concrete ; sometimes they seem like vast and elaborate stage settings for some romantic drama. Occasionally windows and even doorways were carved into Gargantuan grotesque faces, the mouth representing the aperture. Every device and fancy which can be covered by the word " grotesque " was indulged, and the results were often startling and bizarre.

French sculpture of the seventeenth century, though influenced by Bernini and Baroque ideas, was tempered by the still surviving classical spirit which kept sculpture from some of the excesses of the contemporary Italians. The dominant figure was Louis XIV, and artists, painters, sculptors and architects were almost wholly engaged in ministering to the glorification of the King, his courtiers, mignons, and mistresses. The stupendous Palace of Versailles was occupied by ten thousand people and in the vast gardens there were myriads of fountains, sculptured groups, like Girardon's symbolic " Rivers," and the beautiful marble panels in relief of nymphs bathing, marble portrait statues of court ladies masquerading as Diana or other pagan goddesses, and a group of twenty-two fountains, each with three sculptured children.

All this must have given employment to a vast number of artists, craftsmen and workmen, but it was all for the glorification of the person of the King and the court, and had little relation to the real life of ordinary people ; hence it became, too often, corrupt and effete, echoing the shallow and artificial life of courtiers and sycophants. Art thus dedicated to the glorification of pleasure and pomp became almost a symbol of despotism. The King was not only, as he himself said, " the State," but he decided also what was and what was not art ; and the unparalleled scale and splendours of Versailles had, of course, to be paid for by taxation cruelly exacted from the middle class and the poor. Nothing remained of the free life and art and institutions of the middle ages ; all that was characteristically dismissed by Molière as " those Gothic ages which had made war on the polish of civilization."

Of course, there were forces reacting against this highly artificial external life, and the group of great writers of this age is in striking contrast to the shallow life of courtiers ; there was also a development of spiritual life—the Quietist movement became almost an important and persecuted heresy, and Pascal, turning aside from all the courtly life of the time, sought by his clear thinking and incisive wit to turn men's thoughts towards realities. " Man is nothing but a reed—the most feeble thing in nature, but he is a thinking reed—all our dignity resides in thought. Let us then strive to think well." Words like these strike a strange note in a society so unspiritual. The passion for external splendour reached a climax in this age, when men and women cared intensely about social dignity and precedence ; and all life seemed to be under the " desiccating tyranny " (as Reinach calls it) of the King and his architect Le Brun.

As in the drama, Athalie and Phèdre, however violent the passion represented, however tragic the situation, maintain a great society tradition and die to perfect periods, so with the characteristic works of portraiture of this century, they give a clear picture of this world of fashion. A curious example is the statue by Guérin of " Louis XIV Crushing La Fronde," where the young king is represented in Roman armour and his great court peruke. But in the Louvre is a splendid statue of that " Grand Monarque " and in the spirited and elaborately draped and decorated busts of Condé and of Le Brun, Coysevox achieves a new style and distinction, uniquely artificial yet wholly French, and there is grace and distinction in the statue of Marie Adelaide of Savoie as Diana. Posed with due regard for graceful movement, dressed with elaborate elegance, bewigged and frilled, yet these works are informed with style, and in vigour and technique they set a high standard in the representation of kings and nobles.

The counter-Reformation only temporarily stayed the steady decay of the church ; and the growth of a secular view of life narrowed the scope of ecclesiastical art, limiting it almost to funerary and memorial sculptures. Many of these, though grandiloquent in style and effusive in their inscriptions, are yet stately and impressive.

The tomb of Richelieu in the Sorbonne, by Girardon, is typical. The sculptor was born in Troyes where the Gothic tradition lingered very late and there is still a faint echo of the fifteenth century recumbent effigy with its angels and mourners, but these latter have now become allegorical or symbolic figures, and are usually on the same scale as the central figure. Seldom now are people represented as lying in the repose of death ; that sleep so exquisitely recorded by the Renaissance sculptors has now become a nightmare, and the subject of the monument is now represented either as dying, as Richelieu is here shown—supported by Religion and mourned by Science—or else, as struggling with a shrouded skeleton of Death, or awakening and listening to the trumpets of fame. A high standard of technical skill is everywhere evident, and sculptors wrought new and splendid figures, full of animation and pulsating with life ; but the abandonment of the earlier close relation between architecture and sculpture destroyed the cohesive unity of design which marked both the Gothic and Renaissance monumental effigies. A statue that is a work of art is not just a person " petrified " or turned to stone, and in these earlier monuments the figures preserve not only a quiet dignity but also a sense of stone, or marble, or bronze, for these sculptors were not seeking a complete illusive realism, and they achieved a deeper impression, more moving, and actually more powerful, for emphasis tends always to defeat itself. How quietly impressive, after the rhetorical magniloquence of later inscriptions, is that most moving of epitaphs in all Westminster Abbey— " Jane Lister—deare child."

In Spain, which was the dominant country in Europe in the seventeenth century, the characteristic national intensity—a kind of mental hardness—and the passion for an uncompromising realism, kept the best of their sculpture, however violent in gesture and intricately draped, from the empty emotionalism of much Italian work. A great deal of Spanish sculpture is in wood, a medium which they used superbly and in which they produced some works of unqualified mastery. The St. Francis at Toledo, by Pedro de Mena, the St. Bruno, by Montañez, the Mater Dolorosa now in London, are all wood sculptures of the seventeenth century which can challenge comparison with the work of any period and any race. It is true there is always a tendency with Spanish artists to express something of the militant fanaticism of the race ; in the effort to achieve this they often extended this realism of expression beyond the realm of art, using crystal eyes, real eyelashes and eyebrows, pearly tears, blood stains and wounds, even nightmares of torture and of ecstasy ; the aim seemed to be to frighten people into the church and to force them to devotion, if not by terror at least by lacerating the feelings. Perhaps all this is characteristic of a society where the Inquisition was still dreaded and almost all-powerful, and where, at a corrupt court, Velazquez displayed his superb skill with serene impartiality on kings, princesses, admirals, dwarfs, topers, and a Venus ! In Holland, also, Rembrandt was finding a hitherto undiscovered beauty in the common life and daily actions of ordinary people ; transmuting these by his wide sympathy and marvellous genius into great and moving art for which there is no parallel in the field of sculpture.

In Flanders, so closely allied to Spain that their arts interrelated, there was also a great development of the art of wood sculpture—the most typical examples being the confessionals and the great pulpits which are everywhere conspicuous. These ecclesiastical structures were often on an impressive scale, and though very realistic in design and violent in action, they are evidence of a very high standard of excellence in wood craftsmanship. Wood—and this is almost always oak—is not an easy medium for such sculpture. Stone can be quarried to almost any size, but the limits of wood are much more fixed, and the ingenuity and skill with which these huge erections are built up and carved shows that the workmanship of both joiners and wood sculptors was more than adequate. These closely allied crafts were very obviously flourishing and alive.

The great pulpit of St. Andrew's at Antwerp is typical ; and though one has to note and even admire the skill with which the work is done, the loss of any sense of architectural structure is painfully evident. St. Peter and St. Andrew step from their boat into wooden waves, the priest has to climb up a rockery and an oak tree to enter the pulpit ; the sounding board is a vast cloud, with draperies, over which several very solid cherubs play round a rustic cross of St. Andrew. It is stupendously skilful, and judged by the standards of any other age, entirely wrong !

It has already been suggested that there was a decline in craftsmanship at the Reformation and with the collapse of mediæval institutions and the cessation of ecclesiastical building, which, for four centuries, had been the greatest training school for craftsmen. In England, this decay is most marked in the latter half of the sixteenth century, when the Gothic impulse had almost flickered out. The general level of skill shown in the monumental sculpture of this time is far below the standard set by the mediæval craftsmen. It is a strange and anomalous fact, that the greatest writer of the greatest creative age in English history should be commemorated by a monument which is at once inadequate and incompetent even as to a record of his features. It is true that many other Elizabethan monuments are of much finer quality than that of Shakespeare, for that is possibly the work of a local and not very skilléd craftsman ; but a new school of craftsmen had to be trained and this was assisted by the rise of a distinctly English school of Architecture with Inigo Jones and Nicholas Stone in the seventeenth century.

Inigo Jones was appointed the king's (James I) " Surveyor general " and produced his plan for the great palace of Whitehall just as Shakespeare died. His associate, Nicholas Stone, also held a Royal appointment as " Master Mason to the King," and indeed he is perhaps the last of the craftsmen to describe himself as a " mason " and not as an architect. He probably, as already noted, designed and carved the beautiful Renaissance porch to St. Mary's, Oxford, and also designed and erected the splendid gateway to the botanic garden in that city. These works show that, despite the modesty of his title as " mason," he was an accomplished architect and " designer," as well as a craftsman of real and individual power.

During this century great changes and developments were made and new standards of craftsmanship were achieved ; but the century also saw the final separation of the mason and the sculptor from the architect, and building, instead of being a communal or group work, became a matter of science, mathematics and scholarship, controlled by an individual now designated as Architect. The most notable architect of his age was Christopher Wren who began his career as an architect in the decade of the great plague and Fire of London, and with Wren was associated a master craftsman in the person of Grinling Gibbons.

The association of these two was singularly happy and fruitful, and in their finest work—as in the Chapel of Trinity College, Oxford[1], and St. Paul's Cathedral—there is an impressive unity of style which could only come from a collaboration based on a very real æsthetic understanding. Wren's position, of course, was unchallenged as the greatest architect of his day and he was older than this master craftsman whom he employed for all his important decorative sculpture. Yet Gibbons must have achieved a unique pre-eminence as a working sculptor, for Kneller painted a spirited portrait of him dressed in fine clothes and wearing a full bottomed wig, though he is shown carving a marble head !

The amount of work attributed to Grinling Gibbons is so stupendous that a dozen working lives could not have done it. It is evident that he had associated with him, either as fellow craftsmen or as employees, a considerable group of assistants. In one year, 1695, for his work on St. Paul's he was paid over fifteen hundred pounds, a very great sum in the seventeenth century ; and there are clear evidences in the decorative sculpture of St. Paul's, both in stone and wood, that " Grinling Gibbons " meant not one person but a large group of skilful and accomplished craftsmen working under the direction of an acknowledged master. He first introduced the practice of applying the carved limewood (linden) " drops " and " swags " of fruit and flowers to a darker background of oak panelling. He was a brilliant and inventive designer, and the records of contemporary writers, like Evelyn and Pepys, leave no possible doubt but that he was also, in his own field, unsurpassed as a craftsman.

In the chapel of Trinity College, Oxford, the whole effect of architecture, sculpture and decoration is of a complete unity, and there is no more perfect example, on a small scale, of the beauty achieved by the collaboration of this highly skilled craftsman working for the learned and accomplished architect. As an example of masterly technique in wood carving, this altar ranks with the work at Petworth as among the best works to come from the Gibbons workshop. The combination of darkened oak with the fruit and flower drops and swags of lighter limewood is here used with superb effect—though at some later date the limewood has been painted and thus the carving has lost its original exquisite surface. The walnut screen at the west end, with pierced panels of cherubs' heads and

[1] It is suggested in " A Christ Church Miscellany " by W. G. Hiscock (1946) that this work, though usually attributed to Grinling Gibbons is more probably the work of Jonathan Maine of London.

ornamental foliage, surmounted by broken pediments with life-sized seated figures of walnut wood is a unique and beautiful work, perhaps not yet sufficiently recognized as " sculpture " of a high standard.

Occasionally, Gibbons turned to work on a delicately small scale, in which he showed an almost Chinese fidelity of detail and exactness of workmanship, such as no other craftsman in this field has achieved. Of these works conspicuous examples are two lace cravats, carved in lime-wood, in which even the threads are shown and lace is shown beneath lace so that it seems an incredible feat of craftsmanship.

The bronze statue of James II (in Roman armour) shows that Grinling Gibbons could turn from decorative carving to large-scale sculpture and produce work of at least equal brilliance and distinction. Yet, despite the beauty and invention shown in Gibbons' designs, and the almost unbelievable skill of his workmanship, much of his work fails to sustain our interest. There is a greater vitality, as well as an equally luxuriant beauty in Gothic foliage whose sculptors were working within more clearly defined traditions, and were not seeking the more complete realistic verisimilitude of the Renaissance artists.

The architecture and the decorative arts of the seventeenth century were no longer national, and touching the life of the whole community. With the destruction of the unity of the church, ecclesiastical—or indeed, any—art only affected portions of society. The focal point of the mediæval church was the altar and the mass. With the Reformation and Puritanism the focus became the pulpit and the sermon, and all the splendour of St. Paul's takes the pulpit as its starting point. Yet, in poetry and in art, it is the power to haunt that makes work vital, and St. Paul's, though impressive is not haunting or moving. Burne-Jones, a man of deeply religious nature, asked to design mosaics for it, wrote thus, when he refused the work : " It is nonsense to put mosaic there, nonsense to try to do anything but let it chill, chill, the soul of man, and gently prepare him for the next glacial cataclysm."

There was decay of spiritual life within the church, and there had arisen new forces, like Puritanism, which tended to separate art from religion, or at least to change the outward relation. Even while the new St. Paul's was rising, replacing—as Wren said—" the Gothic rudeness of the old design," Bunyan by the force of his genius in giving concrete and vivid life to abstractions was widening the sphere of art and making a new synthesis of Religion and Art. But there was nothing in art and in sculpture corresponding to that powerful impetus given to literature by Bunyan and Defoe ; the direction in which sculpture developed was alien alike to the prevailing elaboration of the age and to the new and vivid colloquial and racy literature, for sculpture sought to return to the severity of the classical standards of Hellenistic and Roman art and this new movement centred, appropriately enough, in Rome.

> *" There is no way of making an aged art young again ; it must be born anew, and grow up from infancy as a new thing working out its own salvation from effort to effort in all fear and trembling."* SAMUEL BUTLER

THE CLASSICAL REACTION

I T is, perhaps, not strange that in the reaction from the excesses of the Baroque style, sculptors turned towards classicism and endeavoured to revive the ancient Greek and Roman modes. In the previous century, the lingering survival of antique standards (as understood by the Renaissance) had kept French sculpture from the pictorial excesses of the Italian Baroque artists. In the eighteenth century this was reversed, and in the dominance of the widely recognized genius of Houdon, French sculpture remained almost untouched by the arid and barren classicism of his great rival and contemporary, Antonio Canova. The influence of this Italian artist was stupendous, and he gave a direction to sculpture, certainly in Italy and in England, which lasted beyond his own day—till the middle of the nineteenth century.

By another curious reaction French art, early in the nineteenth century under the Napoleonic Empire, turned again towards classicism ; this was conspicuous in official painting, but it was evident also in sculpture, in the design of furniture, and markedly so in the arts of costume.

Jean Antoine Houdon (1744-1828) was born at Versailles, and must have grown up knowing well the vast and splendid sculptures scattered in these great Royal gardens. At the age of 12 he entered the Ecole Royal de Sculpture and at 20 he won the Prix de Rome, and for the next ten years remained in that city, studying and working hard at his sculpture. From Rome he sent his famous statue of " L'homme Ecorché," which is still constantly used in many European art schools for the study and teaching of anatomy. And it was while in Rome that he made the great and beautiful St. Bruno, a marble figure nine feet high, for the church of S. Maria degli Angeli. This statue, of which the Pope said : " he would speak but the order forbids it," with its simplicity of gesture and quiet nobility, is in startling contrast to the violently agitated Baroque figures which Houdon must have seen all round him, and it marks him as an independent artist, uninfluenced by other artists and determinedly individual.

On returning to France, he began immediately to exhibit portrait busts of his contemporaries. He is credited with a list of over two hundred. Some of these, the Voltaire, the Franklin, and the Washington, are known and world famous even today ; and, indeed, many of the portraits are works of profound psychological insight, allied to splendid technical skill. A few of these busts are in bronze, but usually they are either in marble or terracotta. In the latter medium they show well his skilled sensitiveness in handling the clay and his delicacy of perception. In the whole series—whatever the material—they have an unmistakable quality of their own, and in vitality of characterization can hardly be excelled or even rivalled. Houdon, too, devised new techniques, particularly in such details as in the treatment of the eyes and hair, and especially in the terra-cotta models, he seems to have worked with beautiful directness, skill and rapidity. In certain of the marble busts, as in that of Franklin, there is evident some loss of vividness in characterization owing to the translation from clay into marble and the treatment of the hair seems more appropriate to modelling than to carving. Yet the Franklin is extraordinarily life-like, and convincingly " real." I do not know to what extent these marbles may be considered as Houdon's carving, but an examination of the treatment of the hair in the marble bust of the child Alex Brongniart shows a crisp and essentially carver-like treatment of hair, while in the bust of his daughter Sabine, eleven years later, he has returned to a soft and plastic treatment of hair, as in the Franklin.

The statue called The Bather in the Metropolitan Museum, New York, is a work of great technical merit and interest. It preserves a beautiful carved stylism, and the observant may note many drill holes and other traces of the technique of marble carving. The figure has real beauty and distinction, especially in the treatment of the head, and the hair. Such treatment is in no sense entirely realistic ; it has far finer qualities than the artificial figures in the similar subject pictures of Boucher. Houdon's art has its roots in a deeper sense of reality than Boucher and has some relation, perhaps, with the more robust art of the contemporary painter Fragonard. Houdon's famous bronze statue of Diana was made for the Empress of Russia, and, strangely enough, though so much admired today, it was unrecognized as a masterpiece by his contemporaries and was refused by the Salon. In 1785, at the invitation of Benjamin Franklin, the sculptor came to America to make a statue of Washington. He stayed for some months at Mount Vernon, made studies, drawings, and took some casts of details of the President's face. He also modelled a terra-cotta bust of Washington, as a preparation for the statue ; this bust is still at Mount Vernon. It is a vivid and brilliant piece of characterization with more vitality than the finished marble statue which, three years later, Houdon sent from France, and which is now treasured at Richmond, Virginia. Yet this statue, which has been much criticized, has an unmistakable " grand manner " ; and, though the devices by which the necessary stability is achieved—the great fasces, and the cloak—are a little obvious, yet the figure has a distinction and nobility all its own.

A little later Jefferson persuaded the legislature of North Carolina to commission Canova to make the statue of Washington for the State Capitol. Of course, Canova dressed Washington in Roman armour and made him look like a Roman Emperor—though seated in a somewhat negligent attitude—so the first sponsors and guides for sculpture in the new Republic were the brilliant French realist and the great Italian classicist. Together they gave a direction to American sculpture from which, till the twentieth century, her sculptors have hardly swerved with a few brilliant and sporadic exceptions.

Towards the end of the eighteenth century, the influence of Antonio Canova was all-powerful. It was he who led—or rather forced—sculpture away from the exuberances of Bernini and the Baroque, and from " the false and vicious rules of art that then prevailed," towards what were thought to be the final and irrevocable standards of Greek art. Perhaps behind this new movement lay the influence of Goethe, and his predecessor Winckelmann, who was constantly invoked in its defence— " Greek art brings our conceptions back to the true—and serves as a *rule* whereby to judge our work." It was an age that loved rules !

Antonio Canova (1757-1822), like Bernini, was the son of a sculptor, and grew up among marble and stone carving. He was hard at work as a stone carver at the age of 14, and two years later he carved in stone two statues of Orpheus and Eurydice. These are not a group but two separate, yet related figures. To convey the idea of Eurydice rising from the infernal depths, the young sculptor supported the slender legs of the figure with a very solidly carved cloud of smoke, out of which appears only the hand of the frustrated and despairing Orpheus. Yet the work shows a good deal of skill and a certain robust naturalism of modelling. He himself, as a youth, said that what was required of an artist was " entire devotion to the guidance of Nature " ; a theory of art entirely different, alike from his predecessors, and from his own later practice. But it is interesting as showing that, like so many artists, before finding his own style, he was studiously realistic.

In 1780, at the age of 23, he went to Rome, a pensioner of his native Venetian government, and there he quickly became the greatest leader and the busiest artist in the field of sculpture. It was in Rome that he met Gavin Hamilton who urged him " to unite his exact and beautiful imitation of Nature, with the pure taste and beau ideal of the Ancients." So, for the rest of his long life, all his tremendous energy and powerful influence were directed to guiding sculpture to " a return to those forms which the just taste of the Ancients ever observed in works of this nature." His work included every kind of sculpture : portraits, of which some examples—Cardinal Fesch, General Murat and Mme. Murat—are superbly skilful ; sepulchral monuments sometimes on a great scale ; relief work, at which he excelled, and classical nudes, most of which are somewhat over-refined and the forms emasculate and empty. He also painted twenty-two large ecclesiastical pictures, and he designed and built a temple to house his works—particularly to display his model for a statue of " Religion " on a vast and heroic scale ; about which figure his admiring biographer, Count Cicognara, " draws a veil over the motives which prevented its execution in marble." So, like Michelangelo, Canova was sculptor, painter and architect, and the general opinion of his own age regarded him as the greatest sculptor of all time, while to his biographer he was " unquestionably the superior of Michelangelo."

Perhaps his best known work is the Cupid and Psyche in the

Louvre ; and the graceful half-nude reclining figure of Princess Pauline Borghese as Venus—though of this rather elegant figure Count Cicognara only remarks that " the face is a portrait of the Princess " ! When the French had despoiled Italy of some of its greatest treasures, including the Venus de Medici, Canova was commissioned to make another Venus. He did not attempt to make a replica of the Medici Venus, though his figure shows a good deal of similarity, and he refused to allow his statue to stand in the Rotunda of the Pitti Palace from which the Medici Venus had been taken.

His first visit to Paris was in 1802, at the invitation of Napoleon, when he was summoned to make a colossal statue of the First Consul. This statue is now in England. Five years later he again began work on a colossal mounted bronze statue of Napoleon—more than twice life size— but before this was finished and cast the Emperor had fallen, so the figure was changed into one of King Giovacchino. But once again before the statue was finished another political upheaval ensued and the figure became a statue of the Bourbon King Charles III of Naples ! Late in life Canova was once again sent to Paris on a mission which delighted him for he was an Envoy from the Holy See and his mission was to reclaim for his country the sculptures of which she had been despoiled.

He visited London in 1814 to see the Elgin Marbles, which, strangely enough, he admired, and he referred to " the visible improvement " in his own work—due to his study of these sculptures. Yet the classical antique on which his own sculpture was based was certainly late Hellenistic and Græco-Roman work, and much of his sculpture is only a faint echo of work which was already empty.

His biographer records that for all his work in marble he made full-sized models, apparently implying that this was then an unusual practice. These models were accurately copied into marble by his assistants. In his earlier days, he himself carefully finished the marbles, and in this his early training in carving was of great service ; but, with the great increase of commissions, this personal touch must inevitably have become more and more perfunctory and it is probable that many marble monuments and figures named as his work may never have been touched by him. But in almost all his work there is a good sense of carved stylism. In the famous busts of General and Mme. Murat this stylism is strikingly apparent. Madame is very like a Roman Lady, and the General, in spite of side whiskers, is shown nobly and with a spirited and fine sense of chiselling, particularly in the treatment of the hair. Canova had a retinue of assistants and pupils and he ruled the artistic world of Rome and of Italy ; and Rome in the eighteenth century was the Mecca to which all artists made pilgrimage. He was always generous to visiting artists and sculptors. The tradition that all sculptors had to be trained in Rome lasted on until the middle of the nineteenth century and kept alive a lingering classicism, until there was a reaction, owing to the complete decay of native Italian art, and the rise, especially in England and France, of a School of Sculpture based on a closer study of Nature.

In 1797 there arrived in Rome a young Dane, Bertel Thorwaldsen, to whom Canova showed his characteristic kindness. The Dane was the son of a carver of ships' figureheads and had worked at his father's craft, but, being ambitious, and with the assistance of a grant of money from the city of Copenhagen, he made his way to Rome, where, as he himself said, " he was born."

For some time he subsisted by painting small figure subjects for an English painter, but presently Canova took him into his studio, and very quickly admired Thorwaldsen's " new and grand style " in sculpture. His model for a figure of " Jason " being seen by an English banker, Thorwaldsen was commissioned to make it in marble, but fourteen years later, though half the agreed sum had been paid, the work was still undelivered. Throughout his life Thorwaldsen was dilatory, irregular and avaricious. Even his biographer has to admit that he was " ignorant of everything which had no direct bearing on art." His own country kept urging him to return but he remained in Rome till 1819 (twenty-three years after his " rebirth "). Meanwhile he had become rich and world famous.

In 1815, the sculptures from the temple of Ægina were discovered and brought to Rome. The whole collection was turned over to Thorwaldsen, and for several years—in the immense studio placed at his disposal—he " restored these marbles of Ægina, which procured him, among the learned, as much honour as any of his personal productions." Alas—for such " restorations " and so much " honour " ! He made new legs and arms as required ; he joined up fragments, and supplied any missing parts ; he worked over all the surfaces till, as his biographer E. Plon naively says, " he succeeded so perfectly as to deceive even a practised eye." Today his work on these unfortunate figures is not honoured but execrated.

He did not remain long in Denmark, however, and by 1822, when Canova died, he was back in Rome, with, in addition to all his Roman and classical work, a commission to do a gigantic group of Christ and the twelve Apostles for a Protestant church in Copenhagen. At this time, he had a group of over forty artists and assistants working for and with him in his studio. At the suggestion of Sir John Cam Hobhouse, he made a famous bust of Byron—though the poet was dissatisfied with it. This bust later was refused both by Westminster Abbey and St. Paul's Cathedral. Finally in 1835, it found a home in Trinity College, Cambridge.

Thorwaldsen, like Canova, made a famous Venus statue : like that of his rival, this was a variant of the Medici Venus. For this figure, his biographer records that he used thirty different models. This idea of trying to take various excellencies and beauties from different models and consciously combining them into a sort of synthetic whole is characteristic ; and it is hardly surprising that the results were often unsatisfactory and characterless. In his later life there were challenging spirits who protested against Thorwaldsen, a nominal Protestant, but known as in no way religious or moral, being employed to make the great monument to Pope

Pius VII for St. Peter's, while at the same time he was engaged in making apostles for a Protestant church—and pagan gods and goddesses. On this charge, his biographer, again with extreme naivete, remarks " The admirable intellect with which he was gifted conceived them all, but the feelings of the man had no part in their creation." This absence of the " feelings of the man " is precisely what makes all such sculpture, however " elegant and correct in style," fail to touch or move us today. As Carlyle says, " Let a man speak forth with genuine earnestness, the thought and emotion, the actual conditions of the heart, and other men, so strangely are we all knit together by the tie of sympathy, must and will give heed to him." This attempt to galvanize eighteenth century sculpture into a semblance of life by copying what were thought to be the perfections of classical art was but part of a wide revival of interest in classical life.

Stuart and Revett's *Antiquities of Athens* appeared in 1762, and gave a great impetus to the movement. Fifty years later, the acquisition of the Elgin marbles by a grant from the government to the British Museum brought an entirely new conception of classical art, and gradually, the study of these figures and fragments, influenced, and even transformed, the direction and development of sculpture. These marbles set new standards, for, just as Stuart and Revett had shown that Greek architecture could not be confined within the rules of Vitruvius, so these Parthenon sculptures showed that the so-called rules and formulæ for sculpture so sedulously followed by Canova and Thorwaldsen were in no real sense classical standards at all. How empty now seem the gods and heroes of Thorwaldsen, for whom " the process of making a god or a hero is effected rather by suppression than by addition, gradually fining down angles which are too abrupt in Nature, until the entire form has been carried to a point of fineness of execution, as if spirit alone had wrought it." Figures produced in this way could only be suave and hollow generalities, and the pursuit of this kind of empty perfection was bound to result in the atrophy of creativeness, and in the substitution of a shallow gracefulness for real power. It is only necessary to look at the Parthenon Theseus or Ilyssus to see how differently their creators regarded the process of making men into heroes. Those bold planes and edged contours are in violent contrast to the " fining down " process of Thorwaldsen. But though Canova was regarded in his generation as the greatest sculptor of all time, and though Thorwaldsen was also so regarded, and even succeeded to the coveted heritage of the Presidency of the Academy of St. Luke (a then powerful organization founded by Pope Clement X in 1670, for painters and sculptors)—yet, of the three sculptors who were the most potent exponents of classicism and whose influence tended to keep sculpture based on antique models, the greatest artist—though perhaps not the best sculptor—was neither the Italian Canova nor the Dane Thorwaldsen, but the Englishman John Flaxman.

In the earlier part of the eighteenth century, there was a group of foreign sculptors working in England. These included Cibber, Scheemakers, Rysbruck, and Roubiliac. In their work, though it was very varied, these sculptors all carried on a tradition based largely on the Baroque. Roubiliac maintained in some of the monuments, as that to the Duke of Argyll in Westminster Abbey, a certain splendour, and he modelled with great skill. The most original of the group was Caius Gabriel Cibber, whose best known works are the two pedimental figures of Melancholy and Raving Madness, made for Bethlem Hospital (known as Bedlam). These sculptures are of unique power and force, and they are said by a contemporary artist to have been carved directly in the stone without preliminary models.

A strange work is the terra-cotta bust of Cibber's son, Colley Cibber the actor. This is by some unknown sculptor, and is almost certainly cast from a life mask, on which the sculptor afterwards modelled the open eyes and added the headdress and the drapery, using—as some Renaissance artists did—real drapery dipped in plaster and then working details on this when set. The bust is coloured and the whole effect is very striking and entirely original. All these sculptors were foreigners, and their works were conceived and executed in a spirit rather opposed to the tendency of their age and in no way characteristically English.

In England the supposed antithesis between Classical and Romantic has always been less marked than in other European countries. In certain poets, Keats and Landor for instance, and in an artist like Stothard, these supposedly antithetical qualities are so united as to form a unique and yet typically English amalgam.

In Flaxman, the classical element was stronger, and a study of his numberless drawings (360 were reproduced and published in 1876) will show that Flaxman was not only an artist of great skill and delicacy, but that in his use of the human figure as the primary and most expressive form for all purposes of noble design he was unique—and this power of designing with the human body ranks him among the great artists.

John Flaxman (1755-1826) was the son of a London caster or formatori, who made and sold plaster casts of gems, intaglios, and small relief sculptures, and the child, though frail and deformed, grew up among these examples of classical art. The painter Romney helped the boy in his attempts at drawing and modelling, as well as in other studies. He won a Royal Society of Arts prize at the age of eleven, and another at thirteen, and at the age of fifteen he exhibited a model for a statue of " Neptune " at the Royal Academy. He then became a student at the Royal Academy Schools and won a silver medal for his modelling. Before he was twenty he met, and his work was introduced to, Josiah Wedgwood.

Wedgwood was a scholar, a chemist, and an inventor, and the pottery ware with which his name was, and still is, associated was something quite new and original. The main feature of this ware was the modelled decoration which was based on just such classical reliefs and intaglios as Flaxman had been familiar with from his childhood. He quickly became a very expert designer and modeller of small classical figures in low relief, and for a dozen years he worked for the pottery and many of his models must still be in use on the modern reproductions which are still being produced. Wedgwood ware was immediately popular and successful—and continued to be so, as long as the classical revival lasted—and certainly some of this success was due to the skill and beauty of Flaxman's work. He also modelled medallion portraits, like those of his contemporary John Tassie, and small portrait busts of living celebrities, which were reproduced in pottery. Meanwhile, he was the friend of other artists like Stothard and Blake, and it was he who in 1783, persuaded Blake to publish his first *Poetical Sketches*. The poet's letters to his " dear Sculptor of Eternity " give many characteristic and delightful glimpses of their common interests and expanding life—though subsequently they became estranged.

Flaxman gravitated inevitably to Rome, where Canova, as usual, was kind and generous to the newcomer. The visit to Rome was meant to be short but it lasted for seven years. He lived a busy life, for, besides a great deal of important figure sculpture, most of his outline illustrations to Homer, Hesiod and Dante were done in Rome, and, indeed, to many people his name is inseparably connected with these outline illustrations rather than with his sculpture. The illustrations to Hesiod were engraved by his friend Blake, and are generally regarded as the best of his illustrative work, perhaps largely because of the sympathetic engraving at the hands of his friend. But indubitably his delicate draftsmanship suffered by being translated into a rather harsh and uncompromising engraved line. The drawings themselves show real sensitiveness and grace—as well as power—and he had always a wonderful gift for composition and design.

On his return to England, Flaxman soon achieved recognition as a sculptor. He was elected A.R.A. in 1795—and R.A. in 1800—and the chair of Sculpture was founded at the R.A. Schools, so that he might be the first Professor. The lectures which he gave there were social events of importance and the substance of them was both interesting and valuable, and much of it suggestive and useful today. Somewhat unexpectedly, he urged students to draw from life exactly and realistically, and neither to stylize nor to idealize their figures.

For his generation and training, he had an unusual regard for mediæval work, and he urged students, for instance, to study and draw the beautiful " weepers " on the tomb of Aymer de Valence in Westminster Abbey. As Sir Sidney Colvin says : " Flaxman was not a seer nor a hierophant like Blake," but he was always a competent and sometimes an exquisite craftsman. His largest executed work is the great group of " St. Michael overcoming Satan," a small model of which is in the South Kensington Museum, London. It is a skilfully composed and beautifully designed group, but his real genius is shown in his drawings and in his smaller works.

A committee of the House of Commons was appointed to consider the question of the purchase by the State of the whole collection of the Lord Elgin's marbles, chiefly from the Parthenon. Flaxman's evidence before that committee is of great interest. Indeed, the whole report is valuable as indicating contemporary artistic taste, with its somewhat

138. PROBABLY BY MARTINEZ MONTAÑEZ (D.1649): LA VIRGEN DE LOS DOLORES: PAINTED WOOD: VICTORIA AND ALBERT MUSEUM, LONDON

A good example of Spanish realism

BAROQUE

139. EDWARD PIERCE :
SIR CHRISTOPHER WREN (*c*.1673) :
MARBLE :
ASHMOLEAN MUSEUM, OXFORD
distinguished carving style

140. BERNINI (1598–1680) :
A CARDINAL : MARBLE :
METROPOLITAN MUSEUM OF ART
NEW YORK

141. PELLE :
CHARLES II (1684) :
MARBLE : VICTORIA AND
ALBERT MUSEUM, LONDON

142. GRINLING GIBBONS
(1648–1721) :
CARVAT :
LIMEWOOD CARVING

One of these cravats was
owned by Horace Walpole,
who, of course, delighted in its
virtuosity : he wore it once
with great effect, at a reception
at Strawberry Hill. The scale
might almost be called
microscopic and it is certain
that to do them Grinling
Gibbons must have made new
and delicate tools

143. ATTRIBUTED TO ROUBILIAC (1695–1762) :
COLLEY CIBBER : COLOURED TERRA-COTTA :
NATIONAL PORTRAIT GALLERY, LONDON

144, 145. CAIUS GABRIEL
CIBBER (1630–1700) :
CHARLES II :
SOHO SQUARE, LONDON

146. HOUDON (1741–1828) : BENJAMIN FRANKLIN : MARBLE :
METROPOLITAN MUSEUM OF ART, NEW YORK

THE CLASSICAL REACTION

147. FLEMISH STATUETTE: SEVENTEENTH CENTURY: BOXWOOD
VICTORIA AND ALBERT MUSEUM, LONDON

148. ANTONIO CANOVA (1757–1822): PAULINE BORGHESE:
MARBLE: MUSEO DE VILLA BORGHESE, ROME   149. SLEEPING
NYMPH: MARBLE: VICTORIA AND ALBERT MUSEUM, LONDON

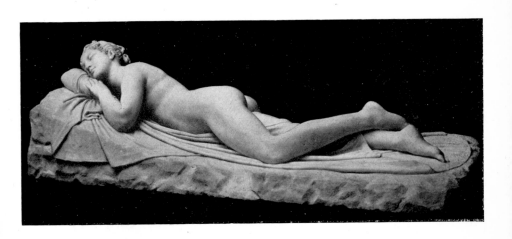

THE CLASSICAL REACTION

50. HOUDON (1741–1828): BATHER: MARBLE: METROPOLITAN MUSEUM OF ART, NEW YORK

In the field of child portraiture in sculpture (see plate 151 opposite), Houdon is unrivalled. He has sympathy, understanding, delicacy of perception, and, above all, exquisite technique.

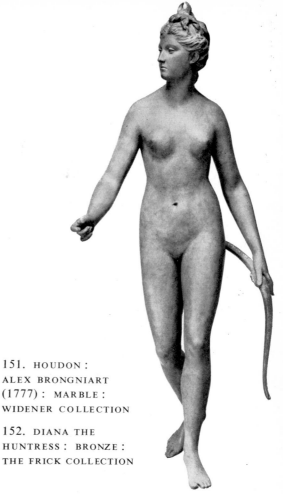

151. HOUDON :
ALEX BRONGNIART
(1777) : MARBLE :
WIDENER COLLECTION

152. DIANA THE
HUNTRESS : BRONZE :
THE FRICK COLLECTION

153. CHINARD (1756–1813) :
MADAME RECAMIER : TERRA-
COTTA : MUSEE DE LYON

154. THORWALDSEN (1770–1844):
VESTAL :
MARBLE : METROPOLITAN
MUSEUM OF ART, NEW YORK

155. JOHN FLAXMAN
(1755–1826) : SELF-
PORTRAIT : TERRA-COTTA

Perhaps his most characteristic sculptures
are the simple memorials,
mostly in high relief,
which are to be found all over England.
In many of these
he showed genuine inventive design
and sensitive feeling ;
the best of them
are a real achievement
in memorial sculpture.

156. JOHN FLAXMAN
PORTRAIT OF A CHILD
WAX MODEL : BOTH VICTORIA
AND ALBERT MUSEUM,
LONDON

157. JOHN
FLAXMAN :
WILLIAM PITT :
MARBLE :
GLASGOW ART
GALLERY

Note
the skilful use
of the official robe
to give
the necessary
support
to the legs.

THE CLASSICAL REACTION

158. MCFARLANE SHANNON :
HENRY ALFRED LONG :
GLASGOW ART GALLERY

The modelled thumb technique is
copied into marble, giving an
entirely false appearance of
plasticity to a hard and brittle
material. In the Macmonnies
monument it is like a dripping
cascade of ice-cream—the result of
thinking only in clay.

159. SIR FRANCIS CHANTRY
(1781–1842) : MARBLE
TOMB OF BISHOP RYDER :
LICHFIELD CATHEDRAL

160. MACMONNIES (b.1863) :
BATTLE MONUMENT,
PRINCETON, U.S.A. STONE

161. RUDE (1784–1855) : LA MARSEILLAISE : STONE : ARC DE TRIOMPHE, PARIS

Vigorous in design and spirited in carving yet keeping a stony quality

162. ARMSTEAD (1828–1905): DETAILS OF MARBLE
FRIEZE ON PODIUM OF ALBERT MEMORIAL, LONDON :
ABOVE, PAINTERS, SCULPTORS AND ARCHITECTS:
BELOW, POETS AND PHILOSOPHERS

163. ALEXANDER MUNRO (1825–1871) :
MRS. HENRY ACLAND : MARBLE RELIEF :
OXFORD CATHEDRAL

164. T. WOOLNER : (1825-1892)
ALFRED TENNYSON (1857): MARBLE:
TRINITY COLLEGE, CAMBRIDGE

165. T. WOOLNER :
PRINCE ALBERT : STONE
NATURAL HISTORY MUSEUM, OXFORD

Spirited realistic modelling with perspective effects yet wholly successful

. J. DALOU (1838–1902) : MIRABEAU ET DE DREUX-BREZE : CHAMBER DES DEPUTIES, PARIS

167. DESIGNED by GEORGE GILBERT SCOTT R.A.
(1811-1878): THE ALBERT MEMORIAL : MARBLE,
BRONZE, MOSAIC : THE FRIEZE IS THE WORK
OF FOLEY, WEEKES, ARMSTEAD ETC : LONDON

168. THOMAS BROCK (1847-1922) :
QUEEN VICTORIA MEMORIAL :
MARBLE AND BRONZE: LONDON

surprising standards and limitations. To all the artists giving evidence the several figures which were upheld as the final standards by which the Elgin sculptures were to be judged, were : the Apollo Belvedere, the Laocoon, and the Belvedere Torso. Even Flaxman gave it as his considered opinion that there was more " ideal beauty " in the Apollo Belvedere than in the Parthenon " Theseus." He insisted that the Apollo had this ideal quality, though he pointed out that he was sure the Apollo was a copy—while the Theseus was the original work of the great artist. He gave as convincing reasons for his view that the Apollo was a copy : " (1) that the treatment of the hair and of the cloak resembles bronze ; (2) that the folds of the cloak, which is over the left arm, do not ' answer ' on the back to the folds of the front." This, he said, truly, was because in the translation into marble a greater thickness and strength was required, so that the folds could not possibly be carved thin, like material, answering each side to the other, as they could be if cast in bronze.

Richard Westmacott, R.A., was the only sculptor among those examined who stated boldly that " the Theseus was infinitely superior to the Apollo Belvedere " and " that the back of the Theseus was the finest thing in the world " and " that the Ilyssus is not surpassed by any work of art." Sir Thomas Lawrence, R.A., made some wise and original comments : " that the Elgin marbles were in the first class of dignified art, wrought out of nature upon uncertain truths, and not on mechanical principles." " The Apollo Belvedere, the Torso, and the Laocoon are systematic art, the Theseus and the Ilyssus stand supreme in art." This shows a surprising judgment and understanding of sculpture on the part of a painter of his school and generation.

Joseph Nollekens, R.A., whose position as a sculptor was then un-challenged, even by Flaxman, and who was twenty years his senior, gave it as his opinion that the marbles should not be touched by restoring or repairing, and in this he showed a very independent judgment. Benjamin Haydon was the most active and vociferous defender of the Elgin marbles, and it was he who interested Keats in them and for whom the poet wrote his great and moving sonnet. The whole controversy about these sculptures is interesting because people took sides so violently and with so much acrimony. Byron's invective against Lord Elgin could hardly have been more excessive had the sculptures been stolen. Yet Lord Elgin received for the collection not much more than half of the sum which he had spent to acquire them : sixty thousand pounds—almost his whole fortune. Actually, the removal of the sculptures by Lord Elgin saved them from being destroyed or used as building material. It is hardly an exaggeration to say that the possession of these marbles changed the development of sculpture not only in England but, in a less degree, also in France and Germany. Their effect, however, was not immediate. Nollekens, Chantrey, Flaxman, Gibson, Bacon, continued to produce monuments even of contemporary figures, which were based on Roman and Græco-Roman models.

Bacon's statue in St. Paul's of Dr. Johnson, half naked and in a sort of Roman toga, is yet dignified and skilful sculpture. But though there was something Roman and senatorial about the Doctor, the statue is conceived and worked in a false idea of the classic spirit. Joseph Nollekens (1737-1823) produced an immense number of memorials and portrait busts ; of these busts his biographer lists 200 as " the more important." The one of Dr. Johnson is perhaps the best-known, and it is a very characteristic work. The fleshy treatment of the face is ably done, and the hair is remarkable, for the Doctor is shown without his usual wig—apparently Nollekens disliked carving wigs ! In this field of portraiture Nolleken's work is of a high standard, though by this time the technique of carving had already been entirely separated from modelling, and it is clear that Nollekens never took any part at all in carving the marble. As a boy he was apprenticed to Scheemakers, but even then he was employed entirely as a modeller.

Nollekens' contemporary biographer, J. T. Smith, gives some curious and interesting particulars of the costs involved in the production of such monuments. For the marble statue of William Pitt, at Cambridge, Nollekens received four thousand pounds. Yet of this sum, the carver, who made the whole figure in the marble, received only three hundred pounds. For portrait busts Nollekens charged 120 to 150 guineas and paid the marble carver only 24 pounds. Nollekens was notoriously mean. Yet these carvers were not " ghosts " but were recognized, known, and named. Apparently each sculptor kept his own trained carvers, and, of course, as this was before the elaboration of the " pointing machine," carving was work requiring great accuracy and skill. In a good sculptor's studio carving was a recognized part of training, but it seems evident that as soon as they reached a certain prosperity and were established, most sculptors (as today) ceased to do anything but make models.

The name of Sir Francis Chantrey has survived partly because he left a large fortune to the Royal Academy to purchase from the annual exhibition works of art for the National Collection and also because he was an admirable sculptor of portrait busts. In that of Sir Walter Scott—though it was done too late in life—there is strength and dignity and noble sculptural style. There is a grave and dignified beauty about the monument to Bishop Ryder in Lichfield Cathedral, though the " Sleeping Children " in the same Cathedral is a better known work of Chantrey's.

John Gibson (1790-1866) who studied under Canova in Rome continued the Classical tradtition in skilful, if not always inspired, works. He made some interesting experiments in using colour on sculpture. In this field he did some unique work. He introduced colour on the Queen Victoria statue at Windsor, an innovation much criticized by other sculptors—few of whom realized that almost all Greek sculpture was coloured. In the famous " Tinted Venus," a marble statue which Gibson exhibited at the second Crystal Palace Exhibition in 1862, the whole figure was slightly tinted, the drapery edged with a pattern in gold and red, the hair darkened and touched with gold, the apple in her hand gilded. The whole effect of the statue (though perhaps quite un-Greek) was probably striking and original. Gibson was an able craftsm skilled in carving as well as in modelling, and was a man of great force and originality. The outline engravings so commonly used to illustrate sculpture at this time give no idea of the quality of his work—and even plaster replicas are very inadequate. Gibson, though not a Flaxman, was a considerable artist ; so, too, was John Henning, a Scottish sculptor who devoted a long life to making reduced copies of the Parthenon frieze and the frieze from Phigalia. These he carved in slate, the scale about an inch to a foot, and they were reproduced in plaster and sold to members of the Dilettante Society and others. These casts are unduly despised today but they deserve recognition as patient, mature and frugal art. Today, when photography is capable of reproductive marvels, we are apt to forget the difficulties under which our predecessors worked.

Wood was not much used for sculpture during this classical age, but wood craftsmanship of rare and exquisite beauty was turned to the making of fine furniture and interior decorative work like overdoors and fireplaces, such as few other ages can show. Chippendale, Sheraton, Heppelwhite, and—in America—Duncan Phyffe, were all craftsmen worthy of real appreciation and regard. It is, perhaps, not surprising that the age in which the Royal Academy was founded, followed the dictum that " the proper study of mankind is man," and was the period of the greatest English school of portrait painting. The seventeenth century had been an age of great development of scientific knowledge ; this knowledge, in the eighteenth century, was turned to material and industrial ends. The study of history in the same age was changed from brave guesses, like Raleigh's, and memoirs like Burnet's, to wide and sweeping reviews like those of Gibbon, Hume, and Robertson. France led Europe intellectually, and before the end of the century there had arisen the new republics of France and America. Of course there were contradictions. The scepticism of Voltaire dominated the intellectual world, and was echoed in England by Gibbon, yet the same age also produced Wesleys and Whitfields and an important growth of religious evangelism. This movement found no expression in art, and English Wesleyan churches are mostly built on the model of pagan temples, and such sculptured monuments as they used are almost always only echoes of pagan classicism. But if one studied a group of characteristic monuments, from the elaborate and often pompous tombs in Westminster Abbey to the simple and genuinely touching marble reliefs of Flaxman, and selected examples of portrait sculpture of this age, the work would show a very high standard of sculptural skill. Much of it has splendid technique, good chiselled qualities and often great nobility and dignity. But, being based on ancient examples and rules rather than on study and observation, the tendency was to substitute archæological knowledge for artistic creation and so there was a gradual atrophy of creative power. The next movement in sculpture, especially in France and England, was towards a greater realism of expression, and was based on a closer study of Nature.

" First follow Nature and your judgment frame
By her just standard, which is still the same ;
Unerring NATURE still divinely bright ;
One clear, unchanged, and universal light.
Life, force, and beauty, must to all impart,
At once the source, and end, and test of Art."

POPE

" What pitfalls there are in the word ' Nature.' "

MATTHEW ARNOLD

THE REVOLT FROM CLASSICISM

THE famous apostrophe to Nature of Pope, seems to echo a sentiment which is associated with Rousseau, and later with Wordsworth, rather than with the " Age of Reason." But the abstraction which Pope called " Nature " connoted something which had little resemblance to the " Nature " of Rousseau, and to Wordsworth the word implied a sense of a mystical union of man with the earth and all earthly things :—

" Rolled round in earth's diurnal course
    With rocks, and stones, and trees."

In his preface to *Lyrical Ballards*, a message of great significance for artists, Wordsworth challenged and then repudiated the view of Pope and his generation that Nature, good taste, and classicism, all meant very much the same thing ; and his insistence that the language of poetry should be that of common speech, and that the subject matter of poetry, (and, by implication, of art) could, and even should, be drawn from the sights, the occupations and the thoughts of the people. These ideas were a potent force in directing men's minds towards a new conception of nature and led inevitably to a break away from the restraints, and so-called rules of classicism.

Art is, and remains essentially a " mystery," but it is evident that Wordsworth took a great step when, as he said, " I have taken as much pains to avoid what is usually called poetic diction as others ordinarily take to produce it."

This attitude or doctrine had a strange tonic effect on literature and art, and the reaction from classical rules towards the freer expression of emotion produced art of new and vital power both in England and France. The intellectual and artistic leadership of France held throughout the eighteenth century and survived even the Revolution. But the new ideas which came to be called the Romantic Movement were there temporarily checked by the Napoleonic Empire with its enforced classicism, and this tended to divert the main currents of the movement, at least for a time, to England. But France was still artistically important, and despite Napoleon, classicism declined, the types and principles of Canova

132

and Thorwaldsen were rejected and the metropolitan centre for sculptors moved from Rome to Paris, where already, by the genius of Houdon, sculpture was seeking and achieving a new and brilliant realism.

This shifting of the artistic centre brought England and France into closer relation, and by the middle of the nineteenth century the " Bonaparte " legend and the " natural enemy " legend were dead or dying and English sculptors were studying in French studios with men whose works were arousing wide interest as marking a New Movement.

" Le Départ " by Francois Rude (1784-1855), carved in stone on the Arc de Triomphe, is perhaps one of the most vigorous and characteristic works of the early nineteenth century, and its influence was great. There is some concession to classicism in the Roman armour of the great bearded warrior, and in the nudity of the youth, both of which seem strange in volunteers of 1792 ! But the whole group is vitalized by a powerful if somewhat turbulent spirit. It is brilliantly composed and the modelling has a robustness and vigour of movement which make it still a splendid epitome in stone of French military spirit.

To appreciate the emotional and technical power of this group one need only compare it with a monument of studiously similar design and setting, Macmonnies' " Washington Battle Monument," at Princeton, N.J., which is an inert mass of soft clay-like forms, dripping into meaningless blobs, totally devoid of any sense of stone ; an eloquent testimony to the devastating effect of thinking in terms of clay and aiming only at realistic modelling.

A. L. Barye (1795-1875) worked chiefly as a sculptor of animals. He studied them anatomically and he achieved, in this somewhat restricted field, works which are often charged with force and power similar to the work of Rude. Long before these vividly modelled animals were fully known in England, and perhaps even in France, they were being eagerly bought by American collectors, and there is a splendid collection of them now in the Corcoran Gallery at Washington.

About mid-nineteenth century, a group of French sculptors exercised considerable influence at first in France and then in England. Of these men, three were conspicuously successful. Paul Dubois (1829-1905), J. B. Carpeaux (1827-1875), and J. Dalou (1838-1902).

Dubois' well known monument at Nantes, an effigy set in a rather overwhelming architectural setting and with four corner figures symbolizing Faith, Charity, Meditation, and Military Courage, is a typical example of the failure of later sculptors to achieve that fusion of architecture, sculpture, and feeling, that cohesion of thought and technique, which marks the best Renaissance monuments. Taken singly, each of the corner figures has some distinction but the power to fuse all the elements of the design into a whole, is lacking. In popular figures, like the child St. John Baptist and the Florentine Singer, Dubois' great skill is evident, but, challenging comparison as they do with Renaissance sculptures, they fail in style and dignity.

Carpeaux carried further the pursuit of realism by loose and fluent modelling and his famous group on the Opera House of " The Dance " shows splendid power, though the plastic, clay-like quality of modelling is too conspicuous in the stone and in this respect the work is less truly sculptural than is Rude's " Le Départ." Dalou, like Carpeaux, pursued realistic modelling as the essential and vitalizing quality in sculpture, apparently not realizing that a Rubens-like softness of form is necessarily unsculptural, except when, as in his large circular relief in South Kensington, London, the work is in terra-cotta. The monument called Triumph of the Republic is too loosely constructed to be successful though it has verve and distinction. One of his finest works, and one in which his skill in composition, and his psychological grasp of character, are shown, is the superb relief of Mirabeau and the Duc de Brézé. Of course, it can be challenged as too pictorial, but this pictorial realism can be justified when it is carried out with such triumphant success. The panels of Ghiberti's gates are also pictorial, yet Michelangelo considered them worthy of Paradise, and though today the representation of perspective in relief-carving is frowned on as unsculptural, this panel by Dalou is a masterpiece such as few sculptors have achieved.

Dalou, having acted as curator of the Louvre during the Commune of 1870, had later to take refuge in England, where he taught at the Royal College of Art, and, both as a teacher and as working sculptor, he exercised a great influence on the group of English sculptors and his inspiration was continued in his pupils well into the twentieth century, and lived on until recent years in his brilliant pupil, Alfred Drury.

The chief characteristic of all this work was its realistic tendency, and the rejection of the stylistic conventions which the classicist sculptors had regarded as binding and final. The leaders of the Romantic Movement, were urging, as an ideal, the " return to nature," and this ideal modified and directed the development of sculpture towards naturalism and realism. The search for personal expression wrought great changes in all the arts of both countries, and it is markedly evident in English architecture, for those who followed the new movement realized that the copying of classical architecture must be abandoned, and that in a revival of Gothic (or even " Gothick ") building there was more scope for the expression of this individuality, and they believed that this greater freedom would revive the arts.

To some of the leaders of this " revival," notably the younger Pugin (son of a French émigré) the whole field of architecture and design divided sharply and finally into only two divisions, " Christian " and " pagan " influence. With all the resolute certainty of his contemporary Macaulay, and with burning intensity and eloquence, Pugin urged the view that all pre-Christian and heathen forms were today irrelevant and should be abandoned, certainly in all buildings of a Christian or religious purpose, and indeed his view was that modern man had nothing to learn from pagan, classical life, and he unremittingly urged that no revival was possible except through a return to the Catholic faith and to the forms associated with mediæval Christian architecture.

He saw with astonishing clearness some truths which have lately been too often propounded as new discoveries. In 1843, in a lecture on church architecture, he notes " Today styles are adopted instead of *generated*, and ornament and design are adapted to, instead of originated by the edifices themselves." Pugin, though he did no actual sculpture, has had less than justice done to his power and influence. At the age of fifteen he was designing, in his father's office, furniture for Windsor Castle and Buckingham Palace. These designs were always based on mediæval work, of which his knowledge was unique, and he quickly found that no craftsmen could be found to translate his drawings into works with any feeling for the mediæval quality which he demanded, so he started a workshop in which men could be trained in all the details of such work.

By the middle of the nineteenth century when the new Houses of Parliament were being built and Barry and Pugin were joint architects (in a very loosely defined partnership), this group of working craftsmen had become important, not only in helping to revive interest in mediæval art, but also in carrying out with skill and understanding the designs for every sculptural and furnishing detail required for the new buildings, which flowed so inexhaustibly from Pugin's studio (which was usually a small fishing boat !). The number of craftsmen so trained must have been considerable and included many men who later became well known as sculptors, and workers in many crafts.

The Pugin tradition still survives. I have myself done ecclesiastical sculpture for Pugin's grandson and I know sons and grandsons of men trained in those workshops who are still working in various branches of architectural design and sculpture.

The best known artistic movement associated with the mid-nineteenth century is that of the Pre-Raphaelite Brotherhood. In 1849 the seven young men who were thus associated and named set themselves to no less a task than to rejuvenate the art of England ; and, though this movement is usually considered as being wholly concerned with painting, it should not be forgotten that one of the original members of the group was a sculptor, Thomas Woolner, and that another sculptor, Alexander Munro, was closely associated with all the members of the Brotherhood.

These men are almost wholly forgotten today yet they both produced some work of singular beauty. If Woolner's name is known it is rather for his few poems, notably " My beautiful lady," which he contributed to the first number of the P.R.B. magazine *The Germ*. Within a very few years of the manifesto of the Brotherhood, Woolner, having failed to get the commission to do the Wordsworth Memorial for Westminster Abbey, departed for Australia to try the goldfields, rather than art. But gold eluded him just as sculpture commissions went to lesser artists, and he returned to Melbourne, where for two years he subsisted by modelling portrait medallions at £25 each. This enabled him to return to England and he quickly made some reputation for his portrait medallions. The one he did of his friend Tennyson was engraved as the frontispiece for the famous 1857 edition of Tennyson's poems, which was illustrated by his

Pre-Raphaelite friends, Millais, Rossetti and Holman Hunt. Woolner was an aggressive and pugnacious man and he made his way as a portrait sculptor, and finally into the Royal Academy, where the Chair of Sculpture, vacant since Flaxman, was revived for him, only to lapse again.

It was soon after his return from Australia that he carved the marble bust of Tennyson now in Trinity College, Cambridge. This is a noble bust, well conveying the strong features and powerful distinction of the poet's head. Later in life, he did a bearded Tennyson. This, too, is distinguished work, but it lacks the fire and power of the earlier head. He designed a doorway for the Natural History Museum in Oxford ; this was never carried out, but he carved a spirited statue in stone of the Prince Consort which has an important place in that Museum.

Woolner also worked as a "carver" in marble for Behnes, a busy and then important sculptor, whose studio was haunted for some years by a young artist, G. F. Watts, who there learned certain noble sculptural stylisms, which later he used with great effect. This carving quality is evident in all the best work of Woolner.

Alexander Munro began carving as a boy in his native Inverness. Coming to London, he worked in Pugin's workshops, carving detail work on the Houses of Parliament, and perhaps it was this training which gave him that precision and firmness of contour which characterize all his work. He was the friend and intimate of all the Brotherhood and, though Millais had admired Woolner's Tennyson, it was Munro who made the relief of "Handsome Johnny," which is now in the Ashmolean Museum in Oxford.

Memorial portrait reliefs by Munro are in many English cathedrals, usually in marble, and seldom have women been carved with such delicacy and distinction. The relief of Mrs. Acland in Oxford is characteristic and, though fashions change and lace and ringlets are outmoded, yet the graciousness remains and the exquisite technique is still challenging to us today when craftsmanship is apt to be underrated. Munro also did several of the stone statues for the Natural History Museum at Oxford, as well as a beautiful high relief portrait, carved in stone, of Woodward, the architect of that unfortunate building. He also made a large and monumental "Hebe" in Grosvenor Square, and a fine statue of James Watt, which is still the best statue in Birmingham.

But, though these large works are spirited and distinguished, his genius lay rather in delicacy of perception and perfection of technique, and these qualities suited his smaller work. That he was an original artist with a very individual outlook may be seen in the carved panel over the door of the Oxford Union, representing King Arthur's round table.

He carved this while his friends, Morris, Rossetti, Prinsep, and Burne-Jones painted the famous frescoes within ; these frescoes faded almost as they were painted, but fortunately they have lately been restored to life by the enthusiasm of the late Sir William Rothenstein and the science and skill of Professor E. W. Tristram, and are now, perhaps, as permanent as works of art can be. This panel must have seemed strangely primitive to a mid-Victorian generation and its orginality and directness are still striking.

The Gothic revival in England, though it began very tenuously with Horace Walpole, ended with Barry and Pugin, and the Houses of Parliament and Parliament Street, and the great law courts of London ; but the "pagan" architects did not immediately give up and the neo-Greek University galleries at Oxford and St. George's Hall at Liverpool are splendid and scholarly examples of work inspired by classical architecture, but, as Pugin found with Gothic detail, this neo-Greek work required the same scholarly knowledge on the part of the sculptors as on the part of the architects and this was not available, so most of the detail had to be rather mechanically copied from ancient examples, and this hastened the separation of the arts and divisions among craftsmen. The division into designer and executant was now accepted as normal and inevitable and this separation was to be fatal to architectural sculpture.

Yet in what might be called almost the last large work to be done in England under the influence of the Gothic revival, the Albert Memorial in London, there is evidence of a collaboration, at once close and salutary, of the architect and his group of sculptors. The great frieze of the podium, with its eighty-four life-sized figures of the world's great poets, artists, and philosophers, is a fine achievement in high relief carving in marble and the sculptors responsible for this, Armstead and Weekes, have had far too little credit for work which is admirably designed and carved with spirit and skill.

This frieze is almost the last work at which the sculptors themselves laboured at the marble carving and in the whole length of the frieze there is no sense of clay or of modelling ; this chiselled quality is rare in modern work (though within the last decade there has been some attempt to return to this direct carving, notably on the additions to the Bank of England).

The Albert Memorial has been the focus of much sarcastic criticism, apparently without any close observation or knowledge on the part of the critics. The sculpture, especially of the frieze, is immeasurably better than that on the Victoria Memorial of half a century later which resembles a wedding cake vastly enlarged and recreated into marble and bronze, and every part of which resembles only clay which has been miraculously petrified or turned to bronze—this falsity is inherent in the whole structure.

H. H. Armstead, who was chiefly responsible for the Albert Memorial frieze, carved a series of panels dealing with the Arthurian legends. These were done for Pugin and are in the Queen's Robing Room at Westminster. He also did some work in the Guards Chapel at Knightsbridge, notably a Samson wrestling with a lion, (since destroyed by enemy bombing) which is strongly designed and rigorously carved, so that it was described as almost " Ninevite in character."

But while these sculptors laboured at the Albert Memorial in the late 'sixties, there was in England one remote and lonely sculptor, Alfred Stevens, who pursued his own course, working for iron founders, and any one who would employ him, but holding tenaciously to his own ideas and resolutely refusing to follow any prevailing style, whether Greek or mediæval.

Alfred Stevens (1818-1875) went as a youth to Italy and spent nine continuous years there, studying and working ; he worked for some time in Thorwaldsen's studio in Rome, but his work remained entirely unaffected by Thorwaldsen's classicism. It was this long sojourn in Italy during which he soaked himself in the spirit, as well as the forms of Renaissance art, which made him ever afterwards use the forms and language of Renaissance art as freely as if it were his native vernacular. No other sculptor has, with such naturalness, adopted and used the forms of Italian fifteenth century art to express his own nineteenth century ideas. Steeped as he was in Renaissance art, he never merely repeated these forms but transformed and vivified them according to his own genius.

The marble mantelpiece made for Dorchester House is a work in which his mastery of design and form is clearly shown. The intricate and beautifully sectioned mouldings are based on those of Italian Renaissance sculpture. The large and ample forms of the caryatid figures echo some trace of the noble types of Michelangelo, yet the whole work is unmistakably modern, and neither a copy nor a pastiche.

The chalk drawings, especially of figures, which he did as studies for sculpture, are among the finest drawings in English art and these alone would give him a high place as an artist, while, among his painted portraits, that of Mrs. Collman would rank him among the great portrait painters of the nineteenth century.

His most important work in sculpture is the monument to the Duke of Wellington in St. Paul's Cathedral. On this great work he laboured for many years, changing details, elaborating mouldings, simplifying, eliminating and yet enriching the design, endlessly studying, working almost unknown and unrecognized, except by a few artist friends, living almost in poverty, and dying, leaving the monument still unfinished. But even as he left it with only the sarcophogus and the noble effigy, and the two allegorical groups in their architectural setting, it was still one of the most impressive monuments in England, a land rich in beautiful sepulchral sculpture. About forty years after his death, the monument was finished, including the equestrian figure of the Duke, by another hand, that of John Tweed.

Stevens must be ranked as the greatest of our nineteenth century sculptors, though he was little known in his own day. He followed his own course, unmoved by the Pre-Raphaelite movement, ignoring the Greek and Gothic revivals, pursuing an ideal of his own, lonely and self-absorbed, knowing that the expression of his conceptions required vast study and persistent eliminating preliminary work. "To be humble before nature, to work unmindful of everything beside, uniquely for the standard of perfection he has set himself ; is the true life of the artist." These wise and searching words of Sir W. Rothenstein may be applied with peculiar force and accuracy to describe the life work of Alfred Stevens.

138

Another artist who followed a lonely path was G. F. Watts (1817-1904), who, though known chiefly as a painter of portraits and of allegorical pictures, yet produced some works of sculpture which give him a definite place in English sculpture. The bust of Clytie, so largely conceived, the ample forms so nobly displayed, was an early work, 1868, but it showed his power. The great equestrian figure of Hugh Lupus, at Eaton Hall must rank among the finest monuments of its kind in England, and closely rivalling it for power and distinction, the later variant of the same theme of horse and man, Physical Energy.

On the technical side, these works are interesting as they were both modelled, not in clay, but in gesso duro. This mixture of plaster, tow and glue was used by Renaissance sculptors. Watts has himself described how he used this mixture, building it over a jointed iron armature ; the joints enabled him to alter or at least modify the action if desired, without destroying the rest of the model, and as the gesso does not perish, or go " sour " like clay, he was able to work on these figures over a number of years, with the result that, in nobility of gesture, in large and splendid sense of style, and variety of surface, these groups show that artist at the height of his great powers, and they are in every way worthy of a very great artist.

But both these men worked against rather than with the prevailing schools and stylisms of their day, and during the last quarter of the nineteenth century, English sculpture developed towards a greater realism. This was partly reaction ; partly it was from the influence of French schools of sculpture, in which many English artists were trained. There was also, especially after 1870, a marked influence from French artists, Legros and Dalou particularly, who were resident in England. There is a torso by Legros in South Kensington Museum, which, in its quiet reserve, is notable and distinguished.

This French influence markedly changed the course of English sculpture and it is clear that the group of sculptors who were prominent in the last two decades of the nineteenth century were seeking ideals in the expression of form very similar to those pursued so effectively by the French schools. A new and searching attention was given to the study of anatomy and of structure generally, and much study was given to the differentiation of surfaces in sculpture. All this tended towards realism, and the writers who wrote about this " new sculpture," as Edmund Gosse called it, show the usual hasty and complacent assumption that the sculpture of the immediately previous decades has been empty, effete and conventional, while that of the " new " men, being based on study from real life and on greater science, was true and vital, and indeed it was hailed as " a revolution in English plastic art."

It *was* revolutionary in the immense extension of the boundaries of the field of sculpture ; but this new freedom led sculptors into the pursuit of such realism that petrified verisimilitude began to be considered as the end and aim of sculpture. Yet the leaders of this school of English sculpture produced some competent, and at times, conspicuously good, work, and though the schools and teachers of France influenced its development, yet somehow the French quality was often transmuted, just as the mediæval builders had done, into something characteristically English.

In spite of widely different personal qualities, the work of Hamo Thornycroft, Onslow Ford, Alfred Gilbert and Thomas Brock has certain general characteristics which mark it as inspired by the ideals and ideas which were current in the latter part of the nineteenth century, however much they are repudiated today.

Both the parents of Hamo Thornycroft were sculptors, and he achieved a recognized position as an artist, while still a very young man. He was always just ahead of a very gifted and versatile rival, Alfred Gilbert, in winning Academy school prizes and honours.

Thornycroft's first conspicuous success was with the Artemis in 1880, the marble version of which is now at Eaton Hall, the seat of the Duke of Westminster. There are lingering traces of classical influence, not only in the subject but also in the action which is reminiscent of the Versailles Artemis, yet the general effect is wholly modern in its realism of modelling and variety of surface textures. The nude figure beneath the Greek garment is carefully studied and is one of great beauty, and, though the statue is to a certain extent realistic, it is informed with style ; so too, is the figure of " Teucer," 1882, another work which aroused great interest and helped to establish his reputation. In his later work, the realistic element rather overpowered the sense of design, as in the Gladstone monument in the Strand, and the lion at the feet of Cromwell which seems to have strayed from the Zoo and is not in any degree stylized or composed into the design. Yet the figure of Cromwell, as he stands outside Westminster Hall, has the quiet brooding power which fits the subject, and the bronze figure of Bishop Creighton in St. Paul's, in cope and with his crozier, has both personality and beauty.

In the work of Onslow Ford, too, this realism led to a loss of " style." His belief, clearly stated in his introduction to Lanteri's *Modelling*, was that the sculptor's job consisted in choosing, with great selective care, a living model and then faithfully and meticulously copying the form into clay, neither selecting nor rejecting, so that the deviations from the ideal should be those of nature rather than of man ; this attitude gave a disturbing and excessive individuality to his figures of what were meant to be romantic or heroic subjects.

But, in spite of his theories, he made a moving and beautiful marble figure of the drowned Shelley for the Shelley Memorial at Oxford, which would be a far better memorial if this tender and pathetic figure were the whole monument ; but the marble slab on which the body lies is itself insecurely balanced on the soft feathers of winged lions, and there is also an incongruous bronze tree amid the branches of which a mourning muse strikes a melancholy lyre. All these vaguely symbolic attributes destroy the pathos of the drowned figure holding in his hand the little copy of Sophocles, which book is now actually in the Bodleian library, not far from the monument.

But Ford produced some admirable portraits, perhaps especially those of his brother Academicians ; memorable for characterization and originality of gesture, are the portrait statues of Henry Irving and Professor Huxley.

Alfred Gilbert holds a curious position among English sculptors. His work is original and always interesting, and its new and unique qualities seduced people into the belief that it was great sculpture ; it was even greatly admired and praised in his time. Today, detached from the contemporary, intensely personal, quarrels and controversies which arose owing to his persistent changes, elaborations and delays over every important commission, his work can be studied dispassionately, and one can see that his predilection for fantastic and exuberant details and, also his excessive sensibility in modelling were essentially unsculptural. On the bronze screen, which surrounds the tomb of the Duke of Clarence, at Windsor, there are small statuettes of exquisite grace and charm ; but their beauty and delicate scale are quite destroyed by the exuberant curvings and squirmings of the rest of the screen ; they are mutually destructive and the whole screen itself completely hides the actual effigy of the Duke, which can only be seen by mounting the step ladder and viewing it from above.

Such confusion of design and of the whole purpose of a monument, makes it evident that Gilbert could not fuse into unity the component parts of his scheme for the memorial. It is this fusion which distinguishes and ennobles the Wellington Monument of Alfred Stevens, stamping it with genius as great art, while the lack of this unity shows the fatal failure of Gilbert as an artist. Much of his work shows eccentricity and virtuosity rather than artistic, or sculptural, power, yet he was indubitably a skilful and sensitive craftsman, seeking new effects and perfecting new processes of sculpture with the ardour of Cellini.

The Royal Academy, as it had done for Woolner, revived the Chair of Sculpture for Professor Gilbert, and his lectures on sculpture (which in one year took the curious scheme of designing and elaborating a gold and silver necklace for the Venus de Milo !) were enthusiastically received, both by the students and the public. He did some few portrait busts ; as with those of Ford, perhaps the best are of fellow artists, notably one of G. F. Watts, for whom he had a real admiration. It is significant, too, that it was Gilbert who urged the President, Sir F. Leighton, to develop his small model of an Athlete with a Python into the large and spirited group now in the Tate Gallery, and recognized as one of Leighton's finest works.

After a long enforced exile from England, Gilbert was invited to return to make the monument to Queen Alexandra in St. James's Park. He was knighted and honoured ; but the memorial is a pathetic failure, and shows convincingly that realistic modelling, no matter how skilful, cannot make a dignified sculptured monument.

In spite of considerable personal divergencies, the works of this group of sculptors have a certain unity. They show a general tendency to fluent and pictorial modelling. In this Gilbert was the most facile, and his work has the greatest sense of personality. But these men were all conscious that they were emancipating sculpture from the trammels and stylisms of the previous generation. This sense of their achieving new aims is constantly reiterated by the contemporary writers of art criticism. Claude Phillips, Cosmo Monkhouse, W. Armstrong and Edmund Gosse all emphasized the artist's search for freedom from convention, but being all literary critics rather than artists, they never sensed that when the work was transferred to marble, the realism of modelling which was the distinguishing characteristic of all this, work, was destructive of the essential quality of chiselled stone.

One man alone had seen this years before, but by the 'eighties Ruskin's influence was waning, and though his Oxford lectures on sculpture dealt with this technical aspect with piercing and analytical skill, yet most people, and certainly most critics and artists, regarded his views on the translation of clay into marble, as mere fantastic pedantry confusing morality with the technical practice of art.

Indeed, a writer in the *Magazine of Art*, probably W. E. Henley, who was then Editor, wrote in 1888 : " When the clay or wax has left the artist's hand, the remainder is, or should be, purely a work for the artizan." It was by that time inconceivable that a figure might be carved as all mediæval statues had been carved, without the preliminary of a full-sized clay model ; it was equally inconceivable that the sculptor should also be the " artizan " and do the carving. The separation into two groups was complete and the strange thing was that this division, and the mechanical measuring of the pointing machine was quite unnoticed or, if noticed, regarded as unimportant.

In the treatment of bronze sculpture, a similar realism of modelling was accepted. Foley's Prince Consort, the central figure of the Albert Memorial, preserved a notable metallic quality of surface, but Brock's Queen Victoria fifty years later made no pretence to be other than a marble translation of clay.

A sculptor, of unique power, who used bronze with a clear understanding of its metallic quality was C. Meunier, a Belgian, whose whole life was spent in making a sort of apotheosis of labour. The noble head, called " Anvers," is a characteristic work.

Adolph Hildebrand in Germany occupies a strange place in sculpture; he continued the classical tradition not only in making his chief subject the ephebe or nude youth, but also in his poses and treatment he constantly echoed the Greek athletic type, but charged with more emotion, and more essentially modern. His search for a classical sculptural stylism led him to write a study of æsthetic problems of proportion, and form, and this work had considerable influence. He also made some quiet and nobly distinguished work in portraiture.

The work of Max Klinger is wholly opposed, in spirit and outlook, to that of his contemporary Hildebrand. The great statue of Beethoven at Leipzig is one of the strange and fantastic creations in sculpture which challenge every accepted tenet, and defy all the so-called rules. The group is in many materials, crystal, gilt bronze, coloured marbles of various kinds, and it attempts by intricate symbolism to express all sides of Beethoven's character. It is wrought with consummate skill and yet it is less impressive than many simpler works of monumental sculpture. Like Alfred Gilbert, he was seduced by a love of virtuosity and display, and in this pursuit his work failed in greatness and dignity.

An even lower form of skill than this virtuosity is seen in the dreadful depths to which Italian sculpture sank during the later nineteenth century. Who that has once seen the cemetery at Genoa, or the sculpture shops of Florence and Rome, can consider their products as " art " in any sense ? Not all the ingenuities of lace carving, or faces under muslin, can redeem such work. Yet Bistolfi produced some work of a tender and poetic feeling, and, in the great monument to Vittorio Emmanuele there is a spirited and powerful frieze by Zanelli which shows the Italian genius continuing a fine tradition. Italian sculpture was less influenced by mechanism (for even the lace carving was human skill !) and by the prevalent French ideas and styles, which were followed in almost all other countries.

But, by a curious paradox, although, as noted before, Houdon visited America to make a portrait of Washington, the early sculptors of the United States were inspired and influenced by Canova and Thorwaldsen, and ignored the more realistic style of Houdon and the French schools.

The absurd half-naked Washington by Greenough in Washington is the counterpart to the classically half-draped Dr. Johnson in St. Paul's. Both have a certain dignity yet both are done under an essentially mistaken view of the sculptor's art.

So, with Hiram Powers' " Greek Slave " (with a real chain !) and " California," Erastus Palmer's " Captive," and Reinhart's " Clytie " ; all these have the limitations, as well as the qualities, of the classical school of Flaxman and Bacon. But after the Civil War, sculpture in America achieved a new life. Perhaps this was in part the result of the great expansion and development of the country, which brought vast wealth to certain families and groups. Splendid private collections of art were formed, like those of the Frick, Altman, Morgan, and Huntington families, and these brought a closer relation with the culture of the older world of Europe, and these examples must have exercised great influence, not only in directing people to the artistic riches of the past, but also by offering standards for study, appreciation and emulation.

New sculpture also came direct from France, for a good many war memorials were the work of French sculptors. Mercie's " General Lee " at Richmond is a spirited example ; and all this tended to increase the French influence. American architecture was largely based on French architecture, and almost all American architects and sculptors were trained in Paris. There was also founded another Ecole des Beaux Arts in New York.

The great architectural firms of Carrère and Hastings, and McKim,

Mead, and White, led to a good collaboration between architects and sculptors. Of these, Daniel French, Paul Bartlett, A. St. Gaudens and F. Macmonnies were all French-trained and worked in a cosmopolitan spirit. Many of their important works were made in Paris and shown first at the Salon ; it was regarded as impossible that an artist could do good work till he had spent some years in France. Poets and artists alike, ignored the clarion call of Whitman to

"migrate from Greece and Ionia.

Placard ' Removed ' and ' to let ' on the rocks of your snowy Parnassus. The same on the walls of your German, French, Spanish castles and Italian collections,

For know, a better, fresher, busier sphere, a wide untried domain awaits—demands you."

It was only later, when, particularly in architecture, Whitman's advice was followed, that America achieved an art at once autochthonous, living and modern.

St. Gaudens was the most accomplished of the group. His Shaw memorial on Boston Common has a noble rhythm in the design of the marching negro troops, and there is a fine distinction in the figure of Colonel Shaw and the horse ; but his finest achievement is the memorial to Mrs. Henry Adams, which makes an impression like that of a great elegiac poem, not personal, but moving. Trained in his youth as a cameo cutter, he excelled in small scale modelled relief portraits, some of which are beautiful in every way. This is especially so when they are in bronze, for the marbles, all too faithfully, copy his delicate plasticity of modelling.

American artists, like those of France and England, were only too ready to take advantage of the great development of mechanism, and everywhere this led to the exact, but insensitive and misunderstood translation of plastic qualities into the hard material. In almost all the varied works of sculpture produced as the century neared its end, the predominant characteristic was a tendency towards plastic realism, which developed and then accelerated into a tremendous impulse, which changed and influenced almost all European sculpture and which was traceable to the compelling force of the work and genius of a single Frenchman, Auguste Rodin.

It is necessary to glance at the sculpture which was so admired, and so successful when Rodin infused new life and vitality into sculpture with his gospel of relentless realism ; and his persistent refusal to alter the forms of nature. " Nature is always right " was his basic idea and he must have felt something like contempt for the works of his immediate confrères, the prosperous academic sculptors, whose work was so acclaimed.

Today it is almost unbelievable that a work like Mercie's " Gloria Victis " should have been, or could ever have been, considered as a masterpiece in the sculptured expression of French national spirit. And the same sculptor's monument to Gounod seems now so banal and childish as to be almost incredible. One recalls also the insipid sentiment of works like Barrias' Nature Unveiling (in various marbles) and

Falguiere's Christian Martyr, and they wake no responsive echo of admiration now.

Against such work the genius of the peasant Rodin offered insistent challenge. The development of his work was consistent enough. He began work under Carrier-Belleuse, a sculptor whose whole output was never more, and seldom less, than graceful and facile. But the genius of Rodin lay not at all in this direction. His first exhibited works, the head of The Man with a Broken Nose," and the nude figure called " The Age of Iron " aroused violent controversy because of their unflinching realism. So completely alive, and anatomical was the modelling of the figure, that the sculptor was accused of having cast it from a living model. This caused the withdrawal of the figure from the Salon ; though later, Rodin convincingly refuted the accusation.

By the 'eighties, Rodin's work was well known not only in France but in England also ; it was violently criticized, and as violently defended ; every work roused a storm of criticism or applause, and all the time the sculptor kept on producing a vast amount of work, and some masterpieces.

There was more unanimity with regard to his portraits, (except that his sitters, particularly the artists, generally disliked them). The best of them, especially those which were reproduced in bronze, can only be rivalled by the Græco-Roman portraits, which they so strongly resemble ; but few portraits in sculpture are so charged with vital life, so filled with creative energy, as those of Rodin's best days. There is the head of Puvis de Chavannes, nobly poised, marvellously alive ; that of Dalou, sensitive, artistic, distinguished in every aspect ; Jean Paul Laurens, powerful and robust, yet imaginative ; Victor Hugo, brooding, intellectual, also creative and energetic. There is too, the amazing terra-cotta head of Balzac in the Metropolitan Museum ; so vivid one expects speech from the open mouth.

All these are in the deepest sense real. His passion was for " reality." Rodin's art and his spirit were rooted in the earth. How significant that in the early 'eighties he was called " the Zola of sculpture." His admirers resented the phrase ; but it was and remains wholly just, and that without disrespect to either artist. Both men were passionately devoted to the pursuit of a certain kind of truth, both sought this tenaciously and un-flinchingly ; both were widely praised and widely blamed, yet neither deviated from his concept of truth, and both were betrayed as artists by a certain earthiness of mind.

Rodin was, and remained, a peasant and simple minded, with a hypersensitive sense of touch, with great sensibility to the stimulus of observing nude figures in action or in repose ; responsive to all physical stimuli, at times erotic, always sensual, endlessly creative in shaping clay or making drawings, yet never able by effort of intellect to discipline his creations into noble forms of serene and changeless beauty, always im-provizing, seizing momentary actions or expressions and recording them in clay with unerring and unwearied skill. He glorified the " clay " of which man is made, but yet, in the most literal sense, his work remained always and immutably only clay.

His mental outlook seems often extraordinarily confused, and the pages of rather wordy rhetoric put into his mouth by admiring biographers are sometimes staggering in their foolishness ! And how incredible are some of his quoted dicta ! Mlle Cladel records his saying of Chartres Cathedral :

" Its two towers, the one carved, the other only of ragstone, plain, bare. How well the architects knew what must be sacrificed to effect ; and what discipline over themselves they must have exercised to build enormous walls like those of a citadel, and to leave the grace and ornament for one single tower."

How fantastic is this ignorance ! Did he know that the two towers were separated by over three hundred years ? Did he know that no " architect " designed any such " effect " ? Did he know that the sixteenth century builders of the carved tower knew, and cared, nothing at all about the builders of the earlier tower, and that no single human being ever " designed " the whole cathedral at all ?

Did Mlle Cladel know ? Yet, she represents Rodin as saying about Chartres and Gothic sculpture, " Though I have thought about their art all my life I do not yet understand it. I feel it profoundly but cannot express it."

How indeed could he understand art so remote from his own age, and his own super-sensual emotions ? He expressed a certain truth when he described Assyrian art as, " terrible as tigers," but he blundered abysmally when he called Egyptian art " savage " for no art is so serene and tranquil and civilized.

The impressive force of his genius may be seen in the fact that in the admirable illustrated *Handbook of Art History* compiled by Mr. F. J. Roos, there are eight illustrations of nineteenth century French sculpture, of which four are by Rodin ; while English sculpture of the nineteenth century is entirely unrepresented.

Surely Rodin was a strange figure ; with fantastic limitations, yet with stupendous powers, gifted with vast creative energy, not inventive or imaginative but phenomenally observant, this man, almost by his own might and genius, gave a direction to sculpture in his age such as, I believe, no other single artist has ever done. But great as were his gifts, persistent as was his energy, so that almost everything he touched he vitalized, his influence on the art of sculpture was to prove profoundly evil.

" Loveliness, magic and grace,
They are here—they are set in the world—
They abide—and the finest of souls
Has not been thrilled by them all
Nor the dullest been dead to them quite
The poet who sings them may die
But they are immortal and live,
For they are the life of the world."

M. ARNOLD

" Dans la morale—comme dans l'art—dire n'est rien. Faire est tout." RENAN

THE TWENTIETH CENTURY
ACTIONS & REACTIONS

At the opening of the century, Rodin was at the height of his powers, and at the pinnacle of his fame. He was applauded as the equal, or even the superior, of Phidias, Donatello, and Michelangelo. Writers, and critics of great authority, and representing many divergent points of view— Havelock Ellis, Arthur Symons, W. E. Henley, R. L. Stevenson, G. Bernard Shaw, Gabriel Mourey—Leonce Benedite (the last a one time Academic enemy) had all written, or were then writing of Rodin's genius as of a splendid and unique phenomenon—and some of them ventured to issue on his behalf, passports to an immortality which reads strangely today when the reaction is at its flood, and Rodin's plasticities are disparaged, and his vivid unstylized realism is derided as unsculptural. That verisimilitude to life pursued by Rodin and his immediate followers tended to lead sculpture into a cul-de-sac from which there was no escape except by a revolt from the whole idea of representation in art ; a revolt which has gathered momentum and is today the most marked characteristic of " the new movement " in art.

Yet it should not be forgotten that within the limits of his genius Rodin produced some works of sculpture of extraordinary skill and vitality. The dynamic power of the walking John the Baptist is striking, and it was brilliantly original when it was done—not even Donatello, or Gian-Bologna had seized on a momentary action and given it form as did Rodin in this unique figure, and although today such realism of surface modelling, and such spontaneity of action are considered as being beyond the range of sculpture, it should be recognized as a work observed with startling clearness and represented with consummate skill and fidelity. The accusation that the " Age of Iron " figure was cast from a living model was a ridiculous one, for no such cast could have the vital power with which this figure is so superbly filled.

It was perhaps this living quality which captivated Stevenson who wrote in 1886 : " The public are weary of statues that say nothing ; well here is a man whose statues live and say things worth uttering." Rodin preached : " Go to nature—nature is always perfect—the artist does not create—that which he does is to represent " ; but in his own work the forms of nature are super-charged, and the result is not a duplication of nature, but Rodin's own art, a re-statement of nature's truth ; which is just what art should be. That browless and brooding pithecanthropos which he calls The Thinker is almost sub-human in type ; but it is superhuman in the amount of vitality that is imprisoned in that gigantic and tortured body.

Any attempt at an assessment of Rodin must consider two aspects of his genius ; first, in relation to the art and ideas of his own age, because though academic French sculptors hated and derided his work, his genius was substantially recognized by writers and critics, both French and English, and secondly, his genius and influence in relation to the wider field of the whole development of sculpture and of the æsthetic and technical principles by which it is controlled and modified. The consideration of these two aspects should be separate, for, though the impression he made on his own age was great, the tendency of today is to belittle his genius. Yet an attempt at an assessment is necessary because of Rodin's immense influence, and also because his very individual and brilliant technique was seized on and copied by his followers, and these included almost every distinguished worker in sculpture during the past fifty years in France, England and America.

Malvina Hoffman and Brenda Putnam, in books dealing with their art of sculpture have lately paid handsome tributes to the galvanizing power of Rodin in freeing his own generation from an empty and academic conception of form, and directing artists towards a constant and searching study of nature. To his own generation, accustomed to suave, academic forms, his works seemed to be supremely naturalistic, hence the accusation of casting from living models. But it would not be difficult to show that, although Rodin studied his models incessantly, and his powers of observation were unique, it is very rarely that his works are merely transcripts from nature. As an artist, he was far too consistent to be thus misled ; and repellent as is the concept and the physical aspect of The Thinker, it is in no sense just a powerful man posed and copied into clay, and then cast in bronze. The whole figure is charged with terrible power, and is the embodiment of male brute strength. If, however, it be compared with a great figure by a supreme sculptural genius, the Day, of Michelangelo, in which the forms are also titanic and brooding, but are disciplined, quiescent, and marble-like, then it is clear that Rodin's too realistic and too undisciplined technique fails by comparison.

I have, in a previous chapter, dealt at some length with the relation between Michelangelo's sculpture and his carving technique, and Rodin's work also deserves close study in this respect, for its qualities, as well as its failures are closely related to his method of working. One of his earliest biographers, F. Lawton, has expressly stated that Rodin was never a " practician " or marble carver—" neither for himself, nor for others, has he ever hewn stone or marble." And a few years ago I was personally assured by Dr. Tait Mackenzie—himself a distinguished sculptor—that in the several years during which he worked in Rodin's studio and under his tuition, he was certain that the master never took the smallest part in the work of carving the marbles. " Why should he," said Dr. Mackenzie, " when his assistants did this work far better than he could ?," and he was puzzled at my implication that this amazingly exact copying of the clay models into marble, was the cause of the falsity of the artistic result. The head of Mlle Cladel, sometimes called Thought is a characteristic work. The exquisitely modelled head is set on a great block of unhewn marble ; the effect is striking and even moving, but had the head been carved directly out of a block of marble, it would never have occurred to any sculptor to complicate his task of carving the head, by leaving this widely projecting block around it. It is true an " effect " is gained, but it is a rhetorical effect only and has no relation to the way a head is carved from a marble block.

Yet this and similar works made a great impression, and were considered comparable to the half hewn figures of Michelangelo ; to those who had no technical knowledge as to their methods of work there seemed to be both similarity and justification. In reality there was neither, for Michelangelo's unfinished work is simply work in process ; while in Rodin's work the rough hewn parts are usually deliberately designed for effect and have no technical justification at all.

Briefly, the rough, unhewn parts of Michelangelo's figures are simply the parts which would be carved away in finishing the figure ; whereas, the roughly hewn parts of Rodin's figures usually bear no relation to the size and shape of stone required for the figure—their function is to offer a violent contrast to the nude figure. Rodin, in this method, provided a dangerous model, for far too many sculptors copied the device of half hewn figures because of its effect. Rodin's failure here was a failure in intellectual integrity ; the result was a mere rhetorical antithesis.

There were several distinct phases in Rodin's development. The early realism, then the great period of portraits and the powerful and forceful Burghers and the Thinker, then a sensual phase of nymphs and fauns, and embracing lovers—a revelling in the physical aspect of love (which indeed was always with Rodin). Perhaps it was of this aspect that Edmund Gosse said, in 1903, when Rodin was elected President of the International Society of Painters, Sculptors and Engravers :

" He sculptured as if he were singing, and this lyrical rapture which marked all that he produced, was one of his most striking characteristics," yet some of these " lyrics " are conceived in a spirit of gross sensuality and are unredeemed by any nobility of style. Again Rodin failed in the intellectual substance of some of his groups. The Hand of God is a conventional idea realistically expressed ; the Beau Dieu of Amiens or the Egyptian Kephren are real concepts conventionally expressed.

149

The last phase of Rodin's art has been acutely noted by Havelock Ellis.

" They are effaced, the details are smoothed out as it were, washed away by the action of running water, so that only the largest and simplest harmonies of line and form remain. He began as a minute realist, and his work caused offence because it was said to be merely photographic ; then he developed his characteristic style of deliberate exaggeration, heightening of natural proportions for the ends of art, the play of light and shade. This last period is of large and simple masses, softened and alleviated of all semblance of reality, gliding into a vast, dim dream."

Unfortunately, this phase was extraordinarily popular, though it too often reduced his marble to an appearance of soap, with a singularly repellent result. It is probable that it is this phase of his work which so distresses the critics today. But the disparagement of Rodin is now a critical game, and the revolt from his plastic conceptions has carried both artists and writers by a reaction to a kind of apotheosis of stone, and quite a few modern sculptors seem so anxious to preserve the " stoneness " of stone, that they can hardly bear to do more than scratch their stone surfaces. One may apply alike to Rodin's realism and to the " stoney " sculptors a remark of Cromwell's, " no one goes so far as he who does not know whither he is going ! " and Rodin may be left with the words with which Ruskin dismissed Michelangelo, " great enough to make praise and blame alike necessary and alike inadequate."

The revolt against Rodin began in a real dissatisfaction with his wilful ignoring of the character of his material, the fact that some of the portrait heads, and a few of the groups, exist both in marble and bronze copies, and the forms are exactly similar, (being, of course, the clay forms) shows that Rodin cared little about his materials, and the reaction was led by men trained in the Rodin tradition and even in his studio, Bourdelle, Maillol, Mestrovic and Despiau.

Many of Bourdelle's works are entirely Rodinesque, the large Rembrandt head, the amazing portrait of Anatole France, are powerfully influenced by Rodin, and in the " Heracles " Bourdelle even adheres to the sub-human physical type of the Thinker and the gilt bronze surface is entirely clay-like. But Bourdelle's monumental sense is shown in the great Virgin of Verdun, carved in stone and with an elemental simplicity which gives it distinction, and there is a beautiful and memorable plaster head of Sir James Frazer, (of the *Golden Bough* and *Pausanias*) in the Luxembourg, which has the noble reserve of great art.

Maillol (1861-1944) spent the latter half of a long life in seeking to achieve a monumental type of female nude. In this type, he turned aside from the realistic nudes of, say, Carpeaux and Dalou, and also from the more carnal figures of some of his predecessors. And he has created a type of woman, monumentally simple in contours and, though formed with a noble amplitude, yet wholly unsensual: disciplined into the simplest gestures, it never lacks an impressive dignity. How far these figures in stone or marble are the work of his own hands, I do not know, but they are not conceived as if their material were clay, translated with mechanical skill into another medium. They give the impression of being the work of an artist of Greek lucidity and directness ; their simplifications are never empty, and in their presence one recalls a sentence of Sir Richard Jebb's about the art of Sophocles, " Simplification consists not in the elimination of detail, but in the subordination and disciplining of it." Maillol achieved this, and his work is thus serene and noble.

The work of Mestrovic (b. 1883) is strangely varied in range of media and scale—portraits of great distinction, occasionally cruel, as in the crouched and lecherous looking " Rodin," nude figures in marble, draped caryatids in wood, reliefs in wood and in plaster ; architecture, and architectural sculpture, emaciated and tortured crucifixes, pure and reverent madonnas and angels, a great bronze Indian at Chicago, and a gigantic and grandly conceived figure of Moses at Spalato. He has essayed every form of sculpture and has produced many masterpieces, with a wide range of feeling, from the profoundly religious to the superb and dynamic energy of the Moses. These sculptures, first shown in London about 1915, were called " ugly," " monstrous," " morbid," yet their power was acknowledged : indeed it was undeniable that here was a genius in the field of sculpture. His influence in the decade after the London exhibition was very great, especially in England, and later his work was much studied and admired in America, where he lived for some years. His influence is still considerable, though it has of late years, somewhat faded before that of Maillol.

Despiau (b. 1874) also began much under the spell of his master Rodin ; but his genius lay in another direction, and skilful as are some of Rodin's busts of women—" Judith Cladel," "Eve Fairfax"—a peculiar beauty and fragrance pervades the heads of those girls so sensitively modelled by Despiau. In spite of the reminiscence of Rodin's modelling, they are informed by a tender and refined spirit to which Rodin never attained. The influence of Despiau has been considerable not only in France but also in England and America.

There are three conspicuous names in German sculpture of the past quarter century, Lehmbruck, Kolbe, and Barlach. The work of both Lehmbruck and Kolbe has been influenced by Rodin, but both have passed through this stage and emancipated themselves in work of moving, and sometimes great beauty. Maillol achieved a certain fine stylism by amplitude. Both Lehmbruck and Kolbe have achieved their ideal adolescent nude type largely by attenuation ; and Kolbe's figures are informed with deep feeling, sensitiveness and exquisite surface. Both these artists have worked chiefly in bronze and though there is little similarity in their types, there is a certain kinship in the grave and reserved spirit which pervades their work. Barlach has used wood as his medium, not indeed wholly, but largely, and in this medium he has produced some great and vigorous works and he is recognized and accepted as a master of wood sculpture. But, powerful and vigorous as are many of these wood carvings, yet it often seems as if the toolmarks did not arise naturally from the shaping of the forms, but are deliberately conspicuous.

There is a prevalent idea today that if wood is carved with due regard for its peculiar and distinctive qualities, the resulting forms will necessarily be somewhat similar to the negro stylisms so admired today. This popular but entirely delusive idea should be dispelled by recalling both Egyptian wood sculpture, and that of fifteenth century Germany, as well as the work of Mestrovic and Barlach.

No one of these sculptors achieved the great pre-eminence of Rodin at the opening of the century, but their cumulative influence gave the impetus which has led to the reaction against the representation and verisimilitude pursued by Rodin and his followers, towards conscious and deliberate stylisms, and towards abstraction and experiment in seeking forms unrelated to nature.

In England the revolt from the dominance of Rodin was slow, but two men took a conspicuous part in this. Jacob Epstein and Eric Gill approached the work of sculpture from entirely different angles but both were revolutionaries. Epstein was born in America but most of his working life has been passed in England. About 1908 he caused a sensation with a series of large figures in high relief on the British Medical Association Building in London. These figures were wildly assailed, and as wildly defended. They were highly skilful architectural sculpture, decoratively simplified in contour and silhouette to suit their position on the building, and they were stylized in a manner very like the vigorous work of Franz Metzner. His next conspicuous and again sensational work was the large memorial to Oscar Wilde, carved in Hopton wood stone. In the Hudson memorial, a few years later, Epstein adopted a carving technique very similar to Gill's, especially in the practice of sinking the background deeply to get a harsh and vigorous outline to the figure of Rima and the birds ; while using only a portion of this relief for modelling the contours within the silhouette. But simultaneously with carved stone and marble sculpture, Epstein developed a facile and highly individual modelling technique which he used in many portrait busts and figures. Using clay loosely and fluently the surfaces of these busts were rough beyond even Rodin's powerful modelling, which indeed they recalled. But vital and even profound as some of these busts are—Tagore is superbly poetic, Hailé Selassie, " twitching with nerves " is skilful and memorable—yet the sense of clay obtrudes itself unpleasantly when, as is usual, they are cast in bronze.

There is no final answer to this problem of the proper treatment of bronze. Ancient bronzes in Egypt, Greece and in the middle ages, usually had smooth surfaces and a marked ductile quality. Modern practice dating from Rodin, has usually allowed the bronze to be an exact reduplication of the clay model with all the heightening of contour and plastic variations of the surface which realist modellers use ; but an opposite instance is found in the brass bust of Osbert Sitwell by Frank Dobson, where the sculptor had deliberately stylized the portrait (with a certain loss to the " likeness ") into beautiful, metallic simplifications which preserve and accentuate the quality of the metal. There are, of course, many halting

169. GEORGE FREDERICK WATTS R.A. (1817-1904):
PHYSICAL ENERGY : BRONZE : KENSINGTON GARDENS, LONDON

170. G. F. WATTS R.A.
CLYTIE : BRONZE :
TATE GALLERY, LONDON

THE REVOLT FROM CLASSICISM

171. ALFRED STEVENS (1818-1875) : MODEL FOR THE CENOTAPH OF THE DUKE OF WELLINGTON : VICTORIA AND ALBERT MUSEUM, LONDON

172. RUDE : MONUMENT TO CAVAIGNAC : MARBLE : MONTMARTRE CEMETERY
A study in rigor mortis—compare with above and with plates 94 and 115

173. ALFRED STEVENS (1817-1875) : CARYATIDS, DORCHESTER HOUSE FIREPLACE :
MARBLE : TATE GALLERY, LONDON

THE REVOLT FROM CLASSICISM

175. A. SAINT GAUDENS (1848-1907):
MEDALLION OF ROBERT LOUIS STEVENSON:
BRONZE: TATE GALLERY, LONDON

176. A. SAINT GAUDENS: MOURNING FIGURE:
BRONZE: FROM A MONUMENT EXECUTED
FOR MR ADAMS, WASHINGTON D.C.

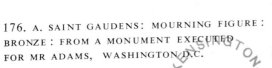

177. RODIN (1840-1917)
DANAIDE : MARBLE

178. RODIN
THOUGHT : MARBLE

The soft and voluptuous figure
contrasted with a rough hewn
mass of marble—a false and
unnecessary contrast. The device
of opening a little space to show
the hand is a mere trick of
ingenuity. The rough marble is
left there only as a foil—it has no
technical reason for its existence.
This desire for "effects" led Rodin
to some very specious devices.
The forms are often more expressive
of modelling than of carving.

179. RODIN: VICTOR HUGO
MARBLE
MUSEE RODIN

180. RODIN: J. P. LAURENS
BRONZE
LUXEMBOURG

181. DELAPLANCHE (1836-1891) MADONNA : MARBLE :
LUXEMBOURG

The entirely banal and stupid work which preceded
Rodin and was so generally accepted and admired.

places between these two treatments ; in the first, the final substance of the bust is ignored ; in the second, the substance is accentuated, with some sacrifice to the portrait which cannot, because of its stylism, have the latent energy of a bust by Rodin or Epstein. Ironically enough many of the most " modern " artists have used this clay-like surface for their bronzes, even while abandoning the realistic modelling ; resulting in a fantastic contradiction. The noble and beautiful mediæval bronze effigies of Beauchamp and Alainor of Castile are surely worthy of consideration as offering examples of exquisite appropriateness in the use of bronze, unsurpassed by any modern sculpture ; and a modern metallic treatment sensitively understood, but not carried to an extreme, is to be seen in Maurice Stern's Bomb Thrower.

Eric Gill's approach to the problems of figure carving was through a long period of letter-cutting and designing. As he achieved figure sculpture in relief and in the round, he also preached, wrote, and reiterated his consistent belief that a modelled model in clay or wax, was necessarily a false and bad preparation for stone or carved sculpture. When he had to do large stone sculpture, as that on The Hague Palace of Peace, and the group of Prospero and Ariel for Broadcasting House, the preliminary models he made and used were carved on a smaller scale in a soft stone ; and few sculptors have felt and expressed such a dislike and distrust of the whole process of modelling as a preliminary for the practice of sculpture, or even as a convenient way of study for students. His insistence on this was, and probably still is by many, considered a mere whimsical fanaticism of practice, but it is not possible to understand his work unless one accepts his method, for he was essentially a carver of stone and marble, and though he often deliberately avoided subtlety of modelling, his carving craftsmanship was superb. But the recognition he gained, and deserved, for his uniquely accomplished workmanship has led to a prevalent idea that his simple contours and archaic manner are necessarily implicit in the technique of direct carving.

This idea should be dispelled by recalling the fact that all the myriad mediæval stone sculptures were equally " direct carving." Where Gothic sculpture shows an archaic stylism, as in the Romanesque work of Moissac and Souillac, it is, as it were, an innocent stylism, and was not the work of men who had mastered the difficulties of form, and then deliberately abandoned this power to seek expressiveness in a stylized formalism, for, in the next century, with growing technical accomplishment there was a marked movement towards naturalism. It is not necessary to assess the artistic power of work so radically different as is that of Souillac in the twelfth century from that of Amiens in the thirteenth century ; it *is* necessary to distinguish between them, and Gill, it is clear, admired and studied the earlier work. This led to a certain similarity of treatment, but he was far too individual an artist to be a mere copyist. One of his greatest works, uniting style with stylization and revealing a sense of formal beauty with superb skill, is the large stone torso which he calls Mankind. This work alone would show him as a great artist. The carving is of peculiar delicacy and sensibility, exquisitely adapted to the Hopton wood stone. This is really an English marble, hard and rather intractable, which Gill often used, seeming to delight in his technical mastery over a resistant material. In his earliest important series of stone relief sculptures, the Westminster, " Stations of the Cross," there is a marked austerity of feeling, but he was responsive to many aspects of life, and that his work is the genuine expression of his personality with its mingled religious didacticism and its frankly expressed sensuality, is made clear by the rather extravagant candour of his *Autobiography*. But the influence of his reiterated plea for better training in the practice of sculpture, and his emphasis on the mastery of carving technique, have had far-reaching consequences in the work of many younger sculptors. But Gill, though he gained a hearing for his views on sculpture by his persistence and persuasiveness, was not in this matter so original as he is often assumed to be, or even as he considered himself to be.

Apart from the already noticed group who carved the Albert Memorial, a good many sculptors, prominent at the end of the nineteenth century had been trained in wood and stone carving, but as soon as success in " sculpture " was achieved they abandoned their practice of carving, whereas Gill regarded this as a defection and would hardly acknowledge as a sculptor, one who only prepared clay models to be carved by others. A few of these men were essentially craftsmen trained in the technique of carving, bronze casting, working in ivory and other media, and some of their work shows a fine standard of workmanship. Sir George Frampton is shown to have been a skilled and patient craftsman in such figures as Dame Alice Owen (an experiment in coloured sculpture) and in the Lamia bust in ivory and bronze. A less well known artist was A. G. Walker, who spent his whole life carving marble, ivory and other media, and produced some very significant works, culminating in a large ivory figure of " Christ at the Pillar." He was, somewhat belatedly, recognized and elected to the Royal Academy, a well deserved honour. Another sculptor whose work is always consistent in craftsmanship is Sir W. Reynolds-Stephens, painter, bronze worker, modeller in plaster, carver in wood, ivory, stone, designer of embroidery and worker in many branches of art ; his work has always grace and skill. The small statuettes of Launcelot and Guinevere shown at a Glasgow Exhibition in 1901 were works of refined sensibility of design and perfect craftsmanship. The figures, perhaps two feet high, were in cast bronze, with ivory and mother-of-pearl additions and enrichments, and despite small scale they showed a notable largeness of style.

Another sculptor whose work is always consistent in technical mastery over many media, is Professor Richard Garbe. Throughout all the various tendencies, movements, and reactions of the past forty years, he has pursued his own course, working in ivory, wood, sometimes enriched with lacquer, stone, terra-cotta, marble, even the hardest coloured marbles ; patiently experimenting with many materials, mastering every craft skill, and amid all the clamant movements and " modernisms " holding quietly to his own conceptions of beauty and fitness. He is an Academician, and in his position as Professor of Sculpture at the Royal College, his influence has been great, and though sculptors, trained under his tuition, are today working, as is right and inevitable, in their own manner and technique, yet their command over materials, and power of invention must have received a wholesome stimulus from Professor Garbe's example. Unspectacular as his work is, it is always consistent and interesting. He has achieved, and may well maintain, a high position in English art by the quality which, Matthew Arnold insisted, gives Gray his place in English poetry that of " distinguished workmanship."

William Simonds and C. d'O. Pilkington-Jackson are two sculptors whose work is characterized by fine craftsmanship, particularly in the field of animal sculpture, in wood and marble. Simmond's group of horses carved in elmwood is a revelation once again that an artist, taking a very simple theme, using a common medium and mastering the technique, can yet produce a work of artistic distinction filled with a sense of spirit and beauty. " Real " as this group seems, it is in no sense only a reduced model of a group of horses ; they are not realistic, neither are the forms forced into a fantastic stylism ; yet dignity and decorative quality are achieved by subtle variations in the scale of all the trappings and harness. These are all recognizable as the usual simple adjuncts to cart-horses, but they are " arranged " into a decorative harmony which is satisfying.

In Pilkington-Jackson's series of Scottish military statuettes, the artist's problem was to combine sculptural style with strict accuracy in all the details of the varied accoutrements ; in this he has achieved a unique success. The figures whether single or mounted are not just reduced men in military costume but are designed for their own scale and a harmony of composition is gained by the design and scale of the accoutrements and by a very simple stylization. Even the rich colour, while " real " enough for military accuracy, is distinctly decorative and harmonious. This is good wood sculpture, good documentary recording and fine craftsmanship.

The work of many English sculptors of today deserves study, but the scale of this book makes it possible to give only a few names : Sir W. Reid Dick, C. S. Jagger, Gilbert Bayes, Cecil Thomas, Gilbert Ledward, Alan Wyon, Derwent Wood, F. Taubman, Ernest Gillick. The list might be enormously extended and yet be very incomplete. Derwent Wood became a successful Academician and his bust in the Tate Gallery, of Henry James, shows his skill in modelling, but the too literal and exact copying of the modelled technique into marble makes the work fatally deficient in style. A work of his student days, carved in wood and with a head-dress of beaten lead, has far more distinction. F. Taubman, in his earlier work, was much under the influence of Rodin (though he studied chiefly in Belgium). The impressive " Adam and Eve " group shows Rodinesque power, but in his later work, notably in " Semiramis," he sought and achieved a more deliberate stylism, and showed his fine sense of design.

With the decline of the dominance of Rodin, English sculpture turned in new directions, but Rodin's influence was powerful in America almost up to his death. A great collection of his works, housed in a splendid museum, was opened in Philadelphia about 1930. The work of Gutson Borglum was obviously much inspired by Rodin, especially in the half-hewn marbles and Rodin's influence is powerfully evident in the sculpture by George Gray Barnard for the Pennsylvania Capital at Harrisburg. Original as this work is in conception, suggestive and thoughtful as is the symbolism, and skilful as is the execution, the plastic realism of the sculpture is too widely different from the architecture. It is not possible to fuse great groups of realistic sculpture on to a classic building, and the result is unsatisfactory. Yet, strangely enough, Barnard knew, understood, and loved mediæval architecture, in which this fusion of masonry and sculpture is beautifully achieved, and it is largely due to his foresight, and taste in collecting, and generosity in giving, that there is housed at the Cloisters in New York a unique and splendid collection of mediæval sculpture.

The Nebraska Capital at Lincoln, is in every way a great and significant contrast, both in architecture and sculpture, to the Harrisburg Capital. The sculpture of Lee Lawrie is admirably adapted to fit into the architecture of Goodhue and the result is a work of singular unity. All the sculpture is conceived and designed as part of the building, and the sense of scale and of chiselled stone is never forgotten, perhaps indeed the simple planes and rigid angularities of the sculpture are a little conscious and over deliberate. Yet the figures on a great scale have a noble and majestic simplicity which recalls—different as is the stylism—the large and impressive figures of Egypt. It is noteworthy that many modern sculptors have regarded great size as offering an opportunity for immense elaboration of detail (as in French's " Lincoln ") whereas the seated Rameses statues at Abu Simbel, and the Colossi are of an almost architectural simplicity and are far less realistic in contours than Egyptian work on a human scale ; this was a right instinct, and it has been wisely followed in the Nebraska sculptures.

Another sculptor who has recognized this is Carl Milles (Swedish born but now American). An admirable example of this simplicity is the great Gustavus Adolphus statue carved in wood. He has many stylisms, but his sense of design is unique, and some of his groups of figures for fountains have a rhythmic beauty that is almost lyrical. Like Maillol, he uses as a theme the youthful nude girl, but Milles' girls are usually in action and grouped in intricate rhythmic patterns of great beauty. Their contours are not very realistic, a certain flattening of all the convexities of the form gives a great sense of firmness and vitality (Watts used a similar stylism which gave nobility to his great fresco figures). Milles' influence has been great and from his Cranbrook group may come a new impetus and revelation of sculptural beauty. There is little doubt that Milles is one of the great living forces in the art of sculpture.

It is perhaps a matter for regret that modern building, especially in America, tends by its scale and simplicity of surface, to leave no place for the sculptor. Yet historically the close association of architects and sculptors has almost always been advantageous. That such an association can still be fruitful may be seen in the sculpture done for the Cathedral of St. John-the-Divine, New York, by John Angel, in collaboration with the architect Ralph Adams Cram. This association, extended now over about twenty years, has produced work covering the whole field of ecclesiastical art, and much of it is of unique beauty and interest. The sculptor (English by birth and training) has a deep and extensive knowledge of sculpture during the three centuries of Gothic art, a retentive memory for all that traditional beauty, and an enviable skill and rapidity of technique. But though this wide knowledge and cultivation gives a definite character to his figures they are never copied, or even obviously derived from mediæval work ; they follow closely on mediæval lines, but they are expressed in an idiom of our own generation. The statues have a convincing simplicity and grace which recalls without imitation, the directness and beauty of the sculpture of Rheims or Lincoln. Altogether the work is a notable contribution to the art of sculpture, and if Gothic architecture is ever again to be used as a vernacular of building, these figures will set a high standard for any successors.

That it is not always in conditions of greatest freedom that the best work is produced may be seen too, in the long series of anthropological studies done for the Field Museum, Chicago, by Malvina Hoffman. These are sculptured records of every type of man, uniting the science of exact recording of anthropological features and facts, with sculptural dignity and power. The whole group of sculptures is of importance both scientifically and artistically, and is a lasting tribute to her unique persistence, accuracy of observation and skill in modelling. I do not doubt that these works are faithful scientific records ; they are also, though necessarily in varying degrees, conceived sculpturally and are carried out in appropriate and often beautiful media.

The work of Paul Manship is always interesting both technically and æsthetically. His works in bronze are unique in that they are entirely firm and metallic in their surfaces, showing no traces of their origin in a clay or wax model. This is perhaps the result of a conviction as to fitness, and of a method of work which is very individual. He begins with a clay or plasticene model, from which, as soon as it has reached an approximation to the conceived form, a mould is made in plaster. This mould is then worked on, smoothing the surfaces, and a cast is made in fine plaster. This cast is then carved into the firm shapes and contours he desires, and which are so characteristic of his work. If important changes are necessary, these can be done either by adding plasticene or plaster, and remoulding a new plaster cast ; the essential thing is that he thus preserves a surface that is never thumbed or plastic and claylike. A work like the Spear Thrower has certain simplifications of contour which recall archaic Greek bronzes, though it is in no sense a copy. I believe the same process is followed in the preparation of models for work in marble, and the firm contours are appropriate and beautiful in the marble bust of Lady

157

Cholmondeley, and in the dignified and stately bust of President Cary Thomas at Bryn Mawr. This same technical beauty is seen in the little Venus of the garden fountain at Andover, with its exquisite design and compact sculptural quality ; the hair acting as a needed attachment to the marble figure, as well as completing the oval composition. The work is usually consciously stylized in a rather neo-Grec manner, though many influences may be traced, as well as a forceful and clear cut individuality.

But though the new schools of sculpture ignore such stylism, the marked tendency of the last two decades, both in England and America, has shown itself not so much in a rejection of stylism, but rather in a definite pursuit of the hitherto unstudied stylisms of negro sculpture, and of the sculptures of remote and little known places like Easter Island, and of barbaric work such as that of neolithic man. All these have been consciously studied, analyzed and imitated ; and proportion, that characteristic quality understood and sought by the white races, tends to be abandoned for the distortion loved and pursued by the black races.

Parallel with this study and imitation of remote and barbaric art forms, and as part of the same revolt from representation, there has been a marked tendency towards abstraction, seeking forms which have no relation to nature, and which " represent " nothing. This has led to the repudiation of almost all our inherited traditions in art and to the pursuit of what is now called " pure form," " organized design," " plastic rhythms," " formal pattern," and the result is, too often, only a series of abstract symbols, arbitrarily chosen and arranged into a pattern, and so, having made their picture or sculpture unintelligible visually they are forced to attempt to convey their meaning by descriptive titles, " femme assise," " nude descending a stair," etc. This is called seeking " significant form " but by a fantastic and ironic paradox this process of eliminating detail and streamlining the figures, seeking " significance " and avoiding any recognizable natural contours, actually often empties these figures of any significance at all !

Yet the idea of seeking for the essentials of form in a stylized and abstract beauty, as conveying the sense of the ultimate beauty inherent in nature, is an idea which has inspired some noble and beautiful historic art. But one must distinguish between the intellectually conscious stylization of forms by the elimination of all individual or secondary characteristics as, for instance, both Brancusi and Archipenko have done, and those other stylisms and simplifications in historic art, where the sculptor worked in a living traditional convention, and with an unconscious or only part-conscious adaptation of style to material and to architecture— as for instance the simple granitic contours of Egyptian sculpture, say in the great Rameses at Turin, or the elongated and pillar-like kings and queens at Chartres, which fuse with the columns and become part of the architecture, and which, when separated from the building, lose so much of their singular beauty, (as is readily seen when photographs of the Museé Trocadero casts are used as illustrations). An artist who simplifies deliberately towards a stylism which ignores all the inheritance of race experience existing behind our concepts of form, achieves something only understandable to the initiated ; and too often the result is only a kind of esoteric infantilism. For the forms, words, colours and sounds used as the language of the arts do not come to us from a celestial vacuum but with a long heritage of traditional association ; they have become, as it were, part of the blood stream of our culture, and to ignore this is to forego the power of communication. An artificial ignorance can only lead to art which bears a superficial resemblance to true primitive art, as indeed Braucusi's small carving bears some resemblance to a neolithic menhir But art is something more than the adoption of a decorative style, whether remote, or contemporary ; it is the giving of form to feeling, and it becomes great and moving art only when the artist has achieved some point of reconciliation between mathematical knowledge which sees the particular in the universal, and the philosophical knowledge which sees the universal in the particular.

This point of reconciliation, this fusion of individual and universal was reached in Greece, and in the lovely spiritualized realism of the finest mediæval sculpture, and again by Michelangelo with his Platonic fusion of intense individuality in universal types. Perhaps, indeed, his greatest significance is in his individual technique allied to the persistent Platonism of his thought.

Plato has been invoked by Professor Herbert Read as a defender of abstract and mathematical art, but it is necessary to remember that Plato expounds two totally divergent views of art, as is seen clearly in the *Republic*. There is first, the splendid and convincing plea for an æsthetic education, so powerfully and convincingly argued in the third book, but by a strange paradox, artists and poets are later dismissed from the Republic, as being engaged in producing replicas of what are not realities, (for what one *sees* is not the reality, instancing a stick refracted in water) and also because the divine afflatus under which they work is inimical to the smooth running of the State ; for artists seek also the expression of their own personalities and this leads to a disturbing diversity, and " change is by far the most dangerous thing in the world," so, like a good authoritarian, he relentlessly sacrifices the artists to preserve the organization. But it appears to suit the defenders of non-representational art to adopt Plato's suggestion that Greek art was concerned only with the external (only a half truth), and that the artist's, or the eye's knowledge is invalid, while the soul's knowledge (that the stick is not bent) is higher and therefore final.

This appeal to Plato is at times used by those who belittle Greek art. Mr. Wilenski argues that Greek art pursued an ideal of empty realism, and illustrates the costumier's dummy as " the Praxitelean ideal." Professor Sheldon Cheney tells us that Phidian sculpture " lacks formal organization " and is " weak in its plastic rhythms." Empty phrases ! Look without prejudice at the Phidian Theseus, and at the Olympian sculptures, at " the music of the marble frieze." Look ! and be not blinded by phrases. Recall the beautiful and strangely exact description by Pater :

"If one had to choose a single product of Hellenic Art, to save in the wreck of all the rest, one would choose from the 'beautiful multitude' of the Panathenaic frieze ; that line of youth on horseback, with their levelled glances, their proud, patient lips, their chastened reins, their whole bodies in exquisite service. This colourless, unclassified purity of life with its blending and interpenetration of intellectual, spiritual and physical elements, still folded together, pregnant with the possibilities of a whole world closed within it, is the highest expression of that indifference which lies beyond all that is relative or partial."

Now here Pater does precisely what he suggests is the function of the critic—"To distinguish, to analyze, to separate the adjuncts— the VIRTUE by which a picture, a landscape, a fair personality in life, or in a book, produces this special impression of beauty or pleasure, and under what conditions it is experienced." Again, he "must be deeply moved by beautiful objects—he must maintain a harmony with that soul of motion in things by a constantly renewed mobility of character." That was what was expected of critics in 1876 !

Today, criticism is, too often, only vague phrases, the point of view subjective, expressed in jargon and violently didactic. This "explanation" attached to a picture by Braque, in a public gallery reads : "He seeks to show the ultimate reality of nature, which is perfect, as contrasted with the imperfect appearances we are accustomed to." How lucid it sounds ! till one asks by what Ithuriel spear of divination does the critic *know* that this picture of an arbitrary rearrangement of natural forms, shows the ultimate reality of nature ? Is it possible to maintain that this concept of an ultimate reality behind the veil of appearance can be perceived, much less than it can be represented by paint on canvas ? Or is the explanation only words, words, words ?

There is, I believe, a law of currency called Gresham's Law, according to which "bad coin tends always to oust the good." Something akin to this seems to prevail in the currency of critical opinions, and much that is accepted as good coinage is only counterfeit. The art itself is subject to a relative assessment by the winnowing of time ; the circulation of counters for words gains power cumulatively, for few people have the courage to challenge a prevalent opinion or phrase, or remember Pater's advice, "never to acquiesce in a facile orthodoxy," or even heterodoxy ! One such instance of critical writing on modern sculpture may usefully be examined because it is typical of much art criticism circulating widely in the journals and books on art in England and America, and it is the more important because the author, Professor Herbert Read, is a learned, scholarly and discriminating writer whose influence on criticism both in literature and art has been great and is today authoritative :

"For the last 400 years artists have said: We will carve a block of stone or marble into the very image of Alderman Jones or Miss Simpkins

182. PILKINGTON JACKSON : DRUM
(HORSE : OAK, COLOURED : THE
SCOTTISH NAVAL AND MILITARY
MUSEUM, EDINBURGH CASTLE
a good blend of documentary art
and technical skill

183. WILLIAM G. SIMMONDS : THE FARM TEAM : ELM : TATE GALLERY, LONDON

ACTIONS AND REACTIONS

184. RODIN (1840-1917) : THE KISS : MARBLE

185. BRANCUSI : ABSTRACT : MARBLE :
COLLECTION OF MRS RESOR, NEW YORK

In the example of abstract stylism afforded by Brancusi's little stone block of two figures embracing, though its theme is essentially the same as Rodin's group, it has by its simplification only the interest of a mnemonic sign or shorthand symbol.

186. LORD LEIGHTON P.R.A. (1830-1896):
ATHLETE STRUGGLING WITH PYTHON :
BRONZE : TATE GALLERY, LONDON

187. JOHN ANGEL : ST JOHN THE
DIVINE : CLAY MODEL FOR CARVING
CATHEDRAL OF ST. JOHN, NEW YORK

188. R. L. GARBE R.A., F.R.B.S.
THE RED SHAWL :
JAPANESE ASH, LACQUERED

189. MESTROVIC : MARBLE RELIEF

THE TWENTIETH CENTURY

190. GEORGE GREY BARNARD
(1863-1938): ABRAHAM LINCOLN
MARBLE
METROPOLITAN MUSEUM OF ART,
NEW YORK

191. EPSTEIN
AMERICAN SOLDIER : BRONZE
METROPOLITAN MUSEUM OF ART,
NEW YORK

192. MAURICE STERNE
THE BOMB THROWER
METROPOLITAN MUSEUM OF ART,
NEW YORK

193. FRANK DOBSON
OSBERT SITWELL
POLISHED BRASS
TATE GALLERY, LONDON

194. DESPIAU
PORTRAIT DE JEUNE FILLE
BRONZE : THE LOUVRE

195. PAUL MANSHIP
LADY CHOLMONDELEY
MARBLE

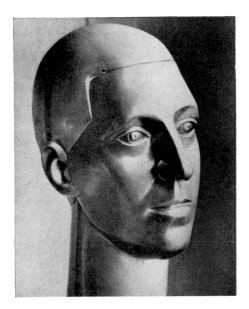

THE TWENTIETH CENTURY

196. MATISSE
RELIEF
PLASTER

197. MALVINA
HOFFMAN
SARA DANCING GIRL
BRONZE
NATURAL HISTORY
MUSEUM, CHICAGO

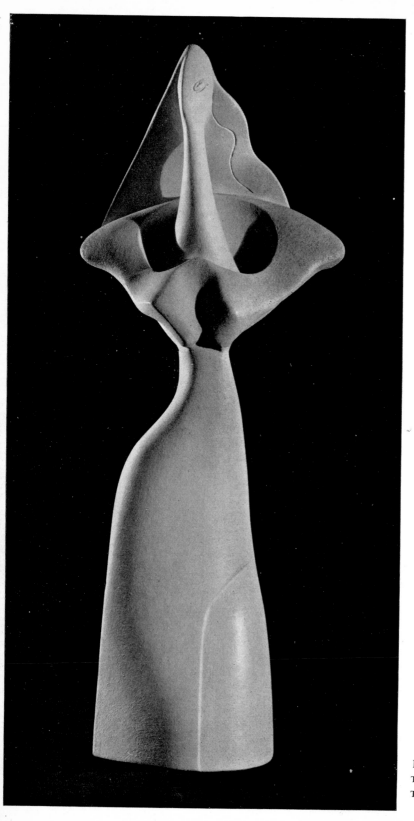

198. ARCHIPENKO
THE BRIDE (1935)
TERRA-COTTA

199. HENRY MOORE : RECLINING WOMAN (1930): HORNTON STONE
COLLECTION PETER WATSON

THE TWENTIETH CENTURY

201. CHARLES WHEELER R.A., F.R.B.S.
APHRODITE : ALABASTER

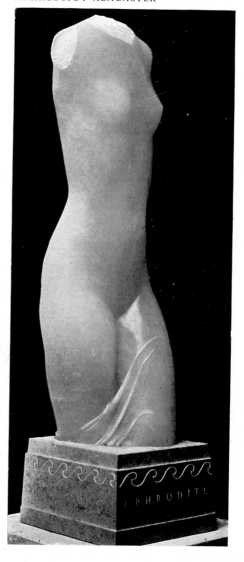

200. ARISTIDE MAILLOL
(1861-1944): NUDE: LEAD:
TATE GALLERY, LONDON

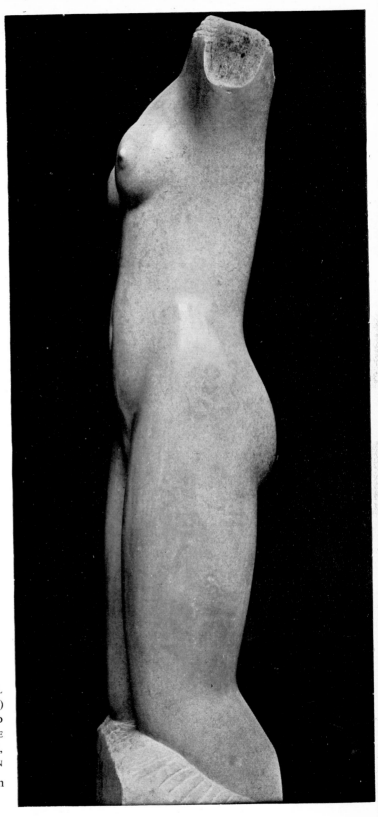

202. ERIC GILL
(1882-1940)
MANKIND
HOPTONWOOD STONE
TATE GALLERY,
LONDON
splendid carved stylism

203. a. Full size template drawing showing figure beneath drapery. This was 'offered' in situ to determine scale.

b. After one day's work chiefly with pitcher and point.

c. After three days' work with claw tools. The heads defined to fix scale.

d. After one week's work. Action of figures fixed, draperies defined in simple moulding sections.

e. Finished statue. Our Lady and Child : 5 feet high. Cotswold stone : Tewkesbury Abbey, Worcs., England.

a

b

f. Wire armature—with "butterflies" to take weight of clay.

g. First stage of modelling.

h. Action of figure defined—and modelling developed.

i. Action of head indicated and suggestion of features.

j. Action defined—surface still quite unfinished.

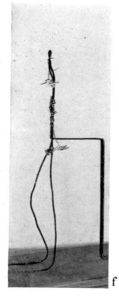

f

d

e

h

i

j

204. ALEC MILLE
ALASTAIR MILLER
LIMEWOOD

205. ALEC MILLER
BETTY BARDSLEY
LIMEWOOD

posing as Venus, of a dying lion or a flying duck ; and man has marvelled at the ingenuity with which the artist has accomplished this difficult aim. The aim of a sculptor like Henry Moore has nothing at all in common with this. He has no regard at all for the appearance of the object (if there is one) which inspires his work of art. His first concern is for his material. If that material is stone he will consider the structure of the stone, its degree of hardness, the way it reacts to the chisel. He will consider how this stone has reacted to natural forces like wind and water, for these in the course of time have revealed the inherent qualities of the stone. Finally he will ask himself what form he can best realize in the particular block of stone he has before him ; and if this form is, say, the reclining figure of a woman he will imagine (and this the act which calls for his peculiar sensibility or insight) what a reclining woman would look like if flesh and blood were translated into stone before him—the stone which has its own principles of form and structure. The woman's body might then, and actually does in some of Moore's figures, take on the appearance of a range of hills, therefore Sculpture is not a *reduplication* of form and nature—it is rather a *translation of meaning* from one material into another material. That . . . is the only key needed for the understanding of sculpture like this of Henry Moore's. . . . Most sculpture —even, for example, ancient Egyptian sculpture, creates mass by a synthesis of two-dimensional aspects. We cannot see all round a cubic mass ; the sculptor therefore tends to walk round his mass of stone and endeavour to make it satisfactory from every point of view. He can thus go a long way towards success, but he cannot be so successful as the sculptor whose act of creation is, as it were, a four-dimensional process growing out of a conception which inheres in the mass itself. Form, then, is an intuition of surface made by the sculptor imaginatively situated at the centre of gravity of the block before him. Under the guidance of this intuition the stone is slowly educated from an arbitrary into an ideal state of existence."

The book is entitled, *The Meaning of Art* and because it is a significant and interesting book, widely circulated and much studied, the passage quoted deserves careful examination, for, in spite of its convincing air of learned commentary it gives no " key to the understanding of sculpture like this of Henry Moore's, it " explains " absolutely nothing. Yet many readers may have been persuaded by it, and by similar passages in *Art Now*, into the feeling that they now understand such sculpture and that this figure is not only explicable, but even beautiful.

But has the critic here fulfilled his function of " isolating the particular virtue " distinguishing the work of art and revealed it to the reader ? Faced by the picture one may legitimately ask for some explanation of the fantastic asymmetry of the head, or a reason for the baleful cross eyes which give the face its truculent malevolence ; what " key " can make us understand the complete disregard for natural forms, while retaining the title " Reclining Woman."

I am not here concerned with the sculpture, but only to question the

161

validity of the proffered explanation. " Form then is an intuition of surface made by the sculptor imaginatively situated at the centre of gravity of the block before him ; under the guidance of this intuition the stone is slowly educated from an arbitrary into an ideal state of existence." Well ! The use of the word " educated " in its Greek sense of something " drawn out " is perhaps a little needless, if impressive, punditry, and the conclusion seems to mean that the figure is first imagined in the block and then " drawn out " into a concrete or real existence ; but that is what all who carve stone do, and to do this one need not be " imaginatively situated at the centre of gravity of the block," whatever that may mean ; one only requires first, the power to visualize the form, then the knowledge and technical skill to reveal this conceived form by cutting away all the unnecessary stone. This is no new sculptural technique. It was used by the sculptors of the Sphinx, and of the Apollo of Sunium, and of the Beau Dieu at Amiens, and it is " the key to the understanding " of all good stone sculpture, equally with this work by Henry Moore.

" We cannot see round a cubic mass," seems to be a truism, but this limitation of human vision is not usually regarded as a reason for the sculptor to " walk round his mass of stone and endeavour to make it satisfactory from every point of view," for it is clear that walking round a block of stone makes no change in it, and the closest study cannot " make it more satisfactory," for the impulse to creation has to come from the stone. " The structure of the stone, its degree of hardness, and how the stone has reacted to natural forces like wind and water, these have revealed the inherent qualities of the stone " and the sculptor then asks himself, " what form he can best realize in the particular block of stone he has before him," this stone which has its own principles of form and structure.

Apparently the meaning of this sentence is that the sculptor should get the initial suggestion from the block of stone before him as to what form his sculpture should take. This is *one* theory of sculpture ; it is very ancient, and was accepted and used by primitive man, who finding a flint which suggested, perhaps, a fishlike shape, may have chipped it into a little closer resemblance. But the sentence is still confusing. One has to ask, is it the shape (often accidental or merely suiting a quarryman's convenience) of the stone which is to suggest the desired form ? Or is it the structure, the hardness, and the evidence of nature's erosion in the stone, which suggest the form, or is it all these ? And in what way do the contours of this Reclining Woman reveal the qualities of blue hornton stone ? (a sandstone in which I have carved many statues) ; or is it that the shape of the stone, as the sculptor first saw it, was already accidentally suggestive of this mountainous lady ? Clearly the proffered theories are far from being " the only key needed for the understanding of such sculpture ! "

And a thoughtful reader may well ask why it is that if " even Egyptian sculpture is a synthesis of two-dimensional aspects " (see the seated Kephren, plate 5), is this Reclining Woman to be regarded as a typical result of " a four-dimensional process growing out of a conception which inheres in the mass itself " (whatever that may mean !) We are told that this figure is the result of " the artist's peculiar sensibility and insight " which revealed to him " what a reclining woman would look like if flesh and blood were translated into stone," and we are glad of the admission that " he has no regard at all for the object which inspires his work of art . . . his first concern is for his material." But it is worth recalling that " the peculiar sensibility and insight " of Michelangelo imagined the form within the block, and then with impetuous energy chiselled his marble into that noble and beautiful reclining woman called Dawn.

We may well ask, did Michelangelo walk round his block of marble and wonder what it might already half resemble? Or did he conceive that mighty figure in his inner vision, and then give it form and permanence by shaping it from a block of beautiful material? His first concern was not for the material, though he used the marble with profound understanding of its qualities ; his first concern was the concept of a noble figure.

This theory of sculptured form as being " dictated " by the material is widely promulgated, and largely accepted. It deserves examination and Henry Moore's work is often defended as exemplifying this way of working.

His work is entirely consistent with his own theories as expressed a few years ago, in a broadcast called " The Sculptor Speaks." In his view the forms of nature, so far as they concern the subject of the sculpture, are deliberately rejected, but somewhat paradoxically, " nature's way of working stone " is held up as showing true sculptural form. He speaks of the " curious shapes and natural holes " in stone which for him " possess the mysterious fascination of caves in hillsides and cliffs " and pebbles " excite his sculptural imagination " ; so in that recurrent theme of a " reclining figure " while the shapes and contours of the natural woman are rejected, the figure emerges as resembling in a considerable degree the contours and eroded shapes and surfaces of stone sculptured by nature.

The late Mr. Stanley Casson, the most acute and perhaps best equipped writer on modern sculpture, has pointed out that this attitude is an inverted one, and answers this theory of the compulsion of material in determining form by reasoning which seems to be inescapable.

" From his observations of nature Mr. Moore draws conclusions which are perfectly clear—as I understand them they amount to one general rule, that the sculptor must not only respect his material, but also recreate the forms and surfaces which nature indicates. Respect for material is a qualification in a sculptor which is to be found in all periods of art when sculpture was best made. It is no new invention as any sculptor who carves can tell us. As I conceive the art of sculpture, it is an art in which man shows his genius for adapting nature to his own human requirements and transforming her works into his ; Mr. Moore prefers to transform his work into hers.

" The first work of sculpture ever made by man was the flint implement.

The earliest flint implements consist of natural flint nodules roughly knocked and chipped to make them serviceable. They have no beauty and do not cause admiration. But the next state in the manufacture of these flint implements shows us forms which are beautiful in themselves. These forms are imposed by man on the natural flint nodules and they bear little relation to it because they are first generated in the mind of man. Sculpture is one of the arts of Humanism, not one of the arts of Nature. The lineal descendant of the flint implement is the head of Amenophis IV. Here an artist has deliberately chosen the most intractable material in the world—obsidian—and from it has made what is the finest portrait ever cut. Had he allowed the material to control his hand without limit, Amenophis would never have emerged and we would have had something which would have looked like a fragment of a natural beer bottle."

I can conceive no valid answer to this admirable and authoritative statement.

I have examined at some length, the views and theories expressed by this distinguished and accepted critic, Professor Herbert Read, because these views have been stated in words which have an appearance of clarity and perspicacity, but which in reality leave the subject unexplained and the issue still confused. Criticism such as this may do harm, especially to youth, for by iteration and reiteration phrases and ideas once accepted, acquire a cumulative impetus. This danger was commented on nearly two thousand years ago by Lucretius (Book 1-6-40 Munro) " For fools admire and like all things the more which they perceive to be concealed under involved language, and determine things to be true which can prettily tickle the ears and are varnished over with finely sounding phrases."

But while a great deal that passes for criticism is useless and delusive, the artist must always be open and sensitive to new impressions and new visions of beauty, and when these take strange forms they are not to be hastily condemned. For the search for new art forms is essential to any living art, and these seekers of strange forms may be functioning like the microbes which devour corrupt matter, and so be serving the life of art. It is quite possible that the next generation will value and preserve some of these products of the " modern outlook on sculpture "; such as survive will serve to show that the desire for " some new things " is recurrent and that the passion for experiment, the exploration of new, or ancient and hitherto unexploited, forms and formulæ will always go on, and it may lead to strange and fantastic, as well as to beautiful and moving forms.

The plea that the traditions of the past lay a dead hand on the present is wholly untrue. That which hampers and confines the artist is far more often a desire to conform to the current conventions of the present. There is a kernel of truth in an aphorism of the historian Burckhardt in *Reflexions on History* : " and then comes the intellectual pest of our time, originality ; it supplies the need tired men feel for sensation."

As a corrective one may set with, rather than against, this some wise words from *The Horizon of Experience* by C. Delisle-Burns. " If the plastic arts do reveal some new aspects of the real world, which no science is able to reveal, then these aspects, these beauties of form and colour must be among the Primordia Rerum ; they are like the ' Semina ' of Lucretius ; they are principles of which philosophy must take account. The continual extension of emotional experience is as necessary for its existence as growth is essential to knowledge, therefore modern art is of the essence of art, and all art is essential to experience."

Our art, like wisdom, has to be a distillation from life and experience, and today when art has turned its vision inwards rather than outwards we must endeavour to unite both aspects of life and to find some compromise between the dominance of intellect and tradition and that sway of impulse and appeal to the blood, which is the cry of D. H. Lawrence and is widely echoed today. " My great religion " he says, " is a belief in the blood, the flesh, as being wiser than the intellect. We can go wrong in our minds, but what our blood feels, and believes, and says, is always true. The intellect is only a bit and bridle. All I want is to answer to my blood, direct, without fribbling intervention of mind or moral, or what not." How characteristic is the resentment of the supersensitive artist at the intellect's " bit and bridle," but is there really this unbridgeable division between the flesh and the mind ? For reason is also an instinct, and tradition and intellect are not just things we inherit from the past, for they have entered into our blood and have thus become part of the living stream of life which may not be denied or eluded.

To be static is to be dead, and all our values have with imaginative effort, to be tested, and retested, for an unteachable spirit is a tragic thing, but let us not too readily assume that all the old values which make up our inheritance from the past are to be swept away as something obstructing the movement and limiting the freedom by which life and art must live. As Santayana says with refreshing clearness :

" The life of reason is also our heritage, and exists only through tradition. Now the misfortune of our revolutionaries is that they are disinherited, and their folly is that they wish to be disinherited even more than they are."

I have endeavoured to trace briefly this inheritance of sculpture, to follow the development of tradition, and to note the tributary streams by which it has been fed and enriched. The importance of art and of æsthetic sensibility, as a part of the spiritual experience of man, is widely recognized today, yet one of the strange and tragic aspects of what is called "the new movement in art" is that many artists seem to be seeking to enter spheres remote from the daily life of man, and this tends to hasten the separation of the arts from life and from each other. The cohesion of mediæval life, reflected in a singularly unified art, is today not possible, nor perhaps desirable, but it is important to recognize that the great art of the past arose in a unity of belief and purpose. Today, owing to the lack of a unifying principle, and the absence of a philosophy of life, artists turn too readily to the expression of individual idiosyncracy, and so our art is no longer what it was to Dante, " visible speech," but is confined to a very

165

limited group of people. The artist must return to the idea of service, and instead of making his art a sterile and esoteric expression of himself, make it a revelation of his love of earth, that neglected Demeter mother from which we spring and to which we go.

Perhaps we must regard rather as a wish than as an attainment, these recent words of Maritain :

" As the world breaks up we see the things of the spirit draw together, art and poetry, metaphysics and wisdom." Yet surely such a drawing together is desirable, and we as artists, by the personal integrity of our minds and art, have our part, small or large, in the effort towards achieving this goal of service and unity.

There is a profound and memorable conclusion in Matthew Arnold's preface to the *Poems* of 1853, and though it deals with the art of poetry, it has a unique and living significance for all who seek to follow the arts.

" In the sincere endeavour to learn and practice amid the bewildering confusion of our times, what is sound and true in poetical art, I seemed to myself to find the only sure guidance, the only solid footing, among the ancients. They, at any rate, knew what they wanted in art, and we do not. It is this uncertainty which is disheartening, which makes our difficulty. Two kinds of dilettante, says Goethe, there are in poetry; he who neglects the indispensable mechanical part and thinks he has done enough if he shows spirituality and feeling, and he who seeks to arrive at poetry merely by mechanism in which he can acquire an artizan's readiness and is without soul or matter. And, he adds, the first does most harm to art, the second to himself. If it is impossible for us, under the circumstances amidst which we live, to think clearly, to feel nobly, and to delineate firmly ; if we cannot attain to the mastery of the great artist, let us at least, have so much respect for our art, as to prefer it to ourselves. Let us not bewilder our successors ; let us transmit to them the practice of poetry, with its boundaries and wholesome regulative laws, under which excellent work may again perhaps, at some future time, be produced, not yet fallen into oblivion through our neglect, nor yet condemned and cancelled by the influence of their eternal enemy Caprice."

BIBLIOGRAPHY

General

Fletcher, Sir Banister	*History of Architecture*
Faure, E.	*History of Art : Ancient, Mediaeval, Modern*
Reinach, S.	*Apollo*
Chase and Post	*A History of Sculpture*
Roos, F. J.	*Illustrated Handbook of Art History*
Parsons, G.	*The Stream of History*
Fisher, H. A.	*History of Europe*
Rostovtzeff, M. I.	*History of the Ancient World*
Statham, H. H.	*Short Critical History of Architecture*
Lubke	*History of Art*
March Phillips, L.	*Works of Man*
	Form and Colour
Marquand and Frothingham	*A History of Sculpture*
Spengler, O.	*The Decline of the West*
Toynbee, A.	*A Study of History*
Mumford, L.	*The Condition of Man*

Definitions and Processes

Lanteri, E.	*Modelling*
Taft, L.	*History of American Sculpture*
Casson, S.	*The Technique of Early Greek Sculpture*
Toft, A.	*Modelling and Sculpture*
Ruskin J.	*Aratra Pentelici*
	Lectures on Art
Jagger, S.	*Modelling and Sculpture in the Making*

Primitive Sculpture

Cartailhac and Breuil	*Caverne d'Altamira*
Stevens, F.	*Stonehenge*
Lynam, E. W.	*Prehistoric Rock Carvings*
Marett, R. R.	*Anthropology**
Windle, Sir B.	*Europe in the Ages of Stone and Bronze*
Huxley, T. H.	*Physiography*
	Essays
Conway, Sir M.	*The Dawn of Art**
" The Antiquary "	
" Antiquity "	

Egyptian Sculpture

Perrot and Chipiez	*Art in Ancient Egypt*
Capart, J.	*Primitive Egyptian Art*
Breasted, J. H.	*History of Egypt*
	Readings in Ancient History
	*The Conquest of Civilization**
Maspero, G.	*Art in Ancient Egypt*
	The Dawn of Civilization
Herodotus	*History*
Peet, E.	*Literature of Egypt and Babylonia*
Wooley, L.	*Ur of the Chaldees*
	Digging Up the Past
Erman, A.	*Life in Ancient Egypt*
Petrie, W. M. F.	*The Pyramids and Temples of Gizeh*
	Religion in Ancient Egypt
	Arts and Crafts of Egypt
	Revolutions of Civilization
	70 Years in Archæology
Weigal, A.	*Egyptian Art*
	Life of Akenaton
	Life of Cleopatra
Fechheimer	*Egyptian Art (Illus.)**
Evans, Sir A.	*Cnossus and the Palace of Minos*
Perry, W. J.	*Growth of Civilization*
Worringer, W.	*Egyptian Art**
British Museum Catalogue	*Egyptian Antiquities*

Babylonian and Assyrian

Perrot and Chipiez	*Art in Ancient Babylonia*
Hall, H. R.	*History of the Near East**
Spence, L.	*Arts of Babylon and Assyria**
British Museum Catalogue	' *Babylonian Antiquities* '
King, L. W.	*The Babylonians and the Assyrians*
Johns, C. H. W.	*Babylonia*
The Bible	

Greek Sculpture

Perrot and Chipiez	*Art in Ancient Greece*
Richter, Gisela	*Greek Sculpture**
Stobart, J. C.	*The Glory that was Greece*

Whibley, L. (ed.)   *Handbook to Greek Studies*

Pater, W.   *Greek Studies**

Thomson, J. A. K.   *Greeks and Barbarians**
The Greek Tradition*

Schliemann   *Troy and Mycenæ*

Livingstone, R. W. (ed.)   *The Legacy of Greece**

Casson, S.   *Ancient Greece**

Glover, T. R.   *The Ancient World Pericles to Philip*

Murray, G.   *Rise of the Greek Epic**
Four Stages of Greek Religion*
Euripides and his Age

Jowett, B.   *Plato's Dialogues*

Jex-Blake and Sellers   *The Elder Pliny's Chapters on the History of Art*

Weyhe   *The Akropolis (illus.)*

Harrison, Jane   *Introductory Studies in Greek Art**
Ancient Art and Ritual*

Gardner, E.   *Six Greek Sculptors*
History of Greek Sculpture

" Cambridge Ancient History "
Vols. III and IV

Dickinson, G. L.   *Greek View of Life**
Plato and his Dialogues

Pausanias (Ed., Fraser)   *Travels in Greece*

Baikie, J.   *Sea-Kings of Crete*

Gardner, P.   *Grammar of Greek Art*

British Museum Catalogue   *The Parthenon*

Newton, Sir C.   *Archæological Essays**

Mackail, J. W. (ed.)   *The Greek Anthology*

Waldstein, C.   *Essays*

Lewes, G. H.   *History of Philosophy**

Mahaffy, J. P.   *The Greek World under Roman Sway*

Wright, W. C.   *History of Greek Literature*

Roman Sculpture

Pliny the younger   *Letters*

Walters, H. B.   *Roman Sculpture*

Marvin, F. S.   *The Living Past*

Glover, T. R.   *The Conflict of Religions in the Ancient World*

Bevan, E.   *Hellenism and Christianity*

Strong, E.   *Roman Art**

Stobart, J. C.   *The Grandeur that was Rome*

Mackail, J. W.   *Latin Literature**
The Aneaid of Virgil

Warde Fowler   *Rome*

Wells, J.   *Roman Life**

The Rise of Christian Art

Davis, H. W. C.   *Mediæval Europe*

Gibbon   *Decline and Fall of the Roman Empire**

Morrison, J. C.   *Life of Bernard of Clairvaux*

Augustine   *Confessions*

Fry, Roger   *Art before Giotto*

Dalton, O. M.   *British Museum Handbook to the Christian Antiquities**

Morey, C. R.   *Christian Art**

Workman, H. B.   *The Papacy*

Baldwin, Brown   *The Arts of the Early Middle Ages**

Dawson, C.   *Enquiries**

Stokes, M.   *Early Christian Art in Ireland**

Gwynn, S.   *Ireland*

Allen, Romily   *Celtic Art in Pagan and Christian Times*

Sullivan, E.   *The Book of Kells*

Mediæval Sculpture

Jacob, E. F. (ed.)   *The Legacy of the Middle Ages**

Male, E.   *French Art in the 13th Century*

Prior, E. S.   *Gothic Architecture*

Lethaby, W. R.   *Mediæval Art**
Westminster Abbey and the King's Craftsmen Architecture*

British Museum   Handbook to the Mediæval Department

Harrison, F.   *The Meaning of History*

Froude, J. A.   *Life and Times of Erasmus*

Prior and Gardner   *Mediæval Figure Sculpture in England*

Lee, V.   *Euphorion*

Morris, W.   *Lectures on Architecture and History**

Coulton, G. G.   *Mediæval Panorama**
Art and the Reformation*
The Black Death

Power, Eileen   *Mediæval People*

Maritain, J.   *Art and Scholasticism*

Bond, F.	*Gothic Architecture in England*
Funck-Brentano, F.	*The Middle Ages*
Waddell, H.	*The Wandering Scholars**
Froissart	*Chronicles*
Gardner, A.	*Mediæval Sculpture in France**
Einstein, L.	*The Renaissance in England*
Maskell, A.	*Wood Sculpture*
Ruskin, J.	*Seven Lamps of Architecture* *The Bible of Amiens*

The Renaissance

Symonds, J. A.	*The Renaissance in Italy : the Fine Arts* *Life of Michelangelo*
Lee, V.	*Renaissance Studies* *Tuscan Sculpture*
Pater, W.	*The Renaissance*
Taylor, R. A.	*Aspects of the Italian Renaissance*
Sichel, W.	*The Renaissance*
Maclehose, L.	*Vasari on Technique**
Holroyd, C.	*Life of Michelangelo**
Cellini, B.	*Autobiography*
Balcarres, Lord	*Evolution of Italian Sculpture**
McCurdy, E.	*Life of Leonardo* *Notebooks of Leonardo* (ed.)
Vasari, G.	*Lives of the Painters and Sculptors*

Baroque

Ricci, C.	*Baroque Architecture and Sculpture*
Blomfield, R.	*Renaissance Architecture in England*
Evelyn, J.	*Diaries*
Symonds, J. A.	*The Catholic Reaction**
Walpole, H.	*Letters*
Pepys, S.	*Diaries*
Eaton, D. C.	*Modern French Sculpture*
Marvin, F. S. (ed.)	*Art and Humanism**
Mac Cartney, M. (ed.)	*Sir Christopher Wren and St. Paul's*
Armstrong, W.	*Art in Great Britain*
Scott, G.	*Architecture of Humanism**

The Classical Reaction

Cicognara, Count	*Antonio Canova, Life and Works*
Colvin, S.	*John Flaxman, Memoir and Drawings**
Smith, J. T.	*Nollekins and his Times**
Gilchrist, A.	*Life of William Blake*
Plon, E.	*B. Thorwaldsen, Life and Works*
Scott, W. Bell	*British Sculpture*
Armstrong, W.	*Art in Great Britain*
Reynolds, Sir J.	*Discourses on Art*

The Nineteenth Century

Holman Hunt	*The P.R.B.*
Gosse, E.	*The New Sculpture*
" The Magazine of Art "	
Ruskin, J.	*The Pre-Raphaelites** *Lectures on Art**
Stannus, H.	*Drawings of Alfred Stevens**
Gsell, P.	*Rodin*
Millais, J. G.	*Life and Letters of Millais*
Woolner, L.	*Life and Work of T. Woolner*
" The Art Journal "	
Catalogue of the Crystal Palace Exhibition	
Pugin, A. W.	*Life of Pugin*
Lawton, F.	*Rodin*
Cladel, M.	*Rodin*

The Twentieth Century

Rindge, A.	*Sculpture**
MacColl, D. S.	*Confessions of a Keeper* *What is Art?**
Read, H.	*The Meaning of Art** *Art Now*
Newton, E.	*European Painting and Sculpture**
Parkes, K.	*The Art of Carved Sculpture**
Mestrovic	*Life and Work of Mestrovic*
Gerald H. Crow	*William Morris, Designer*
Durst, Alan	*Wood Carving*
Fry, R.	*Vision and Design* *Essays**
Symonds, J. A.	*Essays, Speculative and Suggestive*
Wilenski, R. H.	*The Meaning of Modern Sculpture*
Delisle-Burns, C.	*The Horizon of Experience*
Casson, S.	*Some Modern Sculptors* *Sculpture of Today*

* Referred to in text

INDEX

Italic type indicates a plate.

ACKNOWLEDGMENTS

Photographs of the subjects illustrated have been supplied by the following:

Alinari, Florence: plates 20, 22, 23, 25, 31, 44, 45, 47, 48, 49, 51, 53, 54, 55, 113, 114, 115, 117, 120, 125, 126, 128, 129, 134, 135, 148.

Anderson, Rome: plates 30, 43, 111, 127, 13.

Les Archives Photographiques, Paris: plat 1, 7, 11, 12, 13, 14, 38, 69, 70, 71, 72, 73, 74, 75, 76, 95, 101, 102, 103, 110, 112, 161, 166, 172, 179, 180, 181, 184.

The Ashmolean Museum, Oxford: plate 139.

Associated Press, Ltd., London: plates 144, 145.

Bernard Barnard, Lincoln: plate 87.

British Museum: plates 4, 10, 16, 17, 18, 19, 26, 32, 33, 37, 41, 52, 59, 67, 108.

W. A. Call, Monmouth: plates 79, 91, 100. Chicago Natural History Museum: plate 197.

Cleveland Museum of Art, Ohio: plate 60. A. C. Cooper, London: plate 42.

Courtauld Institute, London: plates 15, 62, 66, 99.

Exclusive News Agency, Ltd., London: plate 167.

Giraudon, Paris: plate 153. Glasgow Art Gallery: plates 157, 158.

W. J. Green, York: plate 65.

The Controller of H.M. Stationery Office: plate 82 (from the Herefordshire Inventory of the Royal Commission on Historical Monuments, Vol. I).

R. P. Howgrave-Graham, London: plates 88, 89, 90.

The Louvre: plates 97, 194.

W. F. Mansell, London: plate 40.

Metropolitan Museum of Art, New York: plates 3, 21, 39, 46, 50, 56, 57, 58, 61, 105, 140, 146, 150, 151, 154, 190, 191, 192.

By permission of the Ministry of Works: plate 162.

Musée des Antiquités Nationales, Paris: plate 2.

Museum of Fine Arts, Boston, Mass: plates 24, 28.

National Buildings Record, London: plate 92. National Gallery, London: plate 173.

National Portrait Gallery, London: plates 107, 143.

Oxford Photocrafts, through the courtesy of J. H. Brooks, M.A., J.P.: plate 163.

Sidney Pitcher, Gloucester: plate 93, 94. Princeton University, N.J.: plate 160.

Ruiz Vernacci, Madrid: plate 80.

C. W. Shippam, Chichester: plate 68.

By courtesy of the Trustees of the Tate Gallery, London: plates 170, 173, 175, 183, 186, 193, 200, 202.

The Times, London: plate 29. Topical Press Agency, Ltd., London: plate 169.

Turner & Sons, Cambridge: plate 164.

University College, London: plate 9.

Victoria and Albert Museum, London: plates 77, 98, 104, 109, 118, 138, 141, 147, 149, 155, 156, 171.

Warburg Institute, London: plates 83, 86, 136. Westermann, U.S.A.: plate 119.

Plates 35 and 36 are reproduced from *Hege-Rodenvaldt Akropolis* (Berlin) and plate 85 is reproduced from *Life in the Middle Ages* by G. G. Coulton (Cambridge University Press), also shown in *Didron's Annales Archaeologiques* t. 11, p. 242.

The author wishes also to thank Miss Welsford of The Courtauld Institute of Art, and officials of the French Embassy in London, who have kindly assisted in obtaining illustrative material; also, for help with particular illustrations, Senorita M. Medina of Madrid and Mr. John Munro of Oban.

Thanks are due to Mr. Stanley Cursitor, O.B.E., Director of the National Gallery of Scotland, for interesting data on Michelangelo's wax models; to Dr. Ludlow Bull, of the Metropolitan Museum, New York, for valuable and authoritative help with the Egyptian chapter; to Dr. Gilbert Murray, O.M., and Professor Herbert Read, for permission to quote from their writings; to Messrs. Blackwood & Sons, Messrs. Macmillan & Co., and the Cambridge University Press, for permission to use extracts from Hegel, Sir E. Burne-Jones, Mr. F. Harrison, Mr. G. G. Coulton, Mr. A. J. B. Wace and Professor Beazley.

As the writing of this book has been spread over many years, and notes, quotations and illustrations have been gathered from unremembered sources, it is possible that thanks are due to persons unmentioned. Such thanks are here tendered, with apologies and regret for the lack of explicit mention.   A. M.

ES